Contents

D0517609

A Programmer's
Introduction to PHP 4.0

W. J. Gilmore

Apress™

A Programmer's Introduction to PHP 4.0
Copyright ©2001 by W. J. Gilmore

ISBN (pbk): 1-893115-85-2

Printed and bound in the United States of America 12345678910

Trademarked names may appear in this book. Rather than use a trademark symbol with every occurrence of a trademarked name, we use the names only in an editorial fashion and to the benefit of the trademark owner, with no intention of infringement of the trademark.

Editorial Directors: Dan Appleman, Gary Cornell, Karen Watterson
Technical Editor: Brian Wilson
Project Editor: Carol A. Burbo
Developmental Editor and Indexer: Valerie Perry
Copy Editor: Beverly McGuire
Compositor: Susan Glinert
Artist and Cover and Part Opener Designer: Karl Miyajima

Distributed to the book trade in the United States by Springer-Verlag New York, Inc.,175 Fifth Avenue, New York, NY, 10010
and outside the United States by Springer-Verlag GmbH & Co. KG, Tiergartenstr. 17, 69112 Heidelberg, Germany

In the United States, phone 1-800-SPRINGER; orders@springer-ny.com;
http://www.springer-ny.com
Outside the United States, contact orders@springer.de; http://www.springer.de;
fax +49 6221 345229

For information on translations, please contact Apress directly at 901 Grayson Street, Suite 204, Berkeley, CA, 94710
Phone: 510-549-5931; Fax: 510-549-5939; info@apress.com;
http://www.apress.com

The information in this book is distributed on an "as is" basis, without warranty. Although every precaution has been taken in the preparation of this work, neither the author nor Apress shall have any liability to any person or entity with respect to any loss or damage caused or alleged to be caused directly or indirectly by the information contained in this work.

For my mother and father,
Judith and John Gilmore.

Part Three: Advanced PHP

Acknowledgements

This book would not have been possible without the considerable talent, patience, and endurance of several people. I would like to thank Gary Cornell for contacting me about writing this book; Grace Wong, Valerie Perry, and Beverly McGuire for their tireless editing and suggestions; Brian Wilson for sanity checking the text and code, in addition to listening to my endless ramblings regarding the virtues of PHP programming; Carol Burbo for patiently dealing with my last-minute modifications; The core PHP development team in addition to all of the countless other developers who have made PHP 4.0 such a wonderful success; Randy Cosby for giving me the opportunity to start my writing career; and my family, friends, and colleagues for their endless support.

All of these people have in some way contributed to the creation of a book far better than I could have done alone. I am indebted to them all.

Introduction

Seriously though, was there life before the Web? Growing up today, one would hardly think so. The advent of the Internet has provided a basis for communication unparalleled in the history of mankind, with people both young and not so young using it as a means for shopping, learning, and communicating. In just a few short years following its inception, aspiring entrepreneurs have made it big, corporate empires have been built and lost, and entire economies are booming, all due in part to the vision of Tim Berners-Lee and his colleagues that the world might one day be interconnected via hyperlinks.

Of course, the Web has progressed substantially over the last ten years, beginning largely as a tool for scientific research and soon evolving to one capable of retrieving sometimes mind-boggling amounts of information. Perhaps the single most important contributing agent to the aggregation of this information is the ease in which it can be published to the Web. With minimal knowledge, a person can download a text editor, FTP software, and Web browsers and consequently be "published" to the electronic media.

However, the process behind the creation and maintenance of dynamic, large-scale Web sites tends to be somewhat more complicated. Typically incorporating features such as user interaction, database mining, and multiplatform accessibility, development of a professional Web service can quickly become a major undertaking. If you are interested in learning more about how these types of services can be constructed and deployed, this book is for you.

How To Read This Book

My main goal is to teach PHP in a way that is of immediate benefit to the user; I have no interest in blindly reciting information that can be easily read in the on-line PHP documentation. Rather, I've attempted to provide only information that will be of interest to the majority of Web developers, leaving some of the more obscure concepts to be learned in the interested reader's own time. Concluding projects that relate to the subject matter discussed in the respective chapters are included when deemed necessary, giving the reader some extra insight into how that particular aspect of PHP can be put to practical use.

The PHP scripting language is the culmination of the collaboration of development efforts across the globe, resulting in the creation of a wonderfully rich and powerful Web development language. The sixteen chapters in this book delve into the many features that make this language so popular, beginning with a thorough introduction of the general concepts and constructs of the language, then moving into issues pertaining to Web development, such as building dynamic pages, creating dynamic links, and database interfacing. Finally, attention is directed toward advanced Web development and the role PHP can play in it, discussing XML, JavaScript, COM objects, and security.

Specifically, the book is divided into three parts. Part I, "The Basics," includes Chapters 1 through 8.

Chapter 1, "An Introduction to PHP," introduces PHP, its history, and its key features. Instructions regarding how to install and configure PHP and Apache are also provided. The chapter concludes with a survey of the rudimentary PHP syntax needed to create a basic script.

Chapter 2, "Variables and Data Types," describes the various data formats supported by PHP and how variables are named and used to store information.

Chapter 3, "Expressions, Operators, and Control Structures," expands on the material presented in Chapter 2, introducing how variable values are manipulated. Control structures are also introduced, providing you with the tools to begin creating larger and more complex scripts.

Chapter 4, "Functions," discusses the many underlying details of building modularized, reusable PHP code.

Chapter 5, "Arrays," introduces arrays, providing explanation and examples regarding the creation and manipulation of single and multidimensional arrays of both indexed and associative types.

Chapter 6, "Object-Oriented PHP," highlights PHP's object-oriented features. Although not a full-featured object-oriented language, PHP provides support for several of the basic OOP concepts that can contribute greatly to efficient code development and maintenance.

Chapter 7, "File I/O and the File System," delves into one of PHP's noted features, manipulation of data files. Information is also provided regarding how PHP can interact with the many facets of server directories.

Chapter 8, "Strings and Regular Expressions," discusses string manipulation through the use of predefined functionality and regular expressions. Both POSIX and Perl-type regular expressions are introduced.

Part II, "PHP and the Web," builds on the information covered in the first eight chapters, using it as a basis for developing Web applications. Part II contains Chapters 9 through 13.

Chapter 9, "PHP and Dynamic Site Development," primes the reader on the very basic concepts of using PHP to create dynamic Web sites. Dynamic content, link creation, and basic page templating strategies are covered in this chapter.

Chapter 10, "Forms," describes how PHP can work with HTML forms to gather, display, and manipulate user input.

Chapter 11, "Databases," highlights PHP's vast support for database servers, focusing on the MySQL database to show how PHP can act as an efficient interface between a database and the Web.

Chapter 12, "Templates," introduces advanced page templating strategies.

Chapter 13, "Cookies and Session Tracking," shows how PHP can effectively track site visitors.

Part III, "Advanced PHP," introduces a few of the more advanced implementations of PHP and includes Chapters 14 through 16.

Chapter 14, "PHP and XML," introduces the reader to XML and shows how PHP can parse and convert XML documents.

Chapter 15, "JavaScript and COM," illustrates how PHP can work with JavaScript to produce increasingly user-friendly and interactive Web applications. Information regarding how PHP can interact with Windows COM objects is also covered.

Chapter 16, "Security," describes several of the many facets of Web security and how PHP can be used to implement these features. Advanced PHP configuration, coding issues, data encryption, ecommerce, and user authentication are all topics covered in this chapter.

In an effort to eliminate all possibilities of error in the text and code, I have taken considerable time to verify all facts and code listings. However, as sure as I am human, errors are bound to exist. Should you find a mistake, I would greatly appreciate it if any information regarding the error be sent to book_errata@wjgilmore.com.

The Basics   PART ONE

An Introduction to PHP

The past five years have been fantastic in terms of the explosive growth of the Internet and the new ways in which people are able to communicate with one another. Spearheading this phenomenon has been the World Wide Web (WWW), with thousands of new sites being launched daily and consumers being consistently offered numerous outstanding services via this new communications medium. With this exploding market has come a great need for new technologies and developers to learn these technologies. Chances are that if you are reading this paragraph, you are one of these Web developers or are soon to become one. Regardless of your profession, you've picked this book up because you've heard of the great new technology called *PHP*.

This chapter introduces the PHP language, discusses its history and capabilities, and provides the basic information you need to begin developing PHP-enabled sites. Several examples are provided throughout, hopefully serving to excite you about what PHP can offer you and your organization. You will learn how to install and configure the PHP software on both Linux/UNIX and Windows machines, and you will learn how to embed PHP in HTML. At the conclusion of the chapter, you will be ready to begin delving into the many important aspects of the PHP language. So light the fire, turn on your favorite jazz album, and curl up on the lazyboy; you are about to learn what will be one of the most exciting additions to your resume: PHP programming.

An Abbreviated History

PHP set its roots in 1995, when an independent software development contractor named Rasmus Lerdorf developed a Perl/CGI script that enabled him to know how many visitors were reading his online resume. His script performed two duties: logging visitor information and displaying the count of visitors to the Web page. Because the WWW as we know it today was still so young at that time, tools such as these were nonexistent, and they prompted emails inquiring about Lerdorf's scripts. Lerdorf thus began giving away his toolset, dubbed *Personal Home Page* (PHP), or *Hypertext Preprocessor*.

The clamor for the PHP toolset prompted Lerdorf to begin developing additions to PHP, one of which converted data entered in an HTML form into symbolic variables that allowed for their export to other systems. To accomplish this, he opted to continue development in C code rather than Perl. This addition to the existing PHP toolset resulted in PHP 2.0, or PHP-FI (Personal Home Page—Form Interpreter). This 2.0 release was accompanied by a number of enhancements and improvements from programmers worldwide.

The new PHP release was extremely popular, and a core team of developers soon formed. They kept the original concept of incorporating code directly alongside HTML and rewrote the parsing engine, giving birth to PHP 3.0. By the 1997 release of version 3.0, over 50,000 users were using PHP to enhance their Web pages.

> **NOTE** *1997 also saw the change of the words underlying the PHP abbreviation from Personal Home Page to Hypertext Preprocessor.*

Development continued at a hectic pace over the next two years, with hundreds of functions being added and the user count growing in leaps and bounds. At the onset of 1999, Netcraft (http://www.netcraft.com) reported a conservative estimate of a user base surpassing 1,000,000, making PHP one of the most popular scripting languages in the world.

Early 1999 saw the announcement of the upcoming PHP 4.0. Although one of PHP's strongest features was its proficiency at executing scripts, the developers had not intended that large-scale applications were going to be built using PHP. Thus they set out to build an even-more robust parsing engine, better known as Zend (http://www.zend.com). Development continued rapidly, culminating in the May 22, 2000, release of PHP 4.0.

In addition to the Zend processor, Zend technologies, based in Israel, offers the Zend optimizer, which increases even further the performance benefits of the Zend parsing engine. Available for download free of charge, the benchmarks have shown that the optimizer can result in a 40 to 100 percent overall performance gain. Check out the Zend site for more information.

At the time of this writing, according to Netcraft (http://www.netcraft.com), PHP is installed on over 3.6 million domains, making it one of the most popular scripting languages in the world. The future of PHP indeed looks bright, as major Web sites and personal users alike continue to embrace the product.

PHP is best summarized as an embedded server-side Web-scripting language that provides developers with the capability to quickly and efficiently build dynamic Web applications. PHP bears a close resemblance, both syntactically and grammatically, to the C programming language, although developers haven't been shy to integrate features from a multitude of languages, including Perl, Java, and C++. Several of these valuable borrowed features include regular expression parsing, powerful array-handling capabilities, an object-oriented methodology, and vast database support.

For writing applications that extend beyond the traditional, static methodology of Web page development (that is, HTML), PHP can also serve as a valuable tool for creating and managing dynamic content, embedded directly beside the likes of JavaScript, Stylesheets, WML (Wireless Markup Language) and many other useful languages. Providing hundreds of predefined functions, PHP is capable of handling just about anything a developer can dream of. Extensive support is offered for graphic creation and manipulation, mathematical calculations, ecommerce, and burgeoning technologies such as Extensible Markup Language (XML), open database connectivity (ODBC), and Macromedia Shockwave. This vast range of capabilities eliminates the need for the tedious and costly integration of several third-party modules, making PHP the tool of choice for developers worldwide.

One of the main strengths of PHP is the fact that because it can be embedded directly alongside HTML code, there is no need to write a program that has many commands just to output the HTML. HTML and PHP can be used interchangeably as needed, working alongside one another in unison. With PHP, we can simply do the following:

```
<html>
<title><? print "Hello world!"; ?></title>
</html>
```

And `Hello world!` will be displayed in the Web page title bar. Interestingly, the single line print statement is enclosed in what are commonly known as PHP's escape characters (<?...?>) is a complete program. No need for lengthy prefacing code or inclusion of libraries; the only required code is what is needed to get the job done!

Of course, in order to execute a PHP script, you must first install and configure the PHP software on your server. This process is explained in "Downloading and Installing PHP/Apache," later in this chapter. Immediately preceding that section are a few excerpts from prominent users testifying to the power of PHP, followed by a detailed synopsis of the language and its history. However, before diving into the installation process, take a moment to read more about the characteristics of PHP that make it such a powerful language. This is the subject of the next section, aptly titled "Characteristics of PHP."

Characteristics of PHP

As you may have realized, the PHP language revolves around the central theme of practicality. PHP is about providing the programmer with the necessary tools to get the job done in a quick and efficient fashion. Five important characteristics make PHP's practical nature possible:

- Familiarity

- Simplicity

- Efficiency

- Security

- Flexibility

One final characteristic makes PHP particularly interesting: it's free!

Familiarity

Programmers from many backgrounds will find themselves already accustomed to the PHP language. Many of the language's constructs are borrowed from C and Perl, and in many cases PHP code is almost indistinguishable from that found in the typical C or Pascal program. This minimizes the learning curve considerably.

Simplicity

A PHP script can consist of 10,000 lines or one line: whatever you need to get the job done. There is no need to include libraries, special compilation directives, or anything of the sort. The PHP engine simply begins executing the code after the first escape sequence (<?) and continues until it passes the closing escape sequence (?>). If the code is syntactically correct, it will be executed exactly as it is displayed.

Efficiency

Efficiency is an extremely important consideration for working in a multiuser environment such as the WWW. PHP 4.0 introduced resource allocation mechanisms and more pronounced support for object-oriented programming, in addition to session management features. Reference counting has also been introduced in the latest version, eliminating unnecessary memory allocation.

Security

PHP provides developers and administrators with a flexible and efficient set of security safeguards. These safeguards can be divided into two frames of reference: system level and application level.

System-Level Security Safeguards

PHP furnishes a number of security mechanisms that administrators can manipulate, providing for the maximum amount of freedom and security when PHP is properly configured. PHP can be run in what is known as *safe mode*, which can limit users' attempts to exploit the PHP implementation in many important ways. Limits can also be placed on maximum execution time and memory usage, which if not controlled can have adverse affects on server performance. Much as with a cgi-bin folder, administrators can also place restrictions on the locations in which users can view and execute PHP scripts and use PHP scripts to view guarded server information, such as the passwd file.

Application-Level Security Safeguards

Several trusted data encryption options are supported in PHP's predefined function set. PHP is also compatible with many third-party applications, allowing for easy-integration with secure ecommerce technologies. Another advantage is that the PHP source code is not viewable through the browser because the script is completely parsed before it is sent back to the requesting user. This benefit of PHP's server-side architecture prevents the loss of creative scripts to users at least knowledgeable enough to execute a 'View Source'.

Security is such an important issue that this book contains an entire chapter on the subject. Please read Chapter 16, "Security," for a thorough accounting of PHP's security features.

Flexibility

Because PHP is an embedded language, it is extremely flexible towards meeting the needs of the developer. Although PHP is generally touted as being used in conjunction solely with HTML, it can also be integrated alongside languages like JavaScript, WML, XML, and many others. Additionally, as with most other mainstream languages, wisely planned PHP applications can be easily expanded as needed.

Browser dependency is not an issue because PHP scripts are compiled entirely on the server side before being sent to the user. In fact, PHP scripts can be sent to just about any kind of device containing a browser, including cell phones, personal digital assistant (PDA) devices, pagers, laptops, not to mention the traditional PC. People who want to develop shell-based applications can also execute PHP from the command line.

Since PHP contains no server-specific code, users are not limited to a specific and perhaps unfamiliar Web server. Apache, Microsoft IIs, Netscape Enterprise Server, Stronghold, and Zeus are all fair game for PHP's server integration. Because of the various platforms that these servers operate on, PHP is largely platform independent, available for such platforms as UNIX, Solaris, FreeBSD, and Windows 95/98/NT.

Finally, PHP offers access to external components, such as Enterprise Java Beans and Win32 COM objects. These newly added features put PHP in the big league, truly enabling developers to scale PHP projects upward and outward as need be.

Free

The open source development strategy has gained considerable notoriety in the software industry. The prospect of releasing source code to the masses has resulted in undeniably positive outcomes for many projects, perhaps most notably Linux, although the success of the Apache project has certainly been a major contributor in proving the validity of the open source ideal. The same holds true for the developmental history of PHP, as users worldwide have been a huge factor in the advancement of the PHP project.

PHP's embracing of this open source strategy result in great performance gains for users, and the code is available free of charge. Additionally, an extremely receptive user community numbering in the thousands acts as "customer support," providing answers to even the most arcane questions in popular online discussion groups.

The next section, "User Affirmations," provides testimonies from three noted industry professionals. Each provides keen insight into why they find PHP such an appealing technology.

User Affirmations

"We have for a long time had a personal contact to some of the PHP developers and exchanged a lot of emails with them in the past. When the PHP developers have had any problems with MySQL related issues we have always been ready to help them solve them. We have also on some occasions added new features into MySQL just to get the PHP integration better. The result of this work is that MySQL works extremely well with PHP and we will ensure that it keeps that way!"

Michael "Monty" Widenius, MySQL Developer
http://www.mysql.com

"FAST used PHP to implement mp3.lycos.com for a number of reasons. The most important was time to market; PHP really lets you speed up the development. Another reason was speed, we went from 0 to 1.4 million page impressions in one day, and PHP coped just fine with this. The third reason was of course that I knew that if I found bugs in PHP during this "'stress test",' I could fix them myself since PHP is open source."

Stig Bakken, FAST Search & Transfer ASA
http://www.fast.no

"I've used PHP from the early days when it was PHP/FI 1.x. I loved having the ability to process forms and customize my pages on the fly with such an easy-to-use language. As my company's needs have evolved, so has PHP.

Today, PHP is extremely feature rich. We rely on it for just about every custom web site we develop, including 32bit.com and DevShed.com. We even use it at InfoWest to manage our customer service, account management and port monitoring.

PHP's evolution and acceptance is a textbook example of a successful open source project. Open-mindedness, community contribution, and a well-managed code-base have helped build PHP into a success few commercial entities have been able to emulate. I look forward to the future of PHP. I encourage any budding web developer to give PHP a spin. Like me, you may never want to give it up."

Randy Cosby
President, nGenuity, Inc.
DevShed (http://www.devshed.com)

An Introductory Example

Consider the example shown in Listing 1-1, which illustrates just how easily PHP can be integrated alongside HTML:

Listing 1-1: Dynamic PHP page creation
```
<?
// Set a few variables
$site_title = "PHP Recipes";
$bg_color = "white";
$user_name = "Chef Luigi";
?>


<html>
<head>
<title><? print $site_title; ?></title>
</head>
<body bgcolor="<? print $bg_color; ?>" >
<?
// Display an intro. message with date and user name.
print "
PHP Recipes | ".date("F d, Y")." <br>
Greetings, $user_name! <br>
";
?>
</body>
</html>
```

Figure 1-1 shows how the script appears when it is executed in the browser.

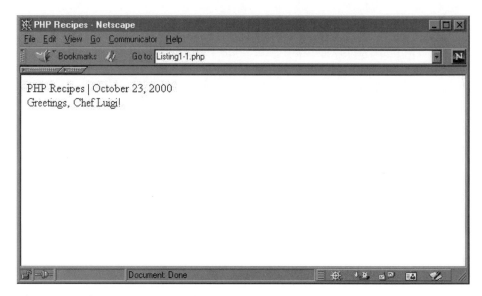

Figure 1-1. The script is executed in the browser.

Not too shabby, huh? I'm sure many a reader's mind is already churning with possibilities. However, before delving further into scripting issues, chances are you may need to install and configure PHP on your machine. This is the subject of the next few sections.

Downloading PHP/Apache

Before you proceed, I recommend that you take some time to download, install, and configure PHP and a Web server on your machine. Although PHP is compatible with a wide variety of Web servers, I'll assume that you will be using Apache, partly because it is currently the Web's most popular Web server and partly because it is the one most widely used with PHP. Regardless, the general installation process will not differ widely between Web servers.

You can download the PHP distribution from the official PHP site or from one of its many worldwide mirror sites. Go to `http://www.php.net` for the most recently updated mirror list. From here, you can download PHP in one of two formats:

- WIN32 Binary

- Source code

The Win32 binary is for Windows 95/98/NT/2000 users. While it is also possible to compile the source code on the Windows platform, for the large majority of users this won't be necessary. However, if you insist on doing so (incidentally, a process that is not discussed within this book), you'll need a recent Visual C++ compiler for doing so. Check out http://www.php.net/version4/win32build.php for more information on this process. The Win32 binary installation process is detailed later in this chapter.

For non-Windows users, you'll need to build the source code. While many beginners may shudder at this thought, it is actually a rather simple process, as you'll soon learn. For those of you interested to know whether or not PHP is offered in RPM (RedHat Package Manager) distribution format; it is, although these RPMs are not available via the official PHP site. Check the discussion groups (some of which are listed at the end of this chapter) for more information regarding distribution locations and instructions. The generalized build process is detailed later in this chapter.

Proceed to http://www.php.net and download the distribution that best suits your needs. Download times will vary with your connection type and speed. Additionally, the documentation is available for download. I strongly recommend downloading the most recent version.

> **TIP**   *PHP 4.0.3 was the current stable version at the time of printing of this book. Of course, this version number is due to change along with the continued development of the PHP package. I recommend always downloading the most recent stable version of the product.*

If you haven't yet installed the Apache server, you will want to download the latest stable version of that as well. These packages are at http://www.apache.org/dist/binaries/, which contains directories for a plethora of operating systems. Download the one that is specific to your needs. Providing instructions regarding PHP configuration specifics for every available platform and Web server is out of the scope of this book. Therefore, I will concentrate on the Apache server. Regardless of the Web server you intend to use, I strongly recommend reading through the configuration sections later in this chapter to gain some insight into the generalized configuration issues that you may encounter.

Installation of new software can sometimes prove to be a daunting process for newcomers. However, the PHP developers have taken extra steps to make PHP installation relatively easy. The following sections highlight the steps you should take to install and configure PHP on both the non-Windows and the Win32 platforms.

> **NOTE**   *In later chapters I'll introduce the MySQL database server, using this popular product as the basis for illustrating Web/database integration. In order to experiment with these examples, you'll need to install the MySQL package, available at* http://www.mysql.com. *Like PHP, MySQL is available for both non-Windows and Windows platforms. Although I defer to the MySQL documentation due to its thorough installation instructions, you may be interested in taking a moment to read through the initial pages of Chapter 11, "Databases," for an introduction of the MySQL database server.*

Installation and Configuration

At this point, I'll assume that you have successfully downloaded PHP and Apache. The next step is deciding how you would like to install the distribution. For non-Windows machines, there three different ways to do so: CGI binary, static Apache module, and the dynamic Apache module. As a non-Windows user, chances are you will not want to build PHP as a CGI binary. Furthermore, there are several advantages to building PHP as a server module, therefore I'll concentrate solely on building PHP both as a static and a dynamic module. As it relates to installation, the main difference between the two is that any subsequent changes to the PHP static module will require the recompilation of both Apache and PHP, while changes to the PHP dynamic module only require the subsequent recompilation of just PHP and not the server.

For Windows machines, PHP can be installed as either a CGI binary or as a static Apache module. In this case, I'll concentrate upon the CGI binary, since a Windows-user might be more prone to use a Web server other than Apache, like Microsoft's Internet Information Server or Microsoft's Personal Web Server. The CGI version can easily be integrated into these servers. Although I illustrate the PHP/Apache Windows installation process, this process is very similar to that which would be used for the above-mentioned Web servers as well.

> **NOTE**   *Recall that PHP4 comes with support for a wide variety of Web servers, including AOL Server, Netscape Enterprise Server, Microsoft IIs, Zeus, and more. However, I will keep the installation process limited to that relating to Apache. For detailed instructions regarding how to install PHP with these other servers, check out the PHP documentation at* http://www.php.net.

Non-Windows

Regardless of the installation variation you choose, you'll need to begin by decompressing the distributions. This is accomplished in two easy steps:

1. Unzip the packages. Once done, you'll see that the files will be left with *.tar extensions:

    ```
    gunzip apache_1.3.9.tar.gz
    gunzip php-4.0.0.tar.gz
    ```

2. Untar the packages. This will unarchive the distributions:

    ```
    tar -zxvf apache_1.3.x.tar
    tar -zxvf php-4.0.x.tar
    ```

    The installation procedure will pick up from this point.

Apache Module

Installing PHP as an Apache module is rather simple. I'll take you through each step here:

1. Change location to the Apache directory:

```
cd apache_1.3.x
```

2. Configure Apache. You can use any path you like. Keep in mind that a slash does *not* follow the pathname:

```
./configure –prefix=[path]
```

3. Change the location to the PHP directory and configure, build, and install the distribution. The option with-config-file-path specifies the directory that will contain PHP's configuration file. Generally, this path is set to be /usr/local/lib, but you can set it to be anything you wish:

```
./configure –with-apache=../apache_1.3.x –with-config-file-path=[config-path]
make
make install
```

4. Change back to the Apache directory. Now you will reconfigure, build, and install Apache. The other-configuration-options option refers to any special configuration options that you would like to pass along to the Apache Web server. This is beyond the scope of this book. I suggest checking out the Apache documentation for a complete explanation of these options:

```
./configure –activate-module=src/modules/php4/libphp4.a
–other-configuration-options
make
make install
```

5. The final step involves modifying Apache's httpd.conf file. Some of these modifications relate specifically to Apache, while others are necessary to ensure that PHP scripts can be recognized and sent to the Web server. First, locate the line that reads:

```
ServerName new.host.name
```

Change this line to read:

```
ServerName localhost
```

Next, locate the following two lines:

```
#AddType application/x-httpd-php .php .php4
#AddType application/x-httpd-php-source .phps
```

These lines need to be uncommented in order for PHP-enabled files to work correctly on the server. To uncomment these lines, simply remove the pound symbol (#) from the beginning of each line. Save the file and move up one directory. Start the Apache server using the following command:

```
./bin/apachectl start
```

Voilà! PHP and Apache are now ready for use. For testing purposes, insert the following code into a file and save the file as phpinfo.php to the Apache's document root directory. This is the directory called htdocs, located in the Apache installation directory.

```
<?
    php_info();
?>
```

Open this file up in a browser on the server. You should see a lengthy list of information regarding PHP's configuration. Congratulations, you've successfully installed PHP as an Apache Module.

Dynamic Apache Module

The Dynamic Module is useful because it allows you to upgrade your PHP distribution without having to recompile the Web server as well. Apache considers it just another one of its many modules, like ModuleRewrite or ModuleSpelling. This idea becomes particularly useful when you want to add some kind of support to PHP later, encryption, for example. All you have to do is reconfigure/compile PHP in accordance with the encryption support, and you can immediately begin using it in your Web applications. Here is the installation process:

1. Change location to the Apache directory:

    ```
    cd apache_1.3.x
    ```

2. Configure Apache. You can use any path you like. Keep in mind that a slash does *not* follow the pathname. The –other-configuration-options option refers to any special configuration options that you would like to pass along to the Apache Web server. This is beyond the scope of this book. I suggest checking out the Apache documentation for a complete explanation of these options:

    ```
    ./configure –prefix=[path] –enable-module=so –other-configuration-options
    ```

3. Build the Apache server. After typing **make**, you will see a bunch of messages scroll by. This is normal.

    ```
    make
    ```

4. Install the Apache server. After you type **make install**, another bunch of messages will scroll by. Again, this is normal. Once this has finished, you'll see a message stating that you have successfully installed the server.

    ```
    make install
    ```

5. Assuming no errors occurred, you're ready to modify Apache's "httpd.con" file. This file is located in the conf directory in the path that

you designated in step 4. Open this file in your favorite text editor. Locate the following line:

```
ServerName new.host.name
```

Modify this line to read:

```
ServerName localhost
```

6. Change location to the directory in which you downloaded PHP. Then, configure, make, and install PHP. You will need to specify the path directory pointing to the apxs file. This file can be found in the bin directory of the path you designated in step 4.

```
./configure –with-apxs=[path/to/apxs]
make
make install
```

7. Reopen Apache's httpd.conf file for another modification. In order for incoming requests for PHP-enabled files to be properly parsed, the file extension must coincide with the one as specified in the Apache server's configuration file, httpd.conf. This file contains a number of options, which can be modified at the administrator's discretion; a few of these options relate directly to PHP. Open the httpd.conf file in your favorite text editor. Towards the end of the file are two lines similar to the following:

```
#AddType application/x-httpd-php .php .php4
#AddType application/x-httpd-php-source .phps
```

8. You must uncomment these in order for PHP-enabled files to work correctly on the server. To uncomment these lines, simply remove the pound symbol (#) from the beginning of each line.

9. Save the file and move up one directory (to cd). Start the Apache server using the following command:

```
./bin/apachectl start
```

Voilà! PHP and Apache are now ready for use.

For testing purposes, insert the following code into a file and save the file as phpinfo.php to the Apache's document root directory. This is the directory called htdocs, located in the Apache installation directory.

```
<?
    php_info();
?>
```

Open this file up in a browser on the server. You should see a lengthy list of information regarding PHP's configuration. Congratulations, you've successfully installed the Dynamic Apache Module.

Installation on Windows 95/98/NT

If you have installed an application on the Windows operating system, you have probably found it to be very easy. Click a few buttons, agree to a few statements, and the application is installed. And so is the case with the installation of Apache and PHP on a Windows machine.

1. Double-click the Apache executable to begin the installation. You will be greeted with an installation wizard. Read attentively and accept the licensing agreement.

2. The wizard will suggest a default installation directory (C:\Program Files\Apache Group\Apache). This is fine, but you may want to shorten it to just C:\Apache\. However, it's up to you.

3. You will then be prompted for what name you would like to have appear in the Start menu. Enter whatever you want, or accept the default.

4. Next you will be prompted for the installation type. Just pick Typical. After you make your choice, the installation process is carried out.

5. Now it is time to modify the "httpd.conf" file, located in the conf directory, which is located in whatever directory you chose to install the Apache server in step 2. Open this file using your favorite text editor. You'll probably want to make at least three basic modifications:

Replace yourname@yoursite.com with the correct information.

`ServerAdmin yourname@yoursite.com`

Uncomment this line and place the correct server name. Just use local-host if you do not have an actual server name:

`ServerName localhost`

6. Attempt to start Apache to ensure that everything is working. At this point you need to make the differentiation as to the type of Windows OS you are using:

   If you're using Windows NT, choose "Install Apache as Service (NT Only)" from the Start menu. Then go to the Control Panel, open up the Services window, choose Apache, and click the "Start" button. Apache will start, and it will start automatically at every subsequent boot of the machine.

   If you're not using Windows NT, choose "Start Apache" from the Start menu. A small window will open. This window must be kept open in order for the server to run.

7. Finally, go to a browser installed on the server and enter **http://localhost/**. You should see a default page stating that the installation has been carried out correctly.

8. Now it's time to install PHP. Change the directory to wherever you down-loaded the PHP package. Extract it to the directory of your choice using an unzipping application.

9. Go to that directory and look for a file entitled "php.ini-dist". Rename this file to php.ini and place it in the C:\Windows\ directory.

10. Go back to the PHP directory. Look for two more files, php4ts.dll and Mscvrt.dll. Place these files in the C:\Windows\System\ directory. You probably already have the Mscvrt.dll file, and you will be prompted to overwrite it. Don't overwrite the file or copy it.

11. Return to the Apache http.conf file, again opening it up in a text editor. There are a few more modifications that you need to make:

Look for this line:

```
ScriptAlias /cgi-bin/ "C:/Apache/cgi-bin/"
```

Directly below this line, add the following:

```
ScriptAlias /php4/ "C:/php4/"
```

Then search for "AddType". You will see the following two commented lines:

```
#AddType application/x-httpd-php3 .phtml
#AddType application/x-httpd-php3-source .phps
```

Directly below these lines, add the following:

```
AddType application/x-httpd-php .phtml .php
AddType application/x-httpd-php-source .phps
```

Keep scrolling down. You will find the following commented lines:

```
#
# Action lets you define media types that will execute a script whenever
# a matching file is called. This eliminates the need for repeated URL
# pathnames for oft-used CGI file processors.
# Format: Action media/type /cgi-script/location
# Format: Action handler-name /cgi-script/location
#
```

Below this, add the following:

```
Action application/x-httpd-php /php4/php.exe
```

12. Voilà! PHP and Apache are now ready for use.

For testing purposes, insert the following code into a file and save the file as "phpinfo.php" to the Apache's document root directory. This is the directory called htdocs located in whatever directory you specified in step 4.

```
<?
    php_info();
?>
```

> **CAUTION** *Although successfully completing the steps outlined above does make it possible for the Web server/PHP configuration to be used for testing purposes, it does not imply that your Web server is accessible via the World Wide Web. Check out the official Apache site (http://www.apache.org) for information regarding this matter. Furthermore, although the preceding steps suffice to get the PHP package up and running, you will probably be interested in modifying PHP's configuration to best suit your needs. See "PHP Configuration," later in this chapter, for details.*

Open this file in a browser on the server. You should see a lengthy list of information regarding PHP's configuration.

PHP Configuration

Although PHP will correctly run given its default configuration setting, you can make quite a few modifications to fine-tune the installation to your needs. The php.ini file, copied by default into the /usr/local/lib/ directory during the installation process, contains all of these configuration settings.

Regardless of the platform and Web server used in conjunction with PHP, the php.ini file will contain the same default set of parameters, from which several

> **NOTE** *The configuration file is entitled php3.ini in the 3.0 version but has been changed to php.ini in the 4.0 version.*

important characteristics of the PHP installation can be administered. This file contains all of the characteristics relevant to how your installation will act when PHP scripts are executed. The PHP engine reads the php.ini file when PHP starts up.

General Configuration Directives

Reiterating all of the configuration directives is beyond the scope of this book, but there are several directives worth mentioning, as most the developers may find them particularly useful. I'll mention other directives as appropriate in subsequent chapters.

short_open_tag [on | off]

The short_open_tag [on | off] configuration directive determines the use of the short PHP escape tags <?...?>, in addition to the default tags.

asp_tags [on | off]

The asp_tags [on | off] configuration directive determines the use of ASP style tags in addition to the default tags. ASP style tags are those that enclose PHP code as follows:

```
<%
print "This is PHP code.";
%>
```

precision [integer]

The precision [integer] configuration directive sets the number of significant digits displayed in floating point numbers.

safe_mode [on | off]

Turning on safe mode is a particularly good idea if you have several users on your system. Essentially, turning on safe mode eliminates the possibility that a user can use a PHP script to gain access to another file on the system, for example, the passwd file on a Linux machine. Safe_mode works solely on the CGI version of PHP. Check out Chapter 16 for more details regarding this matter.

max_execution_time [integer]

The max_execution_time [integer] configuration directive determines the maximum number of seconds that a given PHP script may execute. This prevents runaway scripts from eating up valuable system resources.

error_reporting [1-8]

The error_reporting [1-8] configuration directive gauges to what degree errors will be reported, if any. The higher the bit value, the more sensitive PHP will be to reporting errors:

BIT VALUE	REPORTING SENSITIVITY
1	normal errors
2	normal warnings
4	parser errors
8	notices

display_errors [on | off]

The display_errors [on | off] configuration directive display the errors in the browser.

log_errors

The log_errors configuration directive determines whether or not errors are logged to a file. If log_errors is turned on, the directive error_log designates which file the errors are logged to.

error_log [filename]

If log_errors is turned on, error_log designates the filename to which all errors should be logged.

magic_quotes_gpc

When magic_quotes_gpc is activated, all special characters contained in user or database data will automatically be escaped with the necessary backslash. By the way, "gpc" stands for "get/post/cookie".

Personally, I find it more efficient to keep magic_quotes_gpc turned off and to escape the special characters explicitly. Regardless of the way you ultimately decide to do it, there can be no compromise or your data may be corrupted. If magic_quotes_gpc is "on", then never physically escape special characters with a backslash; otherwise, make it a habit to always do so.

track_vars

The track_vars configuration directive enables the recording of several important session variable arrays, including $HTTP_GET_VARS[], $HTTP_POST_VARS[], $HTTP_POST_FILES, $HTTP_COOKIE_VARS[], $HTTP_ENV_VARS[], and $HTTP_SERVER_VARS[]. These arrays are discussed in further detail in Chapter 13, "Cookies and Session Tracking."

It is important to note that there are many more configuration directives than the ones listed here, although those listed are likely to be the ones that most users will find useful. Many of these directives will be addressed in their respective later chapters.

Basic PHP Constructs

Now I'll introduce several preliminary concepts related to PHP before delving into the core topics of the language that make up the rest of this book.

Escaping to PHP

The PHP parsing engine needs a way to differentiate PHP code from other elements in the page. The mechanism for doing so is known as '*escaping to PHP.*' There are four ways to do this:

- Default tags

- Short tags

- Script tags

- ASP-style tags

Default Tags

The default tags are perhaps those most commonly used by PHP programmers, due to clarity and convenience of use:

```
<?php print "Welcome to the world of PHP!"; ?>
```

These tags may also be the most practical ones because the initial escape characters are followed by php, which explicitly makes reference to the type of code that follows. This can be useful because you may be simultaneously using several technologies in the same page, such as JavaScript, server-side includes, and PHP. Any ensuing PHP code will then follow the initial escape sequence, preceded by the closing escape sequence, "?>".

Short Tags

The short tag style is the shortest available for escaping to PHP code:

```
<? print "Welcome to the world of PHP!"; ?>
```

Short tags must be enabled in order for them to work. There are two ways to do this:

- Include the –enable-short-tags option when compiling PHP.

- Enable the short_open_tag configuration directive found within the php.ini file.

Script Tags

Several text editors will mistakenly interpret PHP code as HTML (that is, viewable) code, interfering with the Web page development process. To eliminate this problem, use the following escape tags:

```
<script language="php">
print "Welcome to the world of PHP!";
</script>
```

ASP-Style Tags

A fourth and final way to embed PHP code is through the use of ASP (Active Server Page)-style tags. This way is much like the short tag way just described, except that a percentage sign (%) is used instead of a question mark.

```
<% print "Welcome to the world of PHP!"; %>
```

A variation of the ASP-style tag that can result in a lesser degree of code clutter is available. This variation eliminates the need to include a 'print' statement in the enclosed PHP code. The equals sign (=) immediately following the opening ASP tag signals the PHP parser to output the value of the variable:

```
<%= $variable %>
```

Making use of this convenient tag style, we could execute the following:

```
<%
// set variable $recipe to something…
$recipe = "Lasagna";
%>
Luigi's favorite recipe is <%=$recipe;%>
```

There are actually two separate PHP scripts in this listing. The first assigns the value "Lasagna" to the variable $recipe. Later on, when it is necessary to display the value of the variable $recipe, you can use the ASP-style variation for this sole purpose. Incidentally, you could also use short tags (<?...?>) in much the same way.

Embedding HTML in PHP Code

Perhaps the most powerful characteristic of PHP is its ability to both output and be written directly alongside other languages, HTML and JavaScript, for example. Listing 1-2 illustrates this concept.

Listing 1-2: Display of HTML using PHP code
```
<html>
<head>
<title>Basic PHP/HTML integration</title>
</head>
<body>
<?
```

Figure 1-2. A simple PHP function, date(), formats the date for display in the browser title bar.

```
// Notice how HTML tags are included in the print statement.
print "<h3>PHP/HTML integration is cool.</h3>";
?>
</body>
</html>
```

Listing 1-2 illustrates how PHP can incorporate HTML code directly in print statements. Notice how level-three header (<h3>…</h3>) tags can be placed right inside the PHP code. These tags will appear in the final document as if they were regular HTML output.

Listing 1-3 illustrates how PHP can dynamically insert information into a Web page. The current date will be inserted into the title, as shown in Figure 1-2.

Listing 1-3: Dynamic date insertion
```
<title>PHP Recipes | <? print (date("F d, Y")); ?></title>
```

The simple PHP function date() can format the current date in several different ways. This formatted date value can then be output into the title.

PHP is also capable of modifying the format of the HTML itself through the designation and subsequent insertion of tag characteristics in the file. Listing 1-4 shows how this is possible, assigning a font characteristic (h3) to a variable ($big_font) and later inserting it as needed in the display text.

Listing 1-4: Dynamic HTML tags
```
<html>
<head>
<title>PHP Recipes | <? print (date("F d, Y")); ?></title>
```

```
</head>
<?
$big_font = "h3";
?>
<body>
<? print "<$big_font>PHP Recipes</$big_font>"; ?>
</body>
</html>
```

Listing 1-4 is a variation of Listing 1-3, this time first assigning level-three header (<h3>...</h3>) tags to a variable and then later using this variable in a print statement. These tags will appear in the final document as if they were regular HTML output.

Multiple-PHP Script Embedding

To allow for flexibility when building dynamic Web applications, you can embed several separate PHP scripts throughout a page. Listing 1-5 illustrates this.

Listing 1-5: Embedding multiple PHP scripts in a single document
```
<html>
<head>
<title>
<?
    print "Another PHP-enabled page";
    $variable = "Hello World!";
?>
</title></head>
<body>
<? print $variable; ?>
</body>
</html>
```

Listing 1-5 begins as a typical (albeit simple) HTML page would. The flexibility offered by this feature is that variables can be assigned in one code section and still used later on in another code section on the same page.

Commenting PHP Code

You should sufficiently comment the code even for relatively short and uncomplicated scripts. There are two commenting formats in PHP:

- *Single-line comments* are generally used for short explanations or notes relevant to the local code.

- *Multiline comments* are generally used to provide pseudocode algorithms and more detailed explanations when necessary.

Both methods ultimately result in the same outcome and have no bearing on the overall performance of the script. Which to use is left up to you.

Single-Line Comments

Two commenting styles are geared toward single-line comments. Both work exactly the same way, but they employ different escape characters. One style uses a double backslash (//) at the beginning of a comment, and the other style uses a pound symbol (#) at the beginning of a comment. Here are examples of each style:

```
<?
// set the color of the roses.
$rose_color = "red";

# set the color of the violets.
$violet_color = "blue";
print "Roses are $rose_color, violets are $violet_color";
?>
```

Of course, it is possible to use single-line comments to build multiline comments using either style, as seen in the following listing:

```
<?
// file: example.php
// author: WJ Gilmore
// date: August 24, 2000

print "An example with comments";
?>
```

Multiline Comments

PHP provides a mechanism for detailed comments that may take up more than one line. This type of comment is enclosed in C-style comments, denoted with an opening '/*' and '*/'.

```
<?
/*
    script: multi_comment_example.php
    purpose: Multiline comment example
    author: wj gilmore
    date: June 14, 2000
*/

print "A multiline comment can be found at the top of this script!";
?>
```

As you can see, multiline comments are useful when you need to provide a relatively lengthy summary of a script or a part of one.

What's Next?

This chapter brought you up to speed regarding several key aspects of PHP, namely:

- PHP's history and features

- Installation and configuration

- "Escaping" to PHP

- Commenting PHP code

These topics serve as the introduction to subsequent chapters, where you will learn more about the developmental issues regarding the PHP language. At the conclusion of the next chapter, you will know enough about PHP to begin writing your own programs. You will apply this knowledge by developing an events calendar that can be easily inserted into an existing Web page. This project will serve as the precursor for further development of the PHP Recipes Web application.

CHAPTER 2

Variables and Data Types

Data types form the backbone of any programming language, providing the programmer with a means by which to represent various types of information. PHP provides support for six general data types:

- Integers

- Floating-point numbers

- Strings

- Arrays

- Objects

- Booleans

One of the pillars of any programming language is its support for numbers. PHP supports both integers and real (double) numbers. Each of these number formats is described in further detail later.

Integer Values

An *integer* is nothing more than a whole number. Integers are represented as a series of one or more digits. Some examples of integers are:

5
591
52

Octals and Hexadecimals

Integers in octal (base 8) and hexadecimal (base 16) formats are supported. Octal values begin with the digit 0, followed by a sequence of digits, each ranging from 0 to 7. Some examples of octal integers are:

```
0422
0534
```

Hexadecimal integers can consist of the digits 0 through 9 or the letters a (A) through f (F). All hexadecimal integers are preceded by 0x or 0X. Some examples of hexadecimal integers are:

```
0x3FF
0X22abc
```

Floating-Point Numbers

A *floating-point number* is essentially a real numbers, that is, a number denoted either wholly or in part by a fraction. Floating-point numbers are useful for representing values that call for a more accurate representation, such as temperature or monetary figures. PHP supports two floating-point formats: standard notation and scientific notation.

Standard Notation

Standard notation is a convenient representation typically used for real numbers, for example, monetary values. Some examples are:

```
12.45
98.6
```

Scientific Notation

Scientific notation is a more convenient representation for very large and very small numbers, such as interplanetary distances or atomic measurements. Some examples include:

```
3e8
5.9736e24
```

String Values

A *string* is a group of characters that are represented as a single entity but can also be examined on a character-by-character basis. Some examples of strings are:

```
thesaurus
49ers
abc
&%/$£
```

Note that PHP doesn't include support for the char data type. Rather, the string data type can be considered the all-encompassing type that represents both single and multiple character sets.

String Assignments

Strings can be delimited in two ways, using either double quotation marks ("") or single quotation marks (''). There are two fundamental differences between the two methods. First, variables in a double-quoted string will be replaced with their respective values, whereas the single-quoted strings will be interpreted exactly as is, even if variables are enclosed in the string.

The following two string declarations produce the same result:

```
$food = "meatloaf";
$food = 'meatloaf';
```

However, the following two declarations result in two drastically different outcomes:

```
$sentence = "My favorite food is $food";
$sentence2 = 'My favorite food is $food';
```

The following string is what exactly will be assigned to $sentence. Notice how the variable $food is automatically interpreted:

```
My favorite food is meatloaf.
```

Whereas $sentence2 will be assigned the string as follows:

```
My favorite food is $food.
```

In contrast with $sentence, the uninterpreted variable $food will appear in the string assigned to $sentence2. These differing outcomes are due to the usage of double and single quotation marks in assigning the corresponding strings to $sentence and $sentence2.

Before discussing the second fundamental difference between double-quoted and single-quoted strings, an introduction of PHP's supported string delimiters is in order. As with most other mainstream languages, a set of delimiters is used to represent special characters, such as the tab or newline characters. Table 2-1 lists the supported delimiters:

Table 2-1. Supported String Delimiters

CHARACTER	SEQUENCE	REPRESENTATION
	\n	Newline
	\r	Carriage return
	\t	Horizontal tab
	\\	Backslash
	\$	Dollar sign
	\"	Double-quotation mark
	\[0-7]{1,3}	Octal notation regular expression pattern
	\x[0-9A-Fa-f]{1,2}	Hexadecimal notation regular expression pattern

With this in mind, the second fundamental difference is that while a double-quoted string recognizes all available delimiters, a single-quoted string recognizes only the delimiters "\\" and "\". Consider an example of the contrasting outcomes when assigning strings enclosed in double and single quotation marks:

```
$double_list = "item1\nitem2\nitem3";
$single_list = 'item1\nitem2\nitem3';
```

If you print both strings to the browser, the double-quoted string will conceal the newline character, but the single-quoted string will print it just as if it were any other character. Although many of the delimited characters will be irrelevant in the browser, this will prove to be a major factor when formatting for various other media. Keep this difference in mind when using double- or single-quoted enclosures so as to ensure the intended outcome.

Here Doc Syntax

A second method with which to delimit strings, introduced in PHP4, is known as *Here doc syntax*. This syntax consists of beginning a string with <<< followed immediately by some identifier of your choice, then the string in which you would like to assign the variable, and finally a second occurrence of the same chosen identifier. Consider this example:

```
$paragraph = <<<DELIM
This is a string that
Will be interpreted exactly
As it is written in the
variable assignment.
DELIM;
```

Be sure to choose an identifier that will not appear in the string being assigned. Furthermore, the first character of the closing identifier *must* appear in the first column of the line following the string.

Character Handling

Strings can be accessed on a character-by-character basis, much like a sequentially indexed array. (Arrays are discussed in the next section.) An example follows:

```
$sequence_number = "04efgh";
$letter = $sequence_number[4];
```

The variable $letter will hold the value g. As you will learn in the next section, PHP begins array position counts from 0. To illustrate this further, consider the fact that $sequence_number[1] would hold the value 4.

Arrays

An *array* is a list of elements each having the same type. There are two types of arrays: those that are accessed in accordance with the index position in which the element resides, and those that are associative in nature, accessed by a key value that bears some sort of association with its corresponding value. In practice, however, both are manipulated in much the same way. Arrays can also be single-dimensional or multidimensional in size.

Single-Dimension Indexed Arrays

Single-dimension indexed arrays are handled using an integer subscript to denote the position of the requested value.

The general syntax of a single-dimension array is:

```
$name[index1];
```

A single-dimension array can be created as follows:

```
$meat[0] = "chicken";
$meat[1] = "steak";
$meat[2] = "turkey";
```

If you execute this command:

```
print $meat[1];
```

The following will be output to the browser:

```
steak
```

Alternatively, arrays may be created using PHP's array() function. You can use this function to create the same $meat array as the one in the preceding example:

```
$meat = array("chicken", "steak", "turkey");
```

Executing the same print command yields the same results as in the previous example, again producing "steak".

You can also assign values to the end of the array simply by assigning values to an array variable using empty brackets. Therefore, another way to assign values to the $meat array is as follows:

```
$meat[] = "chicken";
$meat[] = "steak";
$meat[] = "turkey";
```

Single-Dimension Associative Arrays

Associative arrays are particularly convenient when it makes more sense to map an array using words rather than integers.

For example, assume that you wanted to keep track of all of the best food and wine pairings. It would be most convenient if you could simply assign the arrays using key-value pairings, for example, wine to dish. Use of an associative array to store this information would be the wise choice:

```
$pairings["zinfandel"] = "Broiled Veal Chops";
$pairings["merlot"] = "Baked Ham";
$pairings["sauvignon"] = "Prime Rib";
$pairings["sauternes"] = "Roasted Salmon";
```

Use of this associative array would greatly reduce the time and code required to display a particular value. Assume that you wanted to inform a reader of the best accompanying dish with merlot. A simple call to the pairings array would produce the necessary output:

```
print $pairings["merlot"];                // outputs the value "Baked Ham"
```

An alternative method in which to create an array is via PHP's array() function:

```
$pairings = array(
                    zinfandel => "Broiled Veal Chops",
                    merlot => "Baked Ham",
                    sauvignon => "Prime Rib",
                    sauternes => "Roasted Salmon";
```

This assignment method bears no difference in functionality from the previous $pairings array, other than the format in which it was created.

Multidimensional Indexed Arrays

Multidimensional indexed arrays function much like their single-dimension counterparts, except that more than one index array is used to specify an element. There is no limit as to the dimension size, although it is unlikely that anything beyond three dimensions would be used in most applications.

The general syntax of a multidimensional array is:

```
$name[index1] [index2]..[indexN];
```

An element of a two-dimensional indexed array could be referenced as follows:

```
$position = $chess_board[5][4];
```

Multidimensional Associative Arrays

Multidimensional associative arrays are also possible (and quite useful) in PHP. Assume you wanted to keep track of wine-food pairings, not only by wine type, but also by producer. You could do something similar to the following:

```
$pairings["Martinelli"] ["zinfandel"] = "Broiled Veal Chops";
$pairings["Beringer"] ["merlot"] = "Baked Ham";
$pairings["Jarvis"] ["sauvignon"] = "Prime Rib";
$pairings["Climens"] ["sauternes"] = "Roasted Salmon";
```

Mixing Indexed and Associative Array Indexes

It is also possible to mix indexed and associative arrays indexes. Expanding on the single-dimension associative array example, suppose you wanted to keep track of the first and second string players of the Ohio State Buckeyes football team. You could do something similar to the following:

```
$Buckeyes["quarterback"] [1] = "Bellisari";
$Buckeyes["quarterback"] [2] = "Moherman";
$Buckeyes["quarterback"] [3] = "Wiley";
```

PHP provides a vast assortment of functions for creating and manipulating arrays, so much so that the subject merits an entire chapter. Read Chapter 5, "Arrays," for a complete discussion of how PHP arrays are handled.

Objects

The fifth PHP data type is the object. You can think of an *object* as a variable that is instantiated from a kind of template otherwise known as a *class*. The concept of objects and classes is integral to the notion of object-oriented programming (OOP).

Contrary to the other data types contained in the PHP language, an object must be explicitly declared. It is important to realize that an object is nothing more than a particular instance of a class, which acts as a template for creating objects having specific characteristics and functionality. Therefore, a class must be defined before an object can be declared. A general example of class declaration and subsequent object instantiation follows:

```
class appliance {
            var power;
            function set_power($on_off) {
                            $this->power = $on_off;
            }
}
. . .
$blender = new appliance;
```

A class definition creates several characteristics and functions pertinent to a data structure, in this case a data structure named appliance. So far, the appliance isn't very functional. There is only one characteristic: power. This characteristic can be modified by using the method set_power.

Remember, however, that a class definition is a template and cannot itself be manipulated. Instead, objects are created based on this template. This is accomplished via the new keyword. Therefore, in the preceding listing an object of class appliance named blender is created.

The blender power can then be set by making use of the method set_power:

```
$blender->set_power("on");
```

Object-oriented programming is such an important strategy in today's application development standards that its use with PHP merits its own chapter. Chapter 6, "Object-Oriented PHP," introduces PHP's OOP implementation in further detail.

Boolean, or True/False, Values

The boolean data type is essentially capable of representing only two data types: true and false. Boolean values can be determined in two ways: as a comparison evaluation or from a variable value. Both are rather straightforward.

Comparisons can take place in many forms. Evaluation typically takes place by use of a double equal sign and an if conditional. Here is an example:

```
 if ($sum == 40) :
. . .
```

This could evaluate to only either true or false. Either $sum equals 40, or it does not. If $sum does equal 40, then the expression evaluates to true. Otherwise, the result is false.

Boolean values can also be determined via explicitly setting a variable to a true or false value. Here is an example:

```
$flag = TRUE;
 if ($flag == TRUE) :
   print "The flag is true!";
else :
   print "The flag is false!";
endif;
```

If the variable $flag has been set to true, then print the appropriate statement; Otherwise, print an alternative statement.

An alternative way to represent true and false is by using the values 1 and 0, respectively. Therefore, the previous example can be restated as follows:

```
$flag = 1;
 if ($flag == TRUE) :
   print "The flag is true!";
else :
   print "The flag is false !";
endif;
```

Yet another alternative way to represent the above example follows:

```
$flag = TRUE;
// this implicitly asks "if ($flag == TRUE)"
if ($flag) :
   print "The flag is true!";
else :
   print "The flag is false!";
endif;
```

Identifiers

An *identifier* is a general term applied to variables, functions, and various other user-defined objects. There are several properties that PHP identifiers must abide by:

- An identifier can consist of one or more characters and must begin with an alphabetical letter or an underscore. Furthermore, identifiers can only consist of letters, numbers, underscore characters, and other ASCII characters from 127 through 255. Consider a few examples:

VALID	INVALID
my_function	This&that
Size	!counter
_someword	4ward

- Identifiers are case sensitive. Therefore, a variable named $recipe is different from variables named $Recipe, $rEciPe, or $recipE.

- Identifiers can be any length. This is advantageous, as it enables a programmer to accurately describe the identifier's purpose via the identifier name.

- Finally, an identifier name can't be identical to any of PHP's predefined keywords.

Variables

As a byproduct of examining the examples up to this point, I've introduced you to how variables are assigned and manipulated. However, it would be wise to explicitly lay the groundwork as to how variables are declared and manipulated. The coming sections will examine these rules in detail.

Variable Declaration

A *variable* is a named memory location that contains data that may be manipulated throughout the execution of the program.

A variable always begins with a dollar sign, $. The following are all valid variables:

```
$color
$operating_system
$_some_variable
$model
```

Variable names follow the same naming rules as those set for identifiers. That is, a variable name can begin with either an alphabetical letter or underscore and can consist of alphabetical letters, underscores, integers, or other ASCII characters ranging from 127 through 255.

Interestingly, variables do not have to be explicitly declared in PHP, much as is the case with the Perl language. Rather, variables can be declared and assigned values simultaneously. Furthermore, a variable's data type is implicitly determined by examining the kind of data that the variable holds. Consider the following example:

```
$sentence = "This is a sentence.";    // $sentence evaluates to string.
$price = 42.99;                        // $price evaluates to a floating-point
$weight = 185;                         // $weight evaluates to an integer.
```

You can declare variables anywhere in a PHP script. However, the location of the declaration greatly influences the realm in which a variable can be accessed. This access domain is known as its *scope*.

Variable Scope

Scope can be defined as the range of availability a variable has to the program in which it is declared. PHP variables can be one of four scope types:

- Local variables

- Function parameters

- Global variables

- Static variables

Local Variables

A variable declared in a function is considered *local;* that is, it can be referenced solely in that function. Any assignment outside of that function will be considered to be an entirely different variable from the one contained in the function. Note that when you exit the function in which the local variable has been declared, that variable and its corresponding value will be destroyed.

Local variables are advantageous because they eliminate the possibility of unexpected side effects, which can result from globally accessible variables that are modified, intentionally or not. Consider this listing:

```
$x  = 4;

function assignx () {

            $x = 0;
            print "\$x inside function is $x. <br>";
    }

assignx();

 print "\$x outside of function is $x. <br>";
```

Execution of the above listing results in:

```
$x inside function is 0.
```

$x outside of function is 4.

As you can see, two different values for $x are output. This is because the $x located inside the assignx function is local in nature. Modification of its value has no bearing on any values located outside of the function. On the same note, modification of the $x located outside of the function has no bearing on any variables contained in assignx().

Function Parameters

As is the case with many other programming languages, in PHP any function that accepts arguments must declare these arguments in the function header. Although these arguments accept values that come from outside of the function, they are no longer accessible once the function has exited.

Function parameters are declared after the function name and inside parentheses. They are declared much like a typical variable would be:

```
// multiply a value by 10 and return it to the caller
function x10 ($value) {

            $value = $value * 10;
            return $value;


}
```

It is important to realize that although you can access and manipulate any function parameter in the function in which it is declared, it is destroyed when the function execution ends.

Global Variables

In contrast to local variables, a *global variable* can be accessed in any part of the program. However, in order to be modified, a global variable must be explicitly declared to be global in the function in which it is to be modified. This is accomplished, conveniently enough, by placing the keyword GLOBAL in front of the variable that should be recognized as global. Placing this keyword in front of an already existing variable tells PHP to use the variable having that name. Consider an example:

```
$somevar = 15;

function addit() {
          GLOBAL $somevar;
          $somevar++;
          print "Somevar is $somevar";
}
addit();
```

The displayed value of $somevar would be 16. However, if you were to omit this line:

```
 GLOBAL $somevar;
```

The variable $somevar would be assigned the value 1, since $somevar would then be considered local within the addit() function. This local declaration would be implicitly set to 0, and then incremented by 1 to display the value 1.

An alternative method for declaring a variable to be global is to use PHP's $GLOBALS array. Reconsidering the above example, I use this array to declare the variable $somevar to be global:

```
$somevar = 15;

function addit() {
          $GLOBALS["somevar"];
          $somevar++;
}

addit();
print "Somevar is $somevar";
```

Regardless of the method you choose to convert a variable to global scope, be aware that the global scope has long been a cause of grief among programmers due to unexpected results that may arise from their careless use. Therefore, although global variables can be extremely useful, be prudent when using them.

Static Variables

The final type of variable scoping that I discuss is known as *static*. In contrast to the variables declared as function parameters, which are destroyed on the function's exit, a static variable will not lose its value when the function exits and will still hold that value should the function be called again. You can declare a variable to be static simply by placing the keyword STATIC in front of the variable name.

```
STATIC $somevar;
```

Consider an example:

```
function keep_track() {
            STATIC $count  = 0;
   $count++;
   print $count;
   print "<br>";
}

keep_track();
keep_track();
keep_track();
```

What would you expect the outcome of this script to be? If the variable $count were not designated to be static (thus making $count a local variable), the outcome would be:

```
1
1
1
```

However, since $count is static, it will retain its previous value each time the function is executed. Therefore, the outcome will be:

```
1
2
3
```

Static scoping is particularly useful for recursive functions. *Recursive functions* are a powerful programming concept in which a function repeatedly calls itself until a particular condition is met. Recursive functions are covered in detail in Chapter 4, "Functions."

Type Juggling

From time to time, it may be convenient to use a variable in ways that were not intended when it was first created. For example, you may wish to add the string value "15" to the integer value 12. Fortunately, PHP variable types may be modified without any explicit conversion process. This conversion process, whether explicit or implicit, is known as *type juggling* and is best illustrated with a few examples.

Consider a string and an integer value summed together. What do you think should take place? You may want different actions to take place depending on the contents of the string. For example, if an integer and a numerical string are added together, an integer will result:

```
$variable1 = 1;
$variable2 = "3";
$variable3 = $variable1 + $variable2;
// $variable3 holds the value 4.
```

Another example of type juggling is the attempt to add an integer and a double. Most certainly the integer would be converted to a double, so as not to lose any degree of accuracy provided by the double:

```
$variable1 = 3;
$variable2 = 5.4;
$variable3 = $variable1 + $variable2;
// $variable3 converts to a double, and $variable3 is assigned 8.4
```

A few obscure features of type juggling should be brought to light. What if you attempted to add together an integer and a string *containing* an integer value, assuming the string was not solely numerical in nature? Consider the following example:

```
$variable1 = 5;
$variable2 = "100 bottles of beer on the wall";
$variable3 = $variable1 + $variable2;
// $variable3 holds the value 105.
```

This will result in $variable3 being set to 105. This is because the PHP parser determines the type by looking at only the initial part of a string. However, suppose we modified $variable2 to read "There are 100 bottles of beer on the wall". Since there is no easy way to convert an alphabetical character into an integer value, this string would evaluate to 0, and thus $variable3 would be assigned the value 5.

Although in most cases, PHP's type-juggling strategy will suffice and produce the intended result, it is also possible to explicitly modify a variable to a particular type. This is explained in further detail in the next section, "Type Casting."

Type Casting

Forcing a variable to behave as a type other than the one originally intended for it is a rather straightforward process known as *type casting*. Type modification can be either a one-time occurrence or permanent.

A variable can be evaluated once as a different type by casting it. This is accomplished by placing the intended type in front of the variable to be cast. A type can be cast by inserting one of the casts in front of the variable (see Table 2-2).

Table 2-2. Cast Operators for Variables

CAST OPERATORS	CONVERSION
(int) or (integer)	Integer
(real) or (double) or (float)	Double
(string)	String
(array)	Array
(object)	Object

A simple example of how type casting works is as follows:

```
$variable1 = 13;                 // $variable1 is assigned the integer value 13.
$variable2 = (double) $variable1; // $variable2 is assigned the value 13.0
```

Although $variable1 originally held the integer value 13, the double cast temporarily converted the type to double (and in turn, 13 became 13.0). This value was then assigned to $variable2.

You know from the previous section that an attempt to add an integer and a double together will result in a double. This could be prevented by casting the double to be an integer, as follows:

```
$variable1 = 4.0;
$variable2 = 5;
$variable3 = (int) $variable1 + $variable2;        // $variable3 =  9
```

It is worth noting that type casting a double to an integer will always result in that double being rounded down:

```
$variable1 = 14.7;
$variable2 = (int) $variable1;                      // $variable2 = 14;
```

It is also possible to cast a string or other data type to be a member of an array. The variable being cast simply becomes the first element of the array:

```
$variable1 = 1114;
$array1 = (array) $variable1;
print $array1[0];                                  // The value 1114 is printed.
```

Finally, any data type can also be cast as an object. The result is that the variable becomes an attribute of the object, the attribute having the name scalar:

```
$model = "Toyota";
$new_obj = (object) $model;
```

The value can then be referenced as:

```
 print $new_obj->scalar;
```

Variable Assignment

You've already been exposed to how values can be assigned to variables in a PHP script. However, several nuances to variable assignment are worth reviewing. You might be familiar with *assignment by value*, which simply assigns a particular value, such as the integer 1 or the string ciao, to a named variable. However, there is a second kind of variable assignment, known as *assignment by reference*, which provides a valuable service to the developer. The following sections will consider each of these assignment methods in further detail.

Assignment by Value

This is the most common type of assignment, which simply assigns a value to a memory location represented by a variable name. Some examples of assignments by value are:

```
$vehicle = "car";
$amount = 10.23;
```

These two assignments result in the memory address represented by $vehicle being assigned the string "car" and that represented by $amount receiving the value 10.23.

Assignments by value can also take place through a return call in a function:

```
function simple () {

    return 5;
}

$return_value = simple();
```

The function simple() does nothing more than return the value 5 to the variable that called it. In this case, $return_value will be assigned the value 5.

Assignment by Reference

The other way to assign a value to a variable is by referencing another variable's memory location. Instead of copying an actual value into the destination variable, a pointer (or reference) to the memory location is assigned to the variable receiving the assignment, and therefore no actual copying takes place.

An assignment by reference is accomplished by placing an ampersand (&) in front of the source variable:

```
$dessert = "cake";
$dessert2 = &$dessert;
$dessert2 = "cookies";
print "$dessert2 <br>"; // prints cookies
print $dessert; // Again, prints cookies
```

As you can see by the previous listing, after $dessert2 has been assigned $dessert's memory location reference, any modifications to $dessert2 will result in modification of $dessert or any other variable pointing to that same memory location.

Variable Variables

On occasion it is useful to make use of variables whose contents can be treated dynamically as a variable in itself. Consider this typical variable assignment:

```
$recipe = "spaghetti";
```

Interestingly, we can then treat the value "spaghetti" as a variable by placing a second dollar sign ($) in front of the original variable name and again assigning another value:

```
$$recipe = "& meatballs";
```

This in effect assigns `"& meatballs"` to a variable named `"spaghetti"`.

Therefore, the following two snippets of code produce the same result:

```
print $recipe $spaghetti;
```

```
print $recipe $($recipe);
```

The result of both is the string `"spaghetti & meatballs"`.

Predefined Variables

PHP offers a number of predefined variables geared toward providing the developer with a substantial amount of internal configuration information. PHP itself creates some of the variables, while many of the other variables change depending in which operating system and Web server PHP is running.

Rather than attempt to compile a complete listing of available predefined variables, I will highlight a few of the available variables and functions that most users will find applicable and useful.

To view a comprehensive list of Web server, environment, and PHP variables offered on your particular system setup, simply execute the following code:

```
while (list($var,$value) = each ($GLOBALS)) :

                                echo "<BR>$var => $value";

endwhile;
```

This will return a list of variables similar to the following. Take a moment to peruse through the listing produced by the above code and then check out the examples that immediately follow.

```
GLOBALS =>
HTTP_GET_VARS => Array
HTTP_COOKIE_VARS => Array
HISTSIZE => 1000
HOSTNAME => server1.apress.com
LOGNAME => unstrung
HISTFILESIZE => 1000
REMOTEHOST => apress.com
MAIL => /var/spool/mail/apress
MACHTYPE => i386
TERM => vt100
HOSTTYPE => i386-linux
PATH =>
/usr/sbin:/sbin:/usr/local/bin:/bin:/usr/bin:/usr/X11R6/bin:/usr/local/ja=va/bin
HOME => /root
INPUTRC => /etc/inputrc
SHELL  => /bin/csh
USER => nobody
VENDOR => intel
GROUP  => root
HOST => server1.apress.com
OSTYPE => linux
PWD => /www/bin
SHLVL => 3_ => /www/bin/httpd
DOCUMENT_ROOT  => /usr/local/apress/site.apress
HTTP_ACCEPT => */*
HTTP_ACCEPT_ENCODING => gzip, deflate
HTTP_ACCEPT_LANGUAGE => it,en-us;q=0.5
HTTP_CONNECTION => Keep-Alive
HTTP_HOST => www.apress.com
HTTP_USER_AGENT  => Mozilla/4.0 (compatible; MSIE 5.0; Windows 98;
CNETHomeBuild051099)
REMOTE_ADDR => 127.0.0.1
REMOTE_PORT => 3207
SCRIPT_FILENAME => /usr/local/apress/site.apress/j/environment_vars.php
SERVER_ADDR => 127.0.0.1
SERVER_ADMIN => admin@apress.com
SERVER_NAME => www.apress.com
SERVER_PORT  => 80
SERVER_SIGNATURE =>
Apache/1.3.12 Server at www.apress.com Port 80

SERVER_SOFTWARE => Apache/1.3.12 (Unix) PHP/4.0.1
GATEWAY_INTERFACE => CGI/1.1
```

```
SERVER_PROTOCOL => HTTP/1.1
REQUEST_METHOD => GET
QUERY_STRING =>
REQUEST_URI => /j/environment_vars.php
SCRIPT_NAME => /j/environment_vars.php
PATH_TRANSLATED => /usr/local/apress/site.apress/j/environment_vars.php
PHP_SELF  => /j/environment_vars.php
argv => Array
argc => 0
var => argc
value => argc
```

As you can see, quite a bit of information is available to you, some rather useful, some not so useful. It is possible to display just one of these variables simply by treating it as such; a variable. For example, use this to display the user's IP address:

```
print "Hi! Your IP address is: $REMOTE_ADDR";
```

This returns a numerical IP address, such as 208.247.106.187.

It is also possible to gain information regarding the user's browser and operating system. The following one-liner:

```
print "Your browser is: $HTTP_USER_AGENT";
```

returns information similar to the following:

```
Your browser is: Mozilla/4.0 (compatible; MSIE 5.0; Windows 98;
CNETHomeBuild051099)
```

This is information regarding the browser and the operating system on which it is running. This data can prove quite useful when formatting applications to browser-specific formats.

> **NOTE** *To make use of the predefined variable arrays, track_vars must be turned on in the php.ini file. As of PHP 4.03, track_vars is always enabled.*

Constants

A *constant* is essentially a value that cannot be modified throughout the execution of a program. Constants are particularly useful when working with values that will definitely not require modification, such as pi (3.141592), or a specific distance such as the number of feet in a mile (5,280).

In PHP, constants are defined using the define() function. Once a constant has been defined, it cannot be changed (or redefined) at any other point of the program.

Pi could be defined in a PHP script as follows:

```
define("PI", "3.141592");
```

And subsequently used in the following listing:

```
print "The value of pi is". PI.".<br>";

$pi2 = 2 * PI;

print "Pi doubled equals $pi2.";
```

producing:

```
The value of pi is 3.141592.
Pi doubled equals 6.283184.
```

There are two points to note regarding the previous listing: The first is that use of a constant does not require a dollar sign. The second is that it's not possible to modify the constant once it has been defined (for example, 2*PI); if you need to produce a value based on the constant, the value must be stored in an alternative variable.

What's Next?

Quite a bit of material was covered in this chapter, which introduced many of the details you need to begin understanding and writing the most basic PHP programs. In particular, the following topics were discussed:

- Valid data types (integers, floating points, strings, arrays, objects, booleans)

- Identifiers

- Variables (declaration, scope)

- Type juggling

- Type casting

- Variable assignment (value, reference)

- Constants

This material will serve as the foundation for creating more complicated scripts in the next chapter, which covers PHP's expressions, operators, and control structures in detail. At the conclusion of Chapter 3, you will possess enough knowledge to build your first useful PHP application; namely, a simple Web-based events calendar.

CHAPTER 3

Expressions, Operators, and Control Structures

This chapter will introduce several aspects crucial to any programming language, namely, expressions, operators, and control structures. Knowledge of these topics will prove invaluable for creating large and complex PHP applications, as they will make up much of the code. If you are already familiar with languages such as C and Java, much of this chapter will be a review. If these terms and topics are new for you, comprehension of this chapter will be extremely important for your understanding the later chapters of this book.

Expressions

An *expression* is essentially a phrase representing a particular action in a program. All expressions consists of at least one operand and one or more operators. Before delving into a few examples illustrating the use of expressions, an introduction of operands and operators is in order.

Operands

An *operand* is one of the entities being manipulated in an expression. Valid operands can be of any data type discussed in Chapter 2, "Variables and Data Types." You are probably already familiar with the manipulation and use of operands not only through everyday mathematical calculations, but also through prior programming experience. Some examples of operands follow:

```
$a++; // $a is the operand
$sum = $val1 + val2; // $sum, $val1 and $val2 are operands
```

Operators

An *operator* is a symbol that specifies a particular action in an expression. Many operators may be familiar to you. Regardless, it is important to remember that PHP's automatic type conversion will convert types based on the type of operator placed between the two operands, which is not always the case in other programming languages.

The precedence and associativity of operators are significant characteristics of a programming language (see "Operator Associativity," later in this chapter, for details). Table 3-1 contains a complete listing of all operators, ordered from highest to lowest precedence. Sections following the table discuss each of these topics in further detail.

Table 3-1. PHP's Operators

OPERATOR	ASSOCIATIVITY	PURPOSE
( )	NA	Precedence ordering
new	NA	Object instantiation
! ~	R	Boolean NOT, bitwise NOT
++ —	R	Autoincrement, autodecrement
@	R	Error concealment
/ * %	L	Division, multiplication, modulus
+ - .	L	Addition, subtraction, concatenation
<< >>	L	Shift left, shift right (bitwise)
< <= > >=	NA	Less than, less than or equal to, greater than, greater than or equal to
== != === <>	NA	Is equal to, is not equal to, identical to, is not equal to
& ^ |	L	Bitwise AND, bitwise XOR, bitwise OR
&& ||	L	Boolean AND, boolean OR
?:	R	Ternary operator
= += *= /= .= %=&= |= ^= <<= >>=	R	Assignment operators
AND XOR OR	L	Boolean AND, boolean XOR, boolean OR

Now that the concepts of operands and operators have been introduced, the following examples of expressions will make much more sense:

```php
$a = 5;                  // assign integer value 5 to the variable $a
$a = "5";                // assign string value "5" to the variable $a
$sum = 50 + $some_int;   // assign sum of 50 + $some_int to $sum
$wine = "Zinfandel";     // assign "Zinfandel" to the variable $wine
$inventory++;            // increment the variable $inventory by 1
```

More complex types of expressions that enable the programmer to perform more elaborate calculations are also available. An example follows:

```
$total_cost = $cost + ($cost * 0.06); // cost plus sales tax
```

Operator Precedence

Operator precedence is a characteristic of operators that determines the order in which they will evaluate the operands surrounding them. PHP follows the standard precedence rules used in elementary school math class. Let's consider a few examples:

```
$total_cost = $cost + $cost * 0.06;
```

is the same as writing:

```
$total_cost = $cost + ($cost * 0.06);
```

This is because the multiplication operator has higher precedence than that of the addition operator.

Operator Associativity

The *associativity* characteristic of an operator is a specification of how operations of the same precedence (having the same precedence value as displayed in Table 3-1) are evaluated as they are executed. Associativity can be performed in two directions, left to right and right to left. Left-to-right associativity means that the various operations making up the expression are evaluated from left to right. Consider the following example:

```
$value = 3 * 4 * 5 * 7 * 2;
```

is the same as:

```
$value = ((((3 * 4) * 5) * 7) * 2);
```

resulting in the value 840. This is because the multiplication (*) operator is left-to-right associative. In contrast, right-to-left associativity evaluates operators of the same precedence from right to left:

```
$c = 5;
print $value = $a = $b = $c;
```

is the same as:

```
$c = 5;
$value = ($a = ($b = $c));
```

When this expression is evaluated, variables $value, $a, $b, and $c will all contain the value 5. This is because the assignment operator (=) has right-to-left associativity.

Arithmetic Operators

The arithmetic operators, listed in Table 3-2, perform various mathematical operations and will probably be used frequently in most PHP programs. Fortunately they are easy to use.

Table 3-2. Arithmetic Operators

EXAMPLE	LABEL	OUTCOME
$a + $b	Addition	Sum of $a and $b
$a - $b	Subtraction	Difference of $a and $b
$a * $b	Multiplication	Product of $a and $b
$a / $b	Division	Quotient of $a and $b
$a % $b	Modulus	Remainder of $a / $b

Incidentally, PHP provides a vast assortment of predefined mathematical functions, capable of performing base conversions and calculating logarithms, square roots, geometric values, and more. Check the manual for an updated list of these functions.

Assignment Operators

The *assignment operators* assign a data value to a variable. The simplest form of assignment operator just assigns some value, while others (known as *shortcut assignment operators*) perform some other operation before making the assignment. Table 3-3 lists examples using this type of operator.

Table 3-3. Assignment Operators

EXAMPLE	LABEL	OUTCOME
$a = 5;	Assignment	$a equals 5
$a += 5;	Addition-assignment	$a equals $a plus 5
$a *= 5;	Multiplication-assignment	$a equals $a multiplied by 5
$a /= 5;	Division-assignment	$a equals $a divided by 5
$a .= 5;	Concatenation-assignment	$a equals $a concatenated with 5

Prudent use of assignment operators ultimately result in cleaner, more compact code.

String Operators

PHP's *string operators* (see Table 3-4) provide a convenient way in which to concatenate strings together. There are two such operators, including the concatenation operator (.) and the concatenation assignment operator (.=), discussed in the previous section, "Assignment Operators."

DEFINITION   *Concatenate means to combine two or more objects together to form one single entity.*

Table 3-4. String Operators

EXAMPLE	LABEL	OUTCOME
$a = "abc"."def";	Concatenation	$a equals the concatenation of the two strings $a and $b
$a .= "ghijkl";	Concatenation-assignment	$a equals its current value concatenated with "ghijkl".

Here is an example of usage of the string operators:

```
// $a will contain string value "Spaghetti & Meatballs";
$a = "Spaghetti" . "& Meatballs";

// $a will contain value "Spaghetti & Meatballs are delicious.".
$a .= "are delicious";
```

The two concatenation operators are hardly the extent of PHP's string-handling capabilities. Read Chapter 8, "Strings and Regular Expressions," for a complete accounting of this functionality.

Autoincrement and Autodecrement Operators

The *autoincrement* (++) and *autodecrement* (—) operators listed in Table 3-5 present a minor convenience in terms of code clarity, providing shortened means by which to add 1 to or subtract 1 from the current value of a variable.

Table 3-5. PHP's Autoincrement and Autodecrement Operators

EXAMPLE	LABEL	OUTCOME
++$a, $a++	Autoincrement	Increment $a by 1
—$a, $a—	Autodecrement	Decrement $a by 1

Interestingly, these operators can be placed on either side of a variable, the side on which they are placed providing a slightly different effect. Consider the outcomes of the following examples:

```
$inventory = 15;                  // Assign integer value 15 to $inventory
$old_inv = $inventory—;           // FIRST assign $old_inv the value of
                                  // $inventory, THEN decrement $inventory.
$orig_inventory = ++$inventory;   // FIRST increment inventory, then assign
                                  // the newly incremented $inventory value
                                  // to $orig_inventory
```

As you can see, the order in which the autoincrement and autodecrement operators are used can have profound effects on the value of a variable.

Logical Operators

Much like the arithmetic operators, *logical operators* (see Table 3-6) will probably play a major role in many of your PHP applications, providing a way to make decisions based on the values of multiple variables. Logical operators make it possible to direct the flow of a program and are used frequently with control structures such as the if conditional and the while and for loops.

Table 3-6. Logical Operators

EXAMPLE	LABEL	OUTCOME
$a && $b	And	True if both $a and $b are true.
$a AND $b	And	True if both $a and $b are true.
$a ǁ $b	Or	True if either $a or $b are true.
$a OR $b	Or	True if either $a or $b are true.
! $a	Not	True if $a is not true.
NOT $a	Not	True if $a is not true.
$a XOR $b	Exclusive or	True if only $a or only $b is true.

Logical operators are also commonly used to provide details about the out-come of other operations, particularly those that return a value:

```
file_exists("filename.txt") OR print "File does not exist!";
```

One of two outcomes will occur:

- The file filename.txt exists

- The sentence "File does not exist!" will be output.

Equality Operators

Equality operators (see Table 3-7) are used to compare two values, testing for equivalence.

Table 3-7. Equality Operators

EXAMPLE	LABEL	OUTCOME
$a == $b	Is equal to	True if $a and $b are equivalent.
$a != $b	Is not equal to	True if $a is not equal to $b
$a === $b	Is identical to	True if $a and $b are equivalent *and* $a and $b have the same type.

It is a common mistake for even experienced programmers to attempt to test for equality using just one equal sign (for example, $a = $b). Keep in mind that this will result in the assignment of the contents of $b to $a, in effect *not* produc-ing the expected results.

Comparison Operators

Comparison operators (see Table 3-8), like logical operators, provide a method by which to direct program flow through examination of the comparative values of two or more variables.

Table 3-8. Comparison Operators

EXAMPLE	LABEL	OUTCOME
$a < $b	Less than	True if $a is less than $b
$a > $b	Greater than	True if $a is greater than $b
$a <= $b	Less than or equal to	True if $a is less than or equal to $b
$a >= $b	Greater than or equal to	True if $a is greater than or equal to $b
($a == 12) ? 5 : -1	Trinary	If $a equals 12, then the return value is 5. Otherwise, the return value is –1.

Note that the comparison operators should be used solely for comparing numerical values. While you may be tempted to compare strings with these operators, you will most likely not arrive at the expected outcome if you do so. There is a set of predefined functions that compare string values. These functions are discussed in detail in Chapter 8, "Strings and Regular Expressions."

Bitwise Operators

Bitwise operators examine and manipulate integer values on the level of individual bits that make up the integer value (thus the name). To fully understand this concept, you must have at least an introductory knowledge to the binary representation of decimal integers. Table 3-9 presents a few decimal integers and their corresponding binary representations.

Table 3-9. Decimal Integers and Their Binary Representations

DECIMAL INTEGER	BINARY REPRESENTATION
2	10
5	101
10	1010
12	1100
145	10010001
1,452,012	101100010011111101100

The bitwise operators listed in Table 3-10 are variations on some of the logical operators, but can result in a drastically different outcome.

Table 3-10. Bitwise Operators

EXAMPLE	LABEL	OUTCOME
$a & $b	And	And together each bit contained in $a and $b
$a | $b	Or	Or together each bit contained in $a and $b
$a ^ $b	Xor	Exclusive-or together each bit contained in $a and $b
~ $b	Not	Negate each bit in $b
$a << $b	Shift left	$a will receive the value of $b shifted left two bits.
$a >> $b	Shift right	$a will receive the value of $b shifted right two bits.

If you are interested in learning more about binary encoding, bitwise operators, and why they are important, I suggest Randall Hyde's massive online reference, "The Art of Assembly Language Programming," available at: http://webster.cs.ucr.edu/Page_asm/Page_asm.html. It's by far the best resource I've found thus far on the Web.

Control Structures

Control structures provide programmers with the tools to build complex programs capable of evaluating and reacting to the changing values of various inputs throughout the execution of a program. In summary, these structures control the execution of a program.

True/False Evaluation

Control structures generally evaluate expressions in terms of true and false. A particular action will occur based on the outcome of this evaluation. Consider the comparative expression $a = $b. This expression will evaluate to true if $a in fact is equal to $b, and false otherwise. More specifically, the expression will evaluate to the value 1 if it is true, and 0 if it is false. Consider the following:

```
$a = 5;
$b = 5;
print $a == $b;
```

This would result in 1 being displayed. Changing $a or $b to a value other than 5 would result in 0 being displayed.

if

The if statement is a type of selection statement that evaluates an expression and will (or will not) execute a block of code based on the truth or falsehood of the expression. There are two general forms of the if statement:

```
if (expression) {
    statement block
}
```

and

```
if (expression) {
    statement block
}
else {
    statement block
}
```

As stated in the previous section, "True/False Evaluation," the expression evaluates to either true or false. The execution of the statement block depends on the outcome of this evaluation, where a statement block could be either one or several statements. The following example prints out an appropriate statement after evaluating the string value:

```
if ($cooking_weight < 200) {
    print "This is enough pasta (< 200g) for 1-2 people";
}

else {
    print "That's a lot of pasta. Having a party perhaps?";
}
```

If only one statement is to be executed after the evaluation of the expression, then there is no need to include the bracket enclosures:

```
if ($cooking_weight < 100) print "Are you sure this is enough?";
```

elseif

The elseif statement provides another level of evaluation for the if control structure, adding depth to the number of expressions that can be evaluated:

```
if (expression) {
    statement block
}
elseif (expression) {
        statement block
}
```

> **NOTE** *PHP also allows the alternative representation of the elseif state-
> ment, that is, else if. Both result in the same outcome, and the alternative
> representation is only offered as a matter of convenience. The elseif state-
> ment is particularly useful when it is necessary to more specifically evalu-
> ate values. Note that an elseif statement will only be evaluated if the if and
> elseif statements before it had all evaluated to false.*

```
if ($cooking_weight < 200) {
    print "This is enough pasta (< 200g) for 1-2 people";
}

elseif ($cooking_weight < 500) {
        print "That's a lot of pasta. Having a party perhaps?";
}

else {
        print "Whoa! Who are you cooking for, a football team?";
}
```

Nested if Statements

The ability to nest, or embed, several if statements within one another provides
the ultimate level of control in evaluating expressions. Let's explore this concept
by expanding on the cooking weight example in the previous sections. Suppose
we wanted to evaluate the cooking weight only if the food in question was pasta:

```
// check $pasta value
if ($food == "pasta") {
    // check $cooking_weight value
    if ($cooking_weight < 200) {
        print "This is enough pasta (< 200g) for 1-2 people";
    }
    elseif ($cooking_weight < 500) {
            print "That's a lot of pasta. Having a party perhaps?";
    }
    else {
            print "Whoa! Who are you cooking for, a football team?";
    }
}
```

As you can see from the preceding code listing, nested if statements provide you with greater control over the flow of your program. As your programs grow in size and complexity, you will find nested control statements an indispensable programming tool.

Multiple Expression Evaluation

To further dictate the flow of control in a program, it is possible to simultaneously evaluate several expressions in a control structure:

```
if ($cooking_weight < 0) {
      print "Invalid cooking weight!";
}

elseif ( ($cooking_weight > 0) && ($cooking_weight < 200) ) {
        print "This is enough pasta (< 200g) for 1-2 people";
}

elseif ( ($cooking_weight > 200) && ($cooking_weight < 500) ) {
        print "That's a lot of pasta. Having a party perhaps?";
}

else {
      print "Whoa! Who are you cooking for, a football team?";
}
```

Multiple expression evaluations enable you to set range restrictions, providing greater control over your code flow while simultaneously reducing otherwise redundant control structure calls, resulting in better code readability.

Alternative Enclosure Bracketing

Control structures are enclosed in a set of brackets to clearly signify the various statements making up the structure. Curly brackets ({ }) were introduced earlier. As a convenience for programmers, an alternative format for enclosing control structures exists, as demonstrated here:

```
if (expression) :
   statement block
else :
   statement block
endif;
```

Therefore the following two structures will produce exactly the same outcome:

```
if ($a == $b) {                          if ($a == $b) :

   print "Equivalent values!";              print "Equivalent values!";

                                         endif;

}
```

while

The while structure provides a way to repetitively loop through a statement block. The number of times the statement block is executed depends on the total times the expression evaluates to true. The general form of the while loop is:

```
while (expression) :
   statement block
endwhile;
```

Let's consider an example of the computation of n-factorial (n!), where n = 5:

```
$n = 5;
$ncopy = $n;
$factorial = 1; // set initial factorial value
while ($n > 0) :
             $factorial = $n * $factorial;
    $n-; // decrement $n by 1
endwhile;

print "The factorial of $ncopy is $factorial.";
```

resulting in:

```
The factorial of 5 is 120.
```

In the preceding example, $n will be decremented at the conclusion of each loop iteration. We want to be sure that the evaluation expression does not evaluate to true when $n = 0, because this would cause $factorial to be multiplied by 0, surely an unwanted result.

> **NOTE** *In regard to this particular algorithm, the evaluation expression actually could be optimized to be $n > 1, because any number multiplied by 1 will not change. Although this is an extremely small gain in terms of execution time, these factors should always be considered as programs grow in size and complexity.*

do..while

A do..while structure works in much the same way as the while structure presented in the previous section, except that the expression is evaluated at the *end* of each iteration. It is important to note that a do..while loop will always execute at least once, whereas a while loop might not execute at all if the condition is first evaluated before entering the loop.

```
do :
      statement block
while (expression);
```

Let's reconsider the previous n-factorial example, this time using the do..while construct:

```
$n = 5;
$ncopy = $n;
$factorial = 1; // set initial factorial value
do {

$factorial = $n * $factorial;
      $n--; // decrement $n by 1

} while ($n > 0);

print "The factorial of $ncopy is $factorial.";
```

Execution of the preceding example will have the same results as its counterpart in the example accompanying the explanation of the while loop.

> **NOTE**   *The do..while loop does not support the alternative syntax form (the colon [:] end control enclosure), allowing only usage of curly brackets as an enclosure.*

for

The for loop is simply an alternative means for specifying the duration of iterative loops. It differs from the while loop only in the fact that the iterative value is updated in the statement itself instead of from somewhere in the statement block. As is the case with the while loop, the looping will continue as long as the condition being evaluated holds true. The general form of the for construct is:

```
for (initialization; condition; increment) {
      statement block
}
```

Three components actually make up the conditional. The *initialization* is considered only once, used to assign the initial value of the loop control variable. The *condition* is considered at the start of every repetition and will determine whether or not the next repetition will occur. Finally, the *increment* determines how the loop control variable changes with each iteration. Use of the term *increment* is perhaps misleading because the variable could be either incremented or decremented in accordance with the programmer's intentions. This example illustrates the basic usage of the for loop:

```
for ($i = 10; $i <= 100; $i+=10) :

      print "\$i = $i <br>";            // escaping backslash to suppress
                                        // conversion of $i variable.
endfor;
```

which results in:

```
$i = 10
$i = 20
$i = 30
$i = 40
$i = 50
$i = 60
```

```
$i = 70
$i = 80
$i = 90
$i = 100
```

Summarizing the example, the conditional variable $i is initialized to the value 10. The condition is that the loop will continue until $i reaches or surpasses the value 100. Finally, $i will be increased by 10 on each iteration. The result is that 10 statements are printed, each denoting the current value of $i. It is important to note that an assignment operator is used to increment $i by 10. This is not without reason, as the PHP for loop will not accept the alternative method for incrementation, that is, the form $i = $i + 10.

Interestingly, the above example can be written in a second format, producing the same results:

```
for ($i = 10; $i <= 100; print "\$i = $i <br>", $i+=10) ;
```

Many novice programmers may be questioning the logic behind having more than one method for implementing looping in a programming language, PHP or another language. The reason for this alternate looping implementation is that quite a few variations of the for loop are available.

One interesting variation is the ability to initialize several variables simultaneously, separating each initialization variable with a comma:

```
for ($x=0,$y=0; $x+$y<10; $x++) :

    $y +=2;                         // increment $y by 2
    print "\$y = $y <BR>";          // print value of $y
    $sum = $x + $y;
    print "\$sum = $sum<BR>";       // print value of $sum

endfor;

$y = 2
$sum = 2
$y = 4
$sum = 5
$y = 6
$sum = 8
$y = 8
$sum = 11
```

The example will repeatedly print out both the current value of $y and the sum of $x and $y. As you can see, $sum = 11 is printed, even though this sum surpasses the boundary of the conditional ($x + $y < 10). This is because on the entrance of that particular iteration, $y was equal to 6 and $x equal to 2. This fell within the terms of the condition, and $x and $y were incremented, respectively. The sum of 11 was output, but on return to the condition, 11 surpassed the limit of 10, and the for loop was terminated.

It is also possible to omit one of the components of the conditional expression. For example, you may want to pass an initialization variable directly into the for loop, without explicitly setting it to any particular value. You may also want to change the increment variable based on a particular condition in the loop. Therefore, it would make no sense to include these in the for loop. Consider the following example:

```
$x = 5;

for (; ; $x += 2) :

        print " $x ";
        if ($x == 15) :
        break;      // break out of this for loop
         endif;

endfor;
```

which results in the following outcome:

```
 5 7 9 11 13 15
```

Although there is no difference in function between the for and while looping structures, the for loop arguably promotes a cleaner code structure. This is because a quick glance in the for statement itself provides the programmer with all of the necessary information regarding the mechanics and duration of the structure. Contrast this with the while statement, where one must take extra time to hunt for iterative updates, a task that could be time consuming as a program grows in size.

foreach

The foreach construct is a variation of the for structure, included in the language as a more convenient means to maneuver through arrays. There are two general forms of the foreach statement, each having its own specific purpose:

```
foreach (array_expression as $value) {
        statement
}

foreach (array_expression as $key => $value) {
        statement
}
```

Let's use the first general format in an expression:

```
$menu = array("pasta", "steak", "potatoes", "fish", "fries");

foreach ($menu as $item) {

        print "$item <BR>";

}
```

resulting in:

```
pasta
steak
potatoes
fish
fries
```

In the above example, two points are worth noting. The first is that the foreach construct will automatically reset the array to its beginning position, something that does not occur using other iterative constructs. Second, there is no need to explicitly increment a counter or otherwise move the array forward; This is automatically accomplished through the foreach construct.

The second general format is used for associative arrays:

```
$wine_inventory = array {
    "merlot" => 15,
    "zinfandel" => 17,
    "sauvignon" => 32
}

foreach ($wine_inventory as $i => $item_count) {
    print "$item_count bottles of $i remaining<BR>";
}
```

resulting in:

```
15 bottles of merlot remaining
17 bottles of zinfandel remaining
32 bottles of sauvignon remaining
```

As this example demonstrates, handling arrays becomes rather simple with the foreach statement. For more information regarding arrays, refer to Chapter 5, "Arrays."

switch

The switch statement functions much like an if statement, testing an expression value against a list of potential matches. It is particularly useful when you need to compare many values, as the switch statement provides clean and compact code. The general format of the switch statement is:

```
switch (expression) {
    case (condition) :
        statement block
    case (condition) :
        statement block

        . . .
    default :
        statement block
}
```

The variable to be evaluated is denoted in the expression part of the switch statement. That variable is then compared with each condition, searching for a match. Should a match be found, the corresponding statement block is executed. Should a match not be found, the optional default statement block will execute.

As you will learn in later chapters, PHP is especially valuable for manipulating user input. Assume that the user is presented with a drop-down list containing several choices, each choice resulting in the execution of a different command contained in a case construct. Use of the switch statement would be very practical for implementing this:

```
$user_input = "recipes"; // assume $user_input is passed in to the script

switch ($user_input) :
    case("search") :
        print "Let's perform a search!";
        break;
    case("dictionary") :
        print "What word would you like to look up?";
        break;
    case("recipes") :
        print "Here is a list of recipes…";
        break;
    default:
        print "Here is the menu…";
        break;
endswitch;
```

As you can see, the switch statement offers a clean and concise way in which to order code. The variable denoted in the switch statement (in this case $user_input) will be evaluated by all subsequent case statements in the switch block. If any of the values denoted in a case statement matches the value contained in the variable being compared, the code contained in that case statement block will be executed. The break statement will then cause the execution of subsequent evaluations and code in the switch construct to be terminated. If none of the cases is applicable, the optional default case statement will be activated. If there is no default case and no cases are applicable, the switch statement will simply be exited, and code execution will continue as necessary below it.

It is important to note that the lack of a break statement (discussed in the next section) in a case will cause all subsequent commands in the switch statement to be executed until either a break statement is found or the end of the switch construct is reached. This result of forgetting a break statement is illustrated in the following listing:

```
$value = 0.4;

switch ($value) :
    case (0.4) :
        print "value is 0.4<br>";
    case (0.6) :
        print "value is 0.6<br>";
        break;
    case (0.3) :
        print "value is 0.3<br>";
        break;
```

```
        default :
            print "You didn't choose a value!";
            break;
endswitch;
```

resulting in the following output:

```
value is 0.4
value is 0.6
```

Lack of the break statement will cause not only the print statement contained in the matching case to be output, but also the print statement contained in the following case. Execution of commands in the switch construct then halts due to the break statement following the second print statement.

> **NOTE**   *There are no performance gains to be had in choosing between the switch and if statements. The decision to use one or the other is more or less a matter of convenience for the programmer.*

break

More of a statement than a control structure, break is used to immediately exit out of the while, for, or switch structure in which it is contained. The break statement was already introduced to a certain extent in the preceding section, "switch." However, I'll present one more example to thoroughly introduce the use of the break statement. Let's begin with a review of the rather simple break statement syntax:

```
break n;
```

The optional n proceeding the call to break denotes how many levels of control structures will be terminated should the break statement be executed. For example, if a break statement was nested within two while statements, and the break was preceded by '2', then both while statements would be exited immediately. The default n value is 1, noted either by omitting the n value after the break statement or by explicit inclusion of the value. Interestingly, break does not consider an if statement to be a control statement in the sense that it should be exited in accordance with the depth specified by the n value. Be sure to take this into account when making use of this optional n parameter.

Consider use of the break statement in a foreach loop:

```php
$arr = array(14, 12, 128, 34, 5);

$magic_number = 128;

foreach ($arr as $val) :

    if ($val == $magic_number) :
        print "The magic number is in the array!";
        break;
    endif;

    print "val is $val <br>";

endforeach;
```

If the magic number is in fact found in the array $arr (in this example, it is), there will be no more need to continue looking for the magic number. The following output would result:

```
val is 14
val is 12
The magic number is in the array!
```

Note that the preceding example is provided merely to illustrate usage of the break statement. A predefined array function exists in in_array(), which is capable of searching an array for a given value; in_array() is discussed in further detail in Chapter 5, "Arrays."

continue

The final PHP construct that we will examine is continue. Execution of a continue in an iterative loop will bypass the rest of the current loop iteration, instead immediately beginning a new one. The general syntax of continue is:

```
continue n;
```

The optional n acts as the opposite of the n accompanying the break statement, specifying to the end of how many levels of enclosing loops the continue statement should skip.

Let's consider an example that incorporates the continue statement. Suppose we wanted to count prime numbers between 0 and some designated boundary.

For sake of simplicity, assume that we have written a function capable of determining whether or not a number is prime. We'll call that function is_prime():

```
$boundary = 558;

for ($i = 0; $i <= $boundary; $i++) :

   if ( ! is_prime($i)) :
      continue;
   endif;

   $prime_counter++;

endfor;
```

If the number is in fact prime, then the if statement block will be bypassed, and $prime_counter will be incremented. Otherwise, the continue statement will be executed, resulting in the jump to the beginning of the loop.

The continue statement is certainly not a necessity, as if statements will accomplish the same result.

> **NOTE**   *The use of continue in long and complex algorithms can result in unclear and confusing code. I recommend avoiding use of this construct in these cases.*

Project: Develop an Events Calendar

Putting into practice many of the concepts that have been introduced thus far, I'll conclude this chapter with instructions illustrating how to create a Web-based events calendar. This calendar could store information regarding the latest cooking shows, wine-tasting seminars, or whatever else you deem necessary for your needs. This calendar will make use of many of the concepts you've learned thus far and will introduce you to a few others that will be covered in further detail in later chapters.

A simple file will store the information contained in the calendar. Here are the file's contents:

```
July 21, 2000|8 p.m.|Cooking With Rasmus|PHP creator Rasmus Lerdorf discusses the
wonders of cheese.
July 23, 2000|11 a.m.|Boxed Lunch|Valerie researches the latest ham sandwich
making techniques (documentary)
```

```
July 31, 2000|2:30pm|Progressive Gourmet|Forget the Chardonnay; iced tea is the
sophisticated gourmet's beverage of choice.
August 1, 2000|7 p.m.|Coder's Critique|Famed Food Critic Brian rates NYC's hottest
new Internet cafés.
August 3, 2000|6 p.m.|Australian Algorithms|Matt studies the alligator's diet.
```

Our PHP script shown in Listing 3-1 will produce the output seen in Figure 3-1.

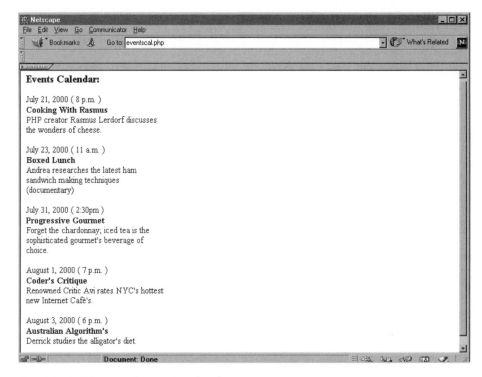

Figure 3-1. The sample events calendar.

Before delving into the code, take a moment to read through the algorithm, which will outline the series of commands executed by the code:

1. Open the file containing the event information.

2. Split each line into four elements: date, time, event title, and event summary.

3. Format and display the event information.

4. Close the file.

Listing 3-1: Script used to display contents of events.txt to browser

```php
<?
// application: events calendar
// purpose: read and parse data from a file and format it
// for output to a browser.

// open filehandle entitled '$events' to file 'events.txt'.
$events = fopen("events.txt", "r");

print "<table border = 0 width = 250>";
print "<tr><td valign=top>";

print "<h3>Events Calendar:</h3>";

// while not the end of the file
while (! feof($events)) :

        // read the next line of the events.txt file
        $event = fgets($events, 4096);

        // separate event information in the current
        // line into array elements.

        $event_info = explode("|", $event);

        // Format and output event information
        print "$event_info[0] ( $event_info[1] ) <br>";
        print "<b>$event_info[2]</b> <br>";
        print "$event_info[3] <br> <br>";

    endwhile;
// close the table
print "</td></tr></table>";

fclose ($events);

?>
```

This short example serves as further proof that PHP enables even novice programmers to develop practical applications while investing a minimum of time and learning. Don't worry if you don't understand some of the concepts introduced; they are actually quite simple and will be covered in detail in later chapters. However, if you just can't wait to learn more about these subjects, jump ahead to Chapter 7, "File I/O and the File System," and Chapter 8, "Strings and Regular Expressions," as much of the unfamiliar syntax is described in those chapters.

What's Next?

This chapter introduced many of the features of the PHP language that you will probably implement in one form or another in almost every script you write: expressions and control structures. Many topics using these features were explained, namely:

- Operators

- Operands

- Operator precedence

- Operator associativity

- Control structures (if, while, do..while, for, foreach, switch, break, continue)

The first three chapters served to introduce you to the core components of the PHP language. The remaining five chapters of this first part of the book will build on these core components, providing you with further information regarding arrays, object-oriented features, file handling, and PHP's string manipulations. This all sets the stage for the second half of the book, serving to highlight PHP's application-building features. So hold on tight and read on!

CHAPTER 4

Functions

This chapter introduces the general concepts of functional programming, one of the most influential advances in application development. Functions enable you to develop reusable and easily modifiable components, which are particularly useful when you need to develop Web applications similar in concept and utility. Functional programming results in shorter, easier to read programs.

In particular, this chapter is concerned with the creation, implementation, and manipulation of PHP functions. Although the general focus is on defining and executing user-defined functions, it is also important to know that PHP offers hundreds of predefined functions. Predefined functions are used exactly as user-defined functions are and save considerable time for developing new applications. For the most up-to-date listing of these functions, check out http://www.php.net.

What Is a Function?

A *function* is a section of code with a specific purpose that is assigned a unique name. The function name can be called at various points in a program, allowing the section of code represented by this name to be repeatedly executed as needed. This is convenient because the same section of code is written only once, but can be easily modified as necessary.

Function Definition and Invocation

Creating a PHP function is a rather straightforward process. You can create a function at any point in a PHP program. However, for organizational purposes you may find it convenient to place all functions intended for use in a script at the very top of the script file. An alternative method for function organization that can greatly reduce redundancy and promote code reuse is the placement of the functions in a separate file (also known as a *library*). This is convenient because you can use the functions repeatedly in various applications without having to make redundant copies and thus risk errors due to rewriting. I explain this process in detail toward the conclusion of this chapter, in "Building Function Libraries."

A function definition generally consists of three distinct parts:

- The name of the function

- Parentheses enclosing an optional set of comma-delimited input parameters

- The body of the function, enclosed in curly brackets

The general form of a PHP function is as follows:

```
function function_name (optional $arg1, $arg2, ..., $argn) {
    code section
}
```

The function name must follow the lexical structure conditions as specified in Chapter 2, "Variables and Data Types." The function name is then followed by a mandatory set of parentheses, enclosing an optional set of input parameters ($arg1, $arg2, ..., $argn). Due to PHP's relatively relaxed perspective on variable definitions, there is no need to specify the data type of the input parameters. While this has its advantages, realize that the PHP engine does not verify that the data passed into the function is intended to be handled by the function. This could result in unexpected results if the input parameter is used in an unintended fashion. (To ensure that the input parameter is being used as intended, you can test it using the predefined gettype() function.) A set of curly brackets ({}) follows the closing parentheses, enclosing the section of code to be associated with the function name.

Let's consider a simple example of practical usage of a function. Suppose you wanted to create a function that outputs a general copyright notice to a Web page:

```
function display_copyright() {
print "Copyright &copy; 2000 PHP-Powered Recipes. All Rights Reserved.";
}
```

Assuming that your Web site contains many pages, you could simply call this function at the bottom of each page, eliminating the need to continually rewrite the same information. Conveniently, the arrival of the year 2001 will bring about one simple modification of the text contained in the function that will result in an updated copyright statement. If functional programming weren't possible, you would have to modify every page in which the copyright statement was included!

Consider a variation of the display_copyright() function in which we pass a parameter. Suppose that you were in charge of the administration of several Web sites, each with a different name. Further imagine that each site had its own administration script, consisting of various variables relative to the specific site, one of the variables being $site_name. With this in mind, the function display_copyright() could be rewritten as follows:

```
function display_copyright($site_name) {
print "Copyright &copy 2000 $site_name. All Rights Reserved.";
}
```

The variable `$site_name`, assigned a value from somewhere outside of the function, is passed into `display_copyright()` as an input parameter. It can then be used and modified anywhere in the function. However, modifications to the variable will not be recognized anywhere outside of the function, although it is possible to force this recognition through the use of special keywords. These keywords, along with a general overview of variable scoping as it relates to functions, were introduced in Chapter 2, "Variables and Data Types."

Nested Functions

It is also possible to nest functions within functions, much as you can insert one control structure (if, while, for, and so on) within another. This is useful for programs large and small, as it adds another level of modularization to the application, resulting in increasingly manageable code.

Revisiting the copyright example described earlier, you can eliminate the need to modify the date altogether by nesting PHP's predefined `date()` function in the `display_copyright()` function:

```
function display_copyright($site_name) {
print "Copyright &copy". date("Y"). " $site_name. All Rights Reserved.";
}
```

The Y input parameter of the `date()` function specifies that the return value should be the current year, formatted using four digits. Assuming that the system date configuration is correct, PHP will output the correct year on each invocation of the script. PHP's `date()` function is extremely flexible, offering 25 different date- and time-formatting flags.

You can also nest function declarations inside one another. However, nesting a function declaration does not imply that it is protected in the sense of it being limited to use only in the function in which it is declared. Furthermore, a nested function does not inherit the input parameters of its parent; they must be passed to the nested function just as they are passed to any other function. Regardless, you may find it useful to do nest function declarations for reasons of code management and clarity. Listing 4-1 gives an example of nesting function declarations.

Listing 4-1: Making efficient use of nested functions

```
function display_footer($site_name) {

        function display_copyright($site_name) {
                print "Copyright &copy ". date("Y"). " $site_name. All Rights
Reserved.";
        }

        print "<center>
        <a href = \"\">home</a> | <a href = \"\">recipes</a> | <a href =
\"\">events</a><br>
        <a href = \"\">tutorials</a> | <a href = \"\">about</a> | <a href =
\"\">contact us</a><br>";

        display_copyright($site_name);

        print "</center>";

}

$site_name = "PHP Recipes";

display_footer($site_name);
```

Executing this script produces the following output:

---

home | recipes | events
tutorials | about | contact us
Copyright © 2000 PHP Recipes. All Rights Reserved.

> **NOTE** *It is important to note that we could also call* display_copyright() *from outside the* display_footer() *function, just as* display_footer() *was called in the preceding example. PHP does not support the concept of protected functions.*

Although nested functions are not protected from being called from any other location of the script, they cannot be called until *after* their parent function has been called. An attempt to call a nested function before calling its parent function results in an error message.

Returning Values from a Function

It is often useful to return a value from a function. This is accomplished by assigning the function call to a variable. Any type may be returned from a function, including lists and arrays. Consider Listing 4-2, in which the sales tax for a given price is calculated and the total cost subsequently returned. Before checking out the code, take a minute to review the pseudocode summary:

- Assume that a few values have been set, in this case some product price, $price, and sales tax, $tax.

- Declare function calculate_cost(). It accepts two parameters, the sales tax and the product price.

- Calculate the total cost and use return to send the calculated cost back to the caller.

- Call calculate_cost(), setting $total_cost to whatever value is returned from the function.

- Output a relevant message.

Listing 4-2: Building a function that calculates sales tax

```
$price = 24.99;
$tax = .06;

function calculate_cost($tax, $price) {
    $sales_tax = $tax;
    return $price + ($price * $sales_tax);
}

// Notice how calculate_cost() returns a value.
$total_cost = calculate_cost ($tax, $price);
// round the cost to two decimal places.
$total_cost = round($total_cost, 2);

print "Total cost: ".$total_cost;
// $total_cost = 26.49
```

> **NOTE**   *A function that does not return a value is also known as a procedure.*

Another way in which to use returned values is to incorporate the function call directly into a conditional/iterative statement. Listing 4-3 checks a user's total bill against a credit limit. The pseudocode is found here:

- Declare function check_limit(), which takes as input two parameters. The first parameter, $total_cost, is the total bill accumulated by the user thus far. The second, $credit_limit, is the maximum cash amount the user is allowed to charge.

- If the total accumulated bill is greater than the credit limit, return a false (0) value.

- If the if statement evaluates to false, then the function has not yet terminated. Therefore, the total cost has not exceeded the credit limit, and true should be returned.

- Use the function check_limit() in an if conditional statement. Check_limit() will return either a true or a false value. This returned value will determine the action that the if statement takes.

If check_limit() evaluates to true, tell the user to keep shopping. Otherwise, inform that user that the credit limit has been exceeded.

Listing 4-3: Comparing a user's current bill against a credit limit

```
$cost = 1456.22;
$limit = 1000.00;

function check_limit($total_cost, $credit_limit) {

    if ($total_cost > $credit_limit) :
        return 0;
    endif;

    return 1;

}

if (check_limit($cost, $limit)) :
// let the user keep shopping
print "Keep shopping!";
else :
print "Please lower your total bill to less than $".$limit."!";
endif;
```

Execution of Listing 4-3 results in the error message being displayed, since $cost has exceeded $limit.

It is also possible to simultaneously return multiple values from a function by using a list. Continuing with the culinary theme, consider a function that returns the three recommended years of a particular wine. This function is illustrated in Listing 4-4. Read through the pseudocode first:

- Declare function best_years(), which takes as input one parameter. The parameter $label is the type of wine in which the user would like to view the three recommended years.

- Declare two arrays, $merlot, and $zinfandel. Each array holds the three recommended years for that wine type.

- Implement the return statement to make wise use of the variable functionality. The statement $$label will first interpret the variable $label and then interpret whatever the value of $label is as another variable. In this case, the merlot array will be returned as a list, each year taking its respective position in the calling list.

- Print out a relevant message, informing the user of these recommended years.

Listing 4-4: Returning multiple values from a function

```
// wine for which best years will be displayed
$label = "merlot";

// This function merely makes use of various arrays and a variable variable to
return multiple values.
function best_years($label) {

    $merlot = array(1987, 1983, 1977);
    $zinfandel = array(1992, 1990, 1989);

    return $$label;

}
// a list() Is used to display the wine's best years.
list ($yr_one, $yr_two, $yr_three) = best_years($label);

print "$label had three particularly remarkable years: $yr_one, $yr_two, and
$yr_three.";
```

Execution of Listing 4-3 results in the following output:

```
merlot had three particularly remarkable years: 1987, 1983, and 1977.
```

Recursive Functions

The act of a function calling on itself again and again to satisfy some operation is indeed a powerful one. Used properly, *recursive* function calls can save undue space and redundancy in a script and are especially useful for performing repetitive procedures. Examples of these repetitive applications include file/array searches and graphic renderings (fractals, for instance). An example commonly illustrated in computer science courses is the summation of integers 1 to N. Listing 4-5 recursively sums all integers between 1 and 10.

Listing 4-5: Using a recursive function to sum an integer set

```
function summation ($count) {
    if ($count != 0) :
        return $count + summation($count-1);
    endif;
}
$sum = summation(10);
print "Summation = $sum";
```

Execution of the Listing 4-5 produces the following results:

```
Summation = 55
```

Using functional iteration (recursion) can result in speed improvements in a program if the function is called often enough. However, be careful when writing recursive procedures, as improper coding can result in an infinite loop.

Variable Functions

An interesting capability of PHP is the possibility to execute *variable functions*. A variable function is a dynamic call to a function whose name is determined at the time of execution. Although not necessary in most Web applications, variable functions can significantly reduce code size and complexity, often eliminating unnecessary if conditional statements.

A call to a variable function is nothing more than a variable name followed by a set of parentheses. In the parentheses an optional set of input parameters can be included. The general form of a variable function is as follows:

```
$function_name();
```

Listing 4-6 illustrates this odd but useful feature. Suppose that users are given the possibility to view certain information in their choice of language. Our example will keep things simple, offering a welcome message tailored to English- and Italian-speaking users. Here is the pseudocode:

- An Italian interface is created in a function entitled "italian".

- An English interface is created in a function entitled "english".

- The choice of language is passed into the script, set in the variable $language.

The variable $language is used to execute a variable function, in this case italian().

Listing 4-6: Using a variable function determined by some input variable

```
// italian welcome message.
function italian() {
    print "Benvenuti al PHP Recipes.";
}

// english welcome message
function english() {
    print "Welcome to PHP Recipes.";
}

// set the user language to italian
$language = "italian";

// execute the variable function
$language();
```

Listing 4-6 illustrates the interesting concept of a variable function and how it can be used to greatly limit code volume. Without the capability of using a variable function, you would be forced to use a switch or if statement to determine which function should be executed. This would take up considerably more space and introduce the possibility of errors due to added coding.

Building Function Libraries

Function libraries are one of the most efficient ways to save time when building applications. For example, you may have written a series of function for sorting arrays. You could probably use these functions repeatedly in various applications. Rather than continually rewrite or copy and paste these functions into new scripts, it is much more convenient to place all relevant sorting functions into a separate file altogether. This file would then be given an easily recognizable title, for example, array_sorting.inc, as shown in Listing 4-7.

Listing 4-7: A sample function library (array_sorting.inc)

```
<?
// file: array_sorting.inc
// purpose: library containing functions used for sorting arrays.
// date: July 17, 2000

function merge_sort($array, $tmparray, $right, $left) {
. . .
}

function bubble_sort($array, $n) {
. . .
}

function quick_sort($array, $right, $left) {
. . .
}

?>
```

This function library, array_sorting.inc, acts as a receptacle for all of my array-sorting functions. This is convenient because I can effectively organize my functions according to purpose, allowing for easy lookup when necessary. As you can see in Listing 4-7, I like to add a few lines of commented header at the top of each library so I have a quick synopsis of the library contents once I open the file. Once you have built your own custom function library, you can use PHP's include() and require() statements to include the entire library file to a script, thus making all of the functions available. The general syntax of both statements is as follows:

```
include(path/filename);
require(path/filename);
```

An alternate syntax is also available:

```
include "path/filename";
require "path/filename";
```

where "path" refers to either the relative or absolute path location of the filename. The include() and require() constructs are introduced in detail in Chapter 9, "PHP and the Web." For the moment, however, you should just understand that these constructs can be used to include a file directly into a script for use.

Suppose you wanted to use the library array_sorting.inc in a script. You could easily include the library, as shown in Listing 4-8.

Listing 4-8: Including a function library (array_sorting.inc) in a script
```
// this assumes that the array_sorting.inc library resides in the same folder as
this script.
include ("array_sorting.inc");

// you are now free to use any function in array_sorting.inc.
$some_array = (50, 42, 35, 46);

// make use of the bubble_sort() function
$sorted_array = bubble_sort($some_array, 1);
```

What's Next?

This chapter introduced functions and their range of uses as applied to PHP. In particular, the following topics were discussed:

- Function definition and invocation

- Nested functions

- Returning values from a function

- Returning multiple values

- Recursive functions

- Variable functions

- Building function libraries

Understanding this chapter will be integral to understanding the concepts discussed throughout the remaining chapters, as functions are used whenever possible. As is the case with every other chapter, I suggest experimenting with the examples in order to strengthen your comprehension of the provided material.

Chapter 5 introduces what will surely become a welcome addition to your PHP knowledge: arrays. Chapter 5 will provide you with your first real taste of data storage, paving the way to more content-oriented and ultimately interesting applications.

CHAPTER 5

Arrays

Chapter 2, "Variables and Data Types," introduced the two types of arrays available for use in your PHP programs, indexed and associative. As you may recall, indexed arrays manipulate elements in accordance with position, while associative arrays manipulate elements in terms of a key/value association. Both offer a powerful and flexible method by which to handle large amounts of data.

This chapter is devoted to the various aspects of PHP's array-manipulation capabilities. By the chapter's conclusion, you will be familiar with single-dimensional and multidimensional arrays, array sorting, array traversal, and various other functions useful in manipulating arrays. It is not in the scope of this book to provide a comprehensive list of all available functions, although this chapter just so happens to cover almost all array functions. For the most up-to-date list, please refer to the PHP home page at http://www.php.net.

Creating Arrays

An *array* is essentially a series of objects all bearing the same size and type. Each object in the array is generally known as an *array element*. Creating an array in PHP is easy. You can create an indexed array by placing a set of square brackets ([ ]) after a variable name:

```
$languages[ ] = "Spanish";
// $languages[0] = "Spanish"
```

You can then add further elements to the array, as seen in the following listing. Notice that there is no explicit reference to index positions. Each array allocation is assigned the position at the length of the array plus 1:

```
$languages[ ] = "English"; // $languages[1] = "English"
$languages[ ] = "Gaelic";  // $languages[2] = "Gaelic"
```

You can also explicitly add elements to a particular location by designating the index key:

```
$languages[15] = "Italian";
$languages[22] = "French";
```

You can create associative arrays in much the same way:

```
$languages["Spain"] = "Spanish";
$languages["France"] = "French";
```

There are also three predefined language constructs that you can use to create an array:

- array()

- list()

- range()

Although all achieve the same result, array creation, there are instances in which a given construct may be more suitable than the others. Descriptions and examples of each construct follow.

array()

The array function takes as input zero or more *elements* and returns an array made up of these input elements. Its syntax is:

```
array array ( [element1, element2 …] )
```

The array() language construct is perhaps nothing more than a more explicit declaration that an array is being created, used for convenience of the programmer. Here is an example of using array() to create an indexed array:

```
$languages = array ("English", "Gaelic", "Spanish");
// $languages[0] = "English", $languages[1] = "Gaelic", $languages[2] = "Spanish"
```

Here is how you would use array() to create an associative array:

```
$languages = array ("Spain" => "Spanish",
                    "Ireland" => "Gaelic",
                    "United States" => "English");
// $languages["Spain"] = "Spanish"
// $languages["Ireland"] = "Gaelic"
// $languages["United States"] = "English"
```

Mapping arrays associatively is particularly convenient when using index values just doesn't make sense. In the preceding example it is useful because it makes sense to associate country names with their language counterparts. Imagine trying to contrive a logical methodology using numbers!

list()

The `list()` language construct is similar to `array()`, though it's used to make simultaneous variable assignments from values extracted from an array in just one operation. Its syntax is:

```
void list (variable1 [, variable2, ...] )
```

It can be particularly useful when extracting information from a database or file. Suppose you wanted to format and output information read from a text file. Each line of the file contains user information, including name, occupation, and favorite color, with each piece of information delimited by a vertical bar (|). The typical line would look similar to the following:

```
Nino Sanzi|Professional Golfer|green
```

If you use `list()`, a simple loop could read each line, assign each piece of data to a variable, and format and display the data as needed. Here's how you could use `list()` to make multiple variable assignments:

```
// While the end-of-file hasn't been reached, get next line
while ($line = fgets ($user_file, 4096)) :

    // use split() to separate each piece of data, assign data to $name,
$occupation, and $color
    list ($name, $occupation, $color) = split ( "|", $line);
    // format and output the data
    print "Name: $name <br>";
    print "Occupation: $occupation <br>";
    print "Favorite color: $color <br>";

endwhile;
```

Each line would in turn be read and formatted similar to this:

```
Name: Nino Sanzi
Occupation: Professional Golfer
Favorite Color: green
```

Reviewing the example, list() depends on the function split() to split each line into three elements. These elements are then assigned to $name, $occupation, and $color, respectively. At that point, it's just a matter of formatting for display to the browser. This is one of the powers of PHP: the ability to easily parse data from text files. This topic is covered in detail in Chapters 7 and 8.

range()

The range() language construct provides an easy way to quickly create and fill an array with a specified range of integers, allowing you to specify a range of low and high integer values. An array containing all integer values making up this range is then returned. Its syntax is:

```
array range (int low, int high)
```

You can see the convenience of this construct in the following example:

```
$lottery = range(0,9);
// $lottery = array(0,1,2,3,4,5,6,7,8,9)
```

As you can observe, the range 0 to 9 was specified as the input parameters of range(), and the array $lottery was subsequently filled with that integer range.

Multidimensional Arrays

As you begin developing more complicated programs, a single-dimensional array may not suffice to store the information that you would like to manipulate. The *multidimensional array* (an array of arrays) offers a much more effective way to store information that requires an extra level of organization. Creating a multidimensional array is easy; simply add an extra set of square brackets to expand the array by one dimension:

```
$chessboard[1] [4] = "King"; // two-dimensional
$capitals["USA"] ["Ohio"] = "Columbus"; // two-dimensional
$streets["USA"] ["Ohio"]["Columbus"] = "Harrison"; // three-dimensional
```

Consider an array that stores information regarding desserts and their preparation details. While this would be rather difficult using a single-dimensional array, a two-dimensional associative array will work just fine:

```
$desserts = array (
                "Fruit Cup" => array (
                                    "calories" => "low",
                                    "served" => "cold",
                                    "preparation" => "10 minutes"
                                    ),
                "Brownies" => array (
                                    "calories" => "high",
                                    "served" => "piping hot",
                                    "preparation" => "45 minutes"
                                    )
                );
```

Once the array has been created, references could be made to each element by indicating the relevant keys:

```
$desserts["Fruit Cup"] ["preparation"] // returns "10 minutes"
$desserts["Brownies"] ["calories"] // returns "high"
```

You can assign elements to a multidimensional array in the same way that you do so with a single-dimensional array:

```
$desserts["Cake"]["calories"] = "too many";
// assigns "too many" to "Cake" property "calories"
```

Although multidimensional arrays introduce another level of complexity to the array structure, creating them is not all that different creating single-dimensional arrays. However, referencing multidimensional arrays in strings requires some special attention. This is the subject of the next section.

Referencing Multidimensional Arrays

You must reference multidimensional arrays in a string slightly differently than you reference other types. You can use the string concatenation operator:

```
print "Brownies are good, but the calorie content is ".
$desserts["Brownies"]["calories"];
```

or you can enclose the multidimensional array in curly brackets ({ }):

```
print "Brownies are good, but the calorie content is
{$desserts[Brownies][calories]}";
```

When using this alternative syntax, take note that there are no quotation marks surrounding the array keys. Furthermore, notice that there is no space between the curly brackets and array reference. If you fail to satisfy both of these requisites, an error will occur.

Either way works fine. I suggest choosing one format and sticking with it to eliminate inconsistencies in your code. The flip side to *not* using either of these formatting rules is that the multidimensional array will be interpreted exactly as it is seen in the string, causing what would most certainly be an unexpected outcome.

Locating Array Elements

The ability to easily locate elements in an array is very important. PHP offers a series of functions that allow for the convenient retrieval of both keys and values constituting an array.

in_array()

The in_array() function provides a convenient way to quickly determine whether or not an element exists in an array, returning true if it does, and false otherwise. Its syntax is:

```
bool in_array(mixed element, array array)
```

This function is particularly convenient because it eliminates the need to create looping constructs to search through each array element. Consider the following example, which uses in_array() to search for the element "Russian" in the array $languages:

```
$languages = array ("English", "Gaelic", "Spanish");
$exists = in_array("Russian", $languages); // $exists set to false
$exists = in_array("English", $languages); // $exists set to true
```

The in_array() function is particularly helpful in a control statement, as the true/false return value can determine the path the conditional construct takes. Here's an example of how you would use in_array() to determine the path of a conditional statement:

```
// user input
$language = "French";
$email = "wjgilmore@hotmail.com";
```

```
// if language exists in the array
if (in_array($language, $languages)) :

    // subscribe the user to the newsletter.
    // . Note that subscribe_user() is not a PHP predefined function. I'm just
using it to simulate the process.
    subscribe_user($email, $language);
    print "You are now subscribed to the $language edition of the newsletter.";

// language does not exist in the array
else :
    print "We're sorry, but we don't yet offer a $language edition of the
newsletter".
endif;
```

What happened in this example? Assume that the variables $language and $email are pieces of data supplied by the user. You want to ensure that their chosen language corresponds to one of those that you offer, and you use in_array() to verify this. If it does exist, then the user is subscribed and receives a message stating so. Otherwise, the user is informed that the newsletter is not offered in that particular language. Of course, chances are you are not going to want to force the user to guess in what languages you offer your newsletter. This problem could be eliminated altogether using a drop-down form list, a subject covered in detail in Chapter 10, "Forms." However, for purposes of illustration, this example does the trick nicely.

array_keys()

The array_keys() function returns an array containing all of the keys constituting the input array. If the optional search_element is included, then only the keys matching that particular element are returned; otherwise, all keys constituting the array are returned. Its syntax is:

```
array array_keys (array array, mixed [search_element])
```

Here's how you could use array_keys() to return the key of a given element:

```
$great_wines = array ("Australia" => "Clarendon Hills 96",
                      "France" => "Comte Georges de Vogue 97",
                      "Austria" => "Feiler Artinger 97");


$great_labels = array_keys($great_wines);
```

```
// $great_labels = array ("Australia", "France", "Austria");

$great_labels = array_keys($great_wines, "Clarendon Hills 96");
// $great_labels = array("Australia");
```

Using array_keys() is a very easy way to retrieve all of the index values of an array, in the preceding example, the names of the countries where the wines are produced.

array_values()

The array_values() function returns an array containing all of the values constituting the input array. Its syntax is:

```
array array_values(array array)
```

Reconsider the previous example, where array_keys() was used to retrieve all of the key values. This time array_values() acts to retrieve all of the corresponding key elements:

```
// $great_wines = array ("Australia" = "Clarendon Hills 96",
                         "France = "Comte Georges de Vogue 97",
                         "Austria = "Feiler Artinger 97");

$great_labels = array_values($great_wines);
// $great_labels = array ("Clarendon Hills 96",
                          "Comte Georges de Vogue 97",
                          "Feiler Artinger 97");
```

The array_keys() and array_values() functions complement each other perfectly, allowing you to retrieve either side of the array as necessary.

Adding and Removing Elements

Thankfully, PHP does not require you to specify the number of elements in an array on its creation. This makes for flexible array manipulation, as there are no worries about surpassing previously designated constraints if an array becomes larger than expected. PHP provides a number of functions for growing an array. Some of these functions are provided as a convenience to programmers wishing to mimic various queue types (FIFO, LIFO, and so on) and stacks, as reflected by their names (push, pop, shift, and unshift). Even if you don't know what queues or stacks are, don't worry; these functions are easy to use.

> **DEFINITION** *A queue is a data structure in which the elements are removed in the same order that they were entered. In contrast, a stack is a data structure in which the elements are removed in the order opposite to that in which they were entered.*

array_push()

The array_push() function appends, or *pushes*, one or more values onto the end of the array. Its syntax is:

```
int array_push(array array, mixed var, [. . . ])
```

The length of the array will increase in direct proportion to the number of values pushed onto the array. This is illustrated in the following example:

```
$languages = array("Spanish", "English", "French");
array_push($languages, "Russian", "German", "Gaelic");
// $languages = array("Spanish", "English", "French",
//                     "Russian", "German", "Gaelic");
```

As is the case with many of PHP's predefined functions, array_push() has a counterpart entitled array_pop(), which acts to pull elements from an array. The main difference between the two is that while array_push() is capable of adding several elements simultaneously, array_pop() can only pull one element off at a time.

array_pop()

The array_pop() function accomplishes a result the exact opposite of that of array_push(), removing, or *popping*, a value from the end of the array. This value is then returned. Its syntax is:

```
mixed array_pop(array array)
```

Each iteration of array_pop() will shorten the length of the array by 1. Consider the following example:

```
$languages = array ("Spanish", "English", "French",
//                     "Russian", "German", "Gaelic");
$a_language = array_pop ($languages); // $a_language = "Gaelic"
$a_language = array_pop ($languages); // $a_language = "German"
// $languages = array ("Spanish", "English", "French", "Russian");
```

The reason for using `array_push()` and `array_pop()` is that they provide for a very clean way to both manipulate array elements and control the length without worrying about uninitialized or empty values. They work much more efficiently than attempting to control these factors on your own.

array_shift()

The `array_shift()` function operates much like `array_pop()`, except that it removes one element from the beginning (the left side) of the array. All remaining array elements are shifted one unit toward the beginning of the array. Notice that `array_shift()` has the same syntax as `array_pop()`:

```
mixed array_shift (array array)
```

The important thing to keep in mind is that `array_shift()` removes the element from the beginning of the array, as shown here:

```
$languages = array("Spanish", "English", "French", "Russian");
$a_language = array_shift($languages); // $a_language = "Spanish";
// $languages = array("English", "French", "Russian");
```

array_unshift()

The `array_unshift()` function is the counterpart to `array_shift()`, instead appending values to the beginning of the array and shifting the array to the right. Its syntax is:

```
int array_unshift(array array, mixed var1 [, mixed var2. . .])
```

You can append one or several values simultaneously, the length of the array increasing in direct proportion to the number of values added. An example of appending multiple values follows:

```
$languages = array ("French", "Italian", "Spanish");
array_unshift ($languages, "Russian", "Swahili", "Chinese");
// $languages = array ("Russian", "Swahili", "Chinese",
//                     "French", "Italian", "Spanish");
```

array_pad()

The array_pad() function enables you to quickly expand an array to a precise size, *padding* it with a default value. Its syntax is:

```
array array_pad(array array, int pad_size, mixed pad_value);
```

The input parameter pad_size specifies the new length of the array. The pad_value parameter specifies the default value to which all of the new array positions should be set. Here are several details regarding array_pad() that you should know:

- If pad_size is positive, then the array will be padded to the right; if negative, the array will be padded to the left.

- If the absolute value of pad_size is less than or equal to the length of the array, then no action will be taken.

> **NOTE** *The absolute value of an integer is its value disregarding any negative signs preceding it. For example, the absolute value of both 5 and –5 is 5.*

Here is an array that is padded from the back:

```
$weights = array (1, 3, 5, 10, 15, 25, 50);
$weights = array_pad($weights, 10, 100);
// The result is $weights = array(1, 3, 5, 10, 15, 25, 50, 100, 100, 100)
```

Here is an array that is padded from the front:

```
$weights = array (1, 3, 5, 10, 15, 25, 50);
$weights = array_pad($weights, -10, 100);
// The result is $weights = array(100, 100, 100, 1, 3, 5, 10, 15, 25, 50)
```

This is an incorrect attempt to pad an array:

```
$weights = array (1, 3, 5, 10, 15, 25, 50);
$weights = array_pad ($weights, 3, 100);
// The array $weights remains $weights = array (1, 3, 5, 10, 15, 25, 50)
```

Traversing Arrays

PHP offers a host of functions for traversing the various elements in an array. Used together, they offer a flexible solution for quickly manipulating and outputting array values. You will probably use these functions frequently, as they form the core of almost every array algorithm.

reset()

The function reset() will rewind the internal pointer of the array back to the first element. It also returns the value of the first element. Its syntax follows:

```
mixed reset (array array)
```

Consider the following array:

```
$fruits = array("apple", "orange", "banana");
```

Suppose the pointer in this array is currently set to the element "orange." Executing:

```
$a_fruit = reset ($fruits);
```

will set the pointer back to the beginning of the array, that is, "apple", and return that value if reset() is used as a function. Alternatively, it could be called as simply:

```
reset ($fruits);
```

This will effectively set the pointer back to the initial array element, but will not return a value.

each()

The each() function performs two distinct operations each time it is executed; It returns the key-value pair residing at the current pointer position and advances the pointer to the next element. The syntax is:

```
array each (array array)
```

For convenience, each() actually returns the key and value in a four-element array, the keys of this array being 0, 1, key, and value. The returned key is associated with the keys 0 and key, while the returned value is associated with the keys 1 and value.

This example uses each() to return the element found at the current pointer position:

```
// declare array of five elements
$spices = array("parsley", "sage", "rosemary", "thyme", "pepper");
// make sure that array is set at first element
reset($spices);
// create array $a_spice, which will hold four values.
$a_spice = each($spices);
```

Executing the preceding listing, the array $a_spice will now contain the following key-value pairs:

- 0 => 0

- 1 => "parsley"

- key => 0

- value => "parsley"

"Parsley" could then be displayed using either of the following statements:

```
print $a_spice[1];
print $a_spice["value"];
```

A common use of the each() function is in conjunction with list() and a looping construct for cycling through some or all of the elements in an array. Each iteration of each() will return either the next key-value pair or false if it has reached the last element in the array. Revisiting the $spices array, you could print all of the values to the screen using the following script:

```
// reset the array pointer
reset ($spices);
// cycle through each key-value pair, printing only the relevant part (the value)
while ( list ($key, $val) = each ($spices) ) :
    print "$val <br>"
endwhile;
```

A more interesting use of each(), along with several other functions introduced in this chapter, follows. Listing 5-1 shows how you could use these functions to display a formatted table of countries and languages.

Listing 5-1: Creating an HTML table from array elements

```
// declare associative array of countries and languages
$languages = array ("Country" => "Language",
                    "Spain" => "Spanish",
                    "USA" => "English",
                    "France" => "French",
                    "Russia" => "Russian");

// begin new table
print "<table border=0>";

// move pointer to first element position
reset ($languages);
// extract the first key and element
$hd1 = key ($languages);
$hd2 = $languages[$hd1];

// Print first key and element as table headers
print "<tr><th>$hd1</th><th>$hd2</th></tr>";

// move to next element set
next($languages);

// Print table rows including keys and elements of array
while ( list ($ctry,$lang) = each ($languages)) :
    print "<tr><td>$ctry</td><td>$lang</td></tr>";
endwhile;

// close table
print "</table>";
```

Execution of the preceding code yields the following HTML table:

COUNTRY	LANGUAGE
Spain	Spanish
USA	English
France	French
Russia	Russian

In this example we truly touched on the power of PHP; that is, the ability to mix dynamic code with HTML to produce clean, formatted results of mined information.

end()

The end() function moves the pointer to the last position of the array. Its syntax is:

```
end (array array)
```

next()

The next() function moves the pointer ahead one position before returning the element found at the pointer position. If an advance in the pointer position will move it past the last element of the array, next() will return false. Its syntax is:

```
mixed next (array array)
```

> **NOTE** *A problem with* next() *is that it will also return false for an array element that exists but is empty. If you are interested in merely traversing the array, use* each() *instead.*

prev()

The prev() function operates just like next(), except that it moves the pointer back one position before returning the element found at the pointer position. If the next retreat in pointer position will move it past the first element of the array, prev() will return false. Its syntax is:

```
mixed prev (array array)
```

> **NOTE** *A problem with prev() is that it will also return false for an array element that exists but is empty. If you are interested in merely traversing the array, use* each() *instead.*

array_walk()

The array_walk() function provides an easy way to apply a function to several or all elements in an array. Its syntax is:

```
int array_walk(array array, string func_name, [mixed data])
```

The function, denoted by the input parameter func_name, could be used for many purposes, for example, searching for elements having a specific characteristic or actually modifying the values of the array itself. At least two values must be passed into func_name: the first is the array value, and the second is the array key. If the optional input parameter data is supplied, then it will be the third value to func_name. Here's how you could use array_walk() to delete duplicates in an array:

```
function delete_dupes($element) {
    static $last="";
    if ($element == $last)
        unset($element);
    else
        $last=$element;
}

$emails = array("blah@blah.com", "chef@wjgilmore.com", "blah@blah.com");

sort($emails);
reset($emails);
array_walk($emails,"delete_dupes");

// $emails = array("chef@wjgilmore.com", "blah@blah.com");
```

array_reverse()

The array_reverse() function provides an easy way to reverse the order of the elements constituting the array. The syntax is:

```
array array_reverse(array array)
```

An example of array_reverse() follows:

```
$us_wine_producers = array ("California", "Oregon", "New York", "Washington");
$us_wine_producers = array_reverse ($us_wine_producers);
// $us_wine_producers = array ("Washington", "New York", "Oregon", "California");
```

Performing array_reverse() on an associative array will retain the key/value matching, but reverse the array order.

array_flip()

The array_flip() function will exchange ("flip") all key and element values for the array. Its syntax is:

```
array array_flip(array array)
```

Here's how you could use array_flip() to flip all key and element values:

```
$languages = array("Spain" => "Spanish",
                        "France" => "French",
                        "Italy" => "Italian");

$languages = array_flip($languages);

// $languages = array("Spanish" => "Spain",
//                         "French" => "France",
//                         "Italian" => "Italy");
```

Keep in mind that array_flip() only flips the key/value mapping and does *not* reverse the positioning. To reverse the positioning of the elements, use array_reverse().

Array Size

Knowledge of the current size of an array has many applications when coding efficient scripts. Other than using the size for simple referential purposes, perhaps the most common use of the array size is for looping through arrays:

```
$us_wine_producers = array ("Washington", "New York", "Oregon", "California");
for ($i = 0; $i < sizeof ($us_wine_producers); $i++) :
     print "$us_wine_producers[$i]";
endfor;
```

Because the $us_wine_producers array is indexed by integer value, you can use a for loop to iteratively increment a counting variable ($i) and display each element in the array.

sizeof()

The function sizeof() is used to return the number of elements contained in an array. Its syntax is:

```
int sizeof (array array)
```

You will probably use the `sizeof()` function often in your Web applications. A brief example of its usage follows. The previous example is another common usage of the `sizeof()` function.

```
$pasta = array("bowties", "angelhair", "rigatoni");
$pasta_size = sizeof($pasta);
// $pasta_size = 3
```

An alternative, extended form of `sizeof()` is `count()`, next.

count()

The `count()` function performs the same operations as `sizeof()`, returning the number of values contained in an array. Its syntax is:

```
int count (mixed variable)
```

The only difference between `sizeof()` and `count()` is that `count()` provides a bit more information in some situations:

- If the variable exists and is an array, `count()` will return the number of elements contained in the array.

- If the variable exists but is not an array, the value '1' will be returned.

- If the variable does not exist, the value '0' will be returned.

array_count_values()

The `array_count_values()` function is a variation of `sizeof()` and `count()`, instead counting the frequency of the values appearing in the array. Its syntax is:

```
array array_count_values (array array);
```

The returned array will use the values as keys and their corresponding frequencies as the values, as illustrated here:

```
$states = array("OH", "OK", "CA", "PA", "OH", "OH", "PA", "AK");
$state_freq = array_count_values($states);
```

The array $state_freq will now contain the following key/value associations:

```
$state_freq = array("OH" => 3, "OK" => 1, "CA" => 1, "PA" => 2, "AK" => 1);
```

Sorting Arrays

The importance of sorting routines can hardly be understated in the realm of programming and can be seen in action in such online applications as ecommerce sites (sorting categories by alphabetical order), shopping bots (sorting prices), and software search engines (sorting software by number of downloads). PHP offers the nine predefined sorting functions listed in Table 5-1, each sorting an array in a unique fashion.

Table 5-1. Sort Function Summary

FUNCTION	SORT BY	REVERSE SORT?	MAINTAIN KEY/VALUE CORRELATION?
sort	Value	No	No
rsort	Value	Yes	No
asort	Value	No	Yes
arsort	Value	Yes	Yes
ksort	Key	No	Yes
krsort	Key	Yes	Yes
usort	Value	?	No
uasort	Value	?	Yes
uksort	Key	?	Yes

? applies to the user-defined sorting functions, where the order in which the array is sorted depends on the results brought about by the user-defined function.

You are not limited to using predefined criteria for sorting your array information, as three of these functions (usort(), uasort(), and uksort()) allow you to introduce array-specific criteria to sort the information any way you please.

sort()

The sort() function is the most basic sorting function, sorting array elements from lowest to highest value. Its syntax is:

```
void sort (array array)
```

Nonnumerical elements will be sorted in alphabetical order, according to their ASCII values. This basic example illustrates use of the sort function:

```
// create an array of cities.
$cities = array ("Aprilia", "Nettuno", "Roma", "Venezia", "Anzio");

// sort the cities from lowest to highest value
sort($cities);

// cycle through the array, printing each key and value.
for (reset ($cities); $key = key ($cities); next ($cities)) :
    print "cities[$key] = $cities[$key] <br>";
endfor;
```

Executing the preceding code yields:

```
cities[0] = Anzio
cities[1] = Aprilia
cities[2] = Nettuno
cities[3] = Roma
cities[4] = Venezia
```

As you can see, the $cities array has been sorted in alphabetical order. A variation on this algorithm is asort(), introduced later in this chapter.

rsort()

The rsort() function operates exactly like the sort() function, except that it sorts the elements in reverse order. Its syntax is:

```
void rsort (array array)
```

Reconsider the $cities array, first introduced in the preceding example:

```
$cities = array ("Aprilia", "Nettuno", "Roma", "Venezia", "Anzio")
rsort($cities);
```

Using rsort() to sort the $cities array results in the following reordering:

```
cities[0] = Venezia
cities[1] = Roma
cities[2] = Nettuno
cities[3] = Aprilia
cities[4] = Anzio
```

Once again, the $cities array is sorted, but this time in reverse alphabetical order. A variation of this function is arsort(), described later in this chapter.

asort()

The asort() function works much like the previously explained sort() function, except that the array indexes maintain their original association with the elements regardless of the new position the element assumes. The function's syntax is:

```
void asort (array array)
```

Revisiting the $cities array:

```
$cities = array ("Aprilia", "Nettuno", "Roma", "Venezia", "Anzio");
asort($cities);
```

Use asort() to sort the $cities array, which yields this new array ordering:

```
cities[4] = Anzio
cities[0] = Aprilia
cities[1] = Nettuno
cities[2] = Roma
cities[3] = Venezia
```

Note the index values and compare them to those in the example accompanying the introduction to sort(). This is the differentiating factor between the two functions.

arsort()

The arsort() function is a variation of asort(), maintaining the original index association but instead sorting the elements in reverse order. Its syntax is:

```
void arsort (array array)
```

Using `arsort()` to sort the `$cities` array:

```
$cities = array ("Aprilia", "Nettuno", "Roma", "Venezia", "Anzio");
arsort($cities);
```

results in the array being sorted in the following order:

```
cities[3] = Venezia
cities[2] = Roma
cities[1] = Nettuno
cities[0] = Aprilia
cities[4] = Anzio
```

Note the index values and compare them to those in the example accompanying the introduction to `rsort()`. This is the differentiating factor between the two functions.

ksort()

The `ksort()` function sorts an array according to its key values, maintaining the original index association. Its syntax is:

```
void ksort (array array)
```

Consider an array slightly different from the original `$cities` array:

```
$wine_producers = array ("America" => "Napa Valley",
                         "Italy" => "Tuscany",
                         "Australia" => "Rutherglen",
                         "France" => "Loire",
                         "Chile" => "Rapel Valley");
```

Sorting this array using `ksort()`, it would be reordered as follows:

```
"America" => "Napa Valley"
"Australia" => "Rutherglen"
"Chile" => "Rapel Valley"
"France" => "Loire"
"Italy" => "Tuscany"
```

Contrast this to the effects of sorting $wine_producers using sort():

```
"America" => "Napa Valley"
"Australia" => "Tuscany"
"Chile" => "Rutherglen"
"France" => "Loire"
"Italy" => "Rapel Valley"
```

Less than optimal results!

krsort()

The krsort() function performs the same operations as ksort(), except that the key values are sorted in reverse order. Its syntax is:

```
void krsort (array $array)
```

Sorting $wine_producers using krsort():

```
$wine_producers = array ("America" => "Napa Valley",
                         "Italy" => "Tuscany",
                         "Australia" => "Rutherglen",
                         "France" => "Loire",
                         "Chile" => "Rapel Valley");
krsort($wine_producers);
```

yields the following reordering of $wine_producers:

```
"Italy" => "Tuscany"
"France" => "Loire"
"Chile" => "Rapel Valley"
"Australia" => "Rutherglen"
"America" => "Napa Valley"
```

For the most part, the sorting functions presented thus far will suit your general sorting requirements. However, occasionally you may need to define your own sorting criteria. This is possible with PHP, through the use of its three predefined functions: usort(), uasort(), and uksort().

usort()

The sorting function usort() provides a way in which to sort an array based on your own predefined criteria. This is possible because usort() accepts as an input parameter a function name that is used to determine the sorting order of the data. Its syntax is:

```
void usort(array array, string function_name)
```

The input parameter array is the name of the array that you are interested in sorting, and the parameter function_name is the name of the function on which the sorting mechanism will be based. To illustrate just how useful this function can be, assume that you had a long list of Greek vocabulary that you needed to learn for an upcoming history exam. You wanted to sort the words according to length, so that you could study the longer ones first, saving the short ones for when you are more fatigued. You could sort them according to length using usort():

Listing 5-2: Defining sorting criteria with usort()
```
$vocab = array("Socrates","Aristophanes", "Plato", "Aeschylus",
"Thesmophoriazusae");

function compare_length($str1, $str2) {
    // retrieve the lengths of the next two array values
    $length1 = strlen($str1);
    $length2 = strlen($str2);

    // Verify which string is shorter in length.
    if ($length1 == $length2) :
        return 0;
    elseif ($length1 < $length2) :
        return -1;
    else :
        return 1;
    endif;
}
// call usort(), defining the sorting function compare_length()
usort($vocab, "compare_length");

// display the sorted list
while (list ($key, $val) = each ($vocab)) {
    echo "$val<br>";
}
```

In Listing 5-2, the function `compare_length()` defines how the array will be sorted, in this case by comparing the lengths of the passed in elements. Note that you must define two input parameters that represent the next two array elements to be compared. Furthermore, take note that these elements are implicitly passed into the criteria function once `usort()` is called and that all elements are passed through this function automatically.

The functions `uasort()` and `uksort()` are variations of `usort()`, each using the same syntax. The function `uasort()` will sort according to the predefined criteria, except that the key->value correlation will remain the same. The function `uksort()` will also sort according to the predefined criteria, except that the keys will be sorted instead of the values.

Other Useful Functions

This section describes a few functions that are obscure enough to not have a section subtitle, but are nonetheless useful.

array_merge()

The `array_merge()` function merges 1 to N arrays together, appending each to another in the order in which they appear as input parameters. The function's syntax is:

```
array array_merge (array array1, array array2, . . ., array arrayN)
```

The `array_merge()` function provides an easy way to merge several arrays, as shown here:

```
$arr_1 = array ("strawberry", "grape", "lemon");
$arr_2 = array ("banana", "cocoa", "lime");
$arr_3 = array ("peach", "orange");

$arr_4 = array_merge ($arr_2, $arr_1, $arr_3);
// $arr_4 = array("banana", "cocoa", "lime", "strawberry",
//                "grape", "lemon", "peach", "orange");
```

array_slice()

The `array_slice()` function will return a piece of the array, the starting and ending points decided by the offset and optional length input parameters. Its syntax is:

```
array array_slice(array array, int offset, int [length])
```

There are several nuances regarding the input parameters:

- If the offset is positive, the returned slice will start that far away from the beginning of the array.

- If the offset is negative, the returned slice will start that far away from the end of the array.

- If the length is omitted, the returned array will consist of everything from the offset to the end of the array.

- If the length is provided and is positive, the returned slice will have length elements in it.

- If the length is provided and is negative, the returned slice will stop length elements away from the end of the array.

array_splice()

The array_splice() function operates somewhat like the function array_slice, except that it replaces the designated elements specified by the offset and the optional length input parameters with the elements in the optional array replacement_array. Its syntax is:

```
array_splice(array input_array, int offset, int [length], array
[replacement_array]);
```

There are several factors to keep in mind regarding the input parameters:

- If offset is positive, then the first element to be removed will be offset elements away from the beginning of the array.

- If offset is negative, then the first element to be removed will be offset elements away from the end of the array.

- If length is not provided, all elements starting from offset to the end of the array will be removed.

- If length is provided and is positive, length elements will be removed from the array.

- If length is provided and is negative, elements from offset to length elements away from the end of the array will be removed.

- If replacement_array is not specified, then the elements from offset to the optional length will be removed from the input array.

- If $replacement_array is specified, it must be enclosed using the array() construct, unless $replacement_array consists of only one element.

A few examples are in order to fully illustrate the capabilities of this function. Consider the array $pasta, below. Each example will manipulate this array in a slightly different manner.

Remove all elements from the fifth element to the end of the array:

```
$pasta = array_splice($pasta, 5);
```

Remove the fifth and sixth elements from the array:

```
$pasta = array_splice($pasta, 5, 2);
```

Replace the third and fourth elements with new elements:

```
$pasta = array_splice($pasta, 5, 2, array("element1", "element2"));
```

Remove all elements from positions 3 to (n 3):

```
$pasta = array_splice($pasta, 5, -3);
```

As illustrated by the preceding examples, array_splice() provides a flexible method to remove specific array elements with a minimal amount of code.

shuffle()

The function shuffle() will sort the elements of an array in random order. Its syntax is:

```
void shuffle(array array);
```

What's Next?

This chapter introduced arrays and the predefined array-handling functions offered by PHP. In particular, the following concepts were discussed:

- Creation of indexed and associative arrays

- Multidimensional arrays

- Display of multidimensional arrays

- Locating array elements

- Adding and removing elements

- Array size

- Sorting arrays

- Other useful array functions

Arrays provide a very convenient and flexible means for managing information in Web applications. There are several instances in later chapters in which I make use of arrays to improve coding efficiency and clarity.

Chapter 6 continues our survey of PHP's basic functionality, discussing PHP's object-oriented capabilities.

CHAPTER 6

Object-Oriented PHP

If you are familiar with programming strategy, object-oriented programming (OOP) is most likely a part of your daily developmental strategy. If you are new to OOP, after reading this chapter and implementing a few of the examples, you will look at coding in a whole new light. This chapter focuses on OOP and PHP's particular implementation of the OOP strategy, introducing the necessary syntax and providing examples that will allow you to begin building your own OO applications.

The OOP strategy can be best summed up as a shift of developmental focus from an application's functional operations to its data structures. This enables programmers to model real world objects and scenarios in the applications that they write. In particular, the OOP strategy offers three advantages:

- Easier to understand: OOP makes it possible to think of programs in terms of everyday objects.

- Improved reliability and maintenance: Designed properly, OO programs are easily expanded and modified. The modular property makes it possible to independently edit various parts of the program, effectively minimizing the risk of programming errors.

- Faster development cycles: Modularity again plays an important role, as various parts of OO programs can be easily reused, eliminating code redundancy and ultimately resulting in the reduction of unnecessarily repeated coding errors.

These intrinsic advantages of OOP have resulted in major efficiency gains for developers, enabling programmers to develop more powerful, scalable, and efficient applications. Many of these advantages are due to one of OOP's foundational concepts known as *encapsulation*, or *information hiding*. Encapsulation is the concept of hiding various elements in a larger entity, causing the programmer to concentrate on the larger object. This results in the overall reduction of program complexity due to the diminution of unnecessary details.

The concept of encapsulation can be correlated to the typical driver's operation of a car. Most drivers are oblivious to the actual mechanical operations of the automobile, yet are capable of operating the vehicle exactly in the way it was intended to be operated. Knowledge of the inner-workings of the engine, brakes, and steering is unnecessary, because proper interfacing has been provided to the driver that makes these otherwise highly complex operations automated and easy. The same idea holds true with encapsulation and OOP, as many of these "inner workings" are hidden from the user, allowing the user to focus on the task at hand. OOP makes this possible through the use of classes, objects, and various means of expressing hierarchical relationships between data entities. (Classes and objects are discussed shortly.)

PHP and OOP

Although PHP offers general object-oriented features, it is not yet a full-featured OO language, like C++ or Java, for example. Unlike OOP, PHP does not explicitly offer the following object-oriented characteristics:

- Multiple inheritance

- Constructor chaining (you must call a parent class constructor explicitly if you would like it to execute on construction of a derived class object)

- Class abstraction

- Method overloading

- Operator overloading (because PHP is a loosely typed language; see Chapter 2, "Variables and Data Types," for more info)

- Concepts of private, virtual, and public

- Destructors

- Polymorphism

However, even without these important OO features, you can still benefit from using those OO features that PHP does support. PHP's OO implementation can aid tremendously in packaging your programming functionality. Read on to learn more.

Classes, Objects, and Method Declarations

The *class* is the syntactical foundation of object-oriented programming and can be considered a container of sorts that holds an interrelated set of data and the data's corresponding functions, better known as *methods* (discussed shortly). A class is a template from which specific instances of the class may be created and used in a program. These instances are also known as *objects*.

One way to grasp the relationship between classes and objects is to consider the class as a general blueprint for a structure. From this blueprint, several structures (or objects) can be built, each sharing the same set of core characteristics (for example, one door, two windows, and a wall thickness). However, each structure is independent of the others in the sense that it is free to change the characteristic values without affecting the values of the others. (For example, one structure might have a wall thickness of five inches, while another has a wall thickness of ten inches.) The important thing to keep in mind is that they all share this characteristic of wall thickness.

A class can also be thought of as a data type (discussed in Chapter 2), much as one would consider a variable entitled $counter to be of type int, or a variable entitled $last_name to be of type string. One could simultaneously manipulate several objects of type class just as one manipulates several variables of type int. The general format of a PHP class is shown in Listing 6-1.

Listing 6-1: PHP class declaration structure

```
class Class_name {
    var $attribute_1;
    . . .
    var $attribute_N;

    function function1() {
    . . .
    }
    . . .
    function functionN() {
    . . .
    }

} // end Class_name
```

To summarize Listing 6-1, a class declaration must begin with the keyword class, much like a function declaration begins with the keyword function. Each attribute declaration contained in a class must be preceded by the keyword var. An attribute can be of any PHP-supported data type and should be thought of as a variable with minor differences, as you will learn throughout the remainder of this chapter. Following the attributes are the method declarations, which bear a close resemblance to typical function declarations.

NOTE   *It is a general convention that OO classes begin with a capital letter, while methods start in lowercase with uppercase separating each word from a multiword function name. Of course, you can use whatever nomenclature you feel most comfortable with; just be sure to choose a standard and stick with it.*

One main use of methods is to manipulate the various attributes constituting the class. However, these attributes are referenced in the methods using a special variable called $this. Consider the following example demonstrating the use of this syntax:

```
<?
class Webpage {
    var $bgcolor;

    function setBgColor($color) {
        $this->bgcolor = $color;
    }

    function getBgColor() {
        return $this->bgcolor;
    }

}
?>
```

The $this variable is referring to the particular object making use of the method. Because there can be many object instances of a particular class, $this is a means of referring to the attribute belonging to the calling (or 'this') object. Furthermore, there are two points regarding this newly introduced syntax worth mentioning:

- The attribute being referenced in the method does *not* have to be passed in as would a functional input parameter.

- A dollar sign ($) precedes only the $this variable and *not* the attribute itself, as would be the case with a normal variable.

Creating and Working with Objects

An object is created using the new operator. An object based on the class Webpage can be instantiated as follows:

```
$some_page = new Webpage;
```

The new object $some_page now has its own set of attributes and methods specified in the class Webpage. The attribute $bgcolor corresponding to this specific object can then be assigned or changed via the predefined method setBgColor():

```
$some_page->setBgColor("black");
```

- Keep in mind that PHP also allows you to retrieve the value by explicitly calling the attribute along with the object name:

```
$some_page->bgcolor;
```

However, this second method of retrieval defeats the purpose of encapsulation, and you should never retrieve a value this way when working with OOP. To better understand why this is the case, take a moment to read the next section.

Why Insufficient Encapsulation Practice Is BAD!

Consider a scenario in which you assign an array as an attribute in a given class. However, instead of calling intermediary methods to control the array (for example, add, delete, modify elements, and so on), you directly call the array whenever needed. Over the period of a month, you confidently design and code a massive "object-oriented" application and revel in the glory of the praise provided to you by your fellow programmers. Ahhhh, a pension plan, paid vacation, and maybe your own office are just around the corner.

But wait, one month after the successful launch of your Web application, your boss decides that arrays aren't the way to go and instead wants all data controlled via a database.

Uh-oh. Because you decided to explicitly manipulate the attributes, you now must go through the code, changing every instance in which you did so to fit the new requirements of a database interface. A time-consuming task to say the least, but also one that could result in the introduction of many new coding errors.

However, consider the result if you had used methods to interface with this data. The only thing you would have to do to switch from an array to a database storage protocol would be to modify the attribute itself and the code contained in the methods. This modification would result in the automatic propagation of these changes to every part of the code in which the relevant methods are called.

Constructors

Often, just creating a new object is a bit inefficient, as you may need to assign several attributes along with each object. Thankfully, the designers of the OOP strategy took this into consideration, introducing the concept of a *constructor*. A constructor is nothing more than a method that sets particular attributes (and can also trigger methods), simultaneously called when a new object is created. For this concurrent process to occur, the constructor method must be given the same name as the class in which it is contained. Listing 6-2 shows how you might use a constructor method.

Listing 6-2: Using a constructor method

```
<?
class Webpage {
    var $bgcolor;

    function Webpage($color) {
        $this->bgcolor = $color;
    }
}

// call the Webpage constructor
$page = new Webpage("brown");
?>
```

Previously, two steps were required for the class creation and initial attribute assignment, one step for each task. Using constructors, this process is trimmed down to just one step.

Interestingly, different constructors can be called depending on the number of parameters passed to them. Referring to Listing 6-2, an object based on the Webpage class can be created in two ways: You can use the class as a constructor, which will simply create the object, but not assign any attributes, as shown here:

```
$page = new Webpage;
```

Or you can create the object using the predefined constructor, creating an object of class Webpage and setting its bgcolor attribute, as you see here:

```
$page = new Webpage("brown");
```

Destructors

As I've already stated, PHP does not explicitly support destructors. However, you can easily build your own destructor by calling the PHP function unset(). This function acts to erase the contents of a variable, thereby returning its resources back to memory. Quite conveniently, unset() works with objects in the same way that it does with variables. For example, assume that you are working with the object *$Webpage*. You've finished working with this particular object, so you call:

```
unset($Webpage);
```

This will remove all of the contents of *$Webpage* from memory. Keeping with the spirit of encapsulation, you could place this command within a method called destroy() and then call:

```
$Website->destroy();
```

Keep in mind that there really isn't a need to use destructors, unless you are using objects that are taking up considerable resources; all variables and objects are automatically destroyed once the script finishes execution.

Inheritance and Multilevel Inheritance

As you are already aware, a class is a template for a real world object that acts as a representation of its characteristics and functions. However, you probably know of instances in which a particular object could be a subset of another. For example, an automobile could be considered a subset of the category vehicle because airplanes are also considered vehicles. Although each vehicle type is easily distinguishable from the other, assume that there exists a core set of characteristics that all share, including number of wheels, horsepower, current speed, and model. Of course, the values assigned to the attributes of each may differ substantially, but nonetheless these characteristics do exist. Consequently, it could be said that the subclasses automobile and airplane both inherit this core set of characteristics from a superclass known as vehicle. The concept of a class inheriting the characteristics of another class is known as *inheritance*.

Inheritance is a particularly powerful programming mechanism because it can eliminate an otherwise substantial need to repeat code that could be shared between data structures, such as the shared characteristics of the various vehicle types mentioned in the previous paragraph. The general PHP syntax used to inherit the characteristics of another class follows:

```
class Class_name2 extends Class_name1 {

    attribute declarations;

    method declarations;

}
```

The notion of a class extending another class is just another way of stating that Class_name2 inherits all of the characteristics contained in Class_name1 and in turn possibly extends the use and depth of the Class_name1 characteristics with those contained in Class_name2.

Other than for reason of code reusability, inheritance provides a second important programming advantage: it reduces the possibility of error when a program is modified. Considering the class inheritance hierarchy shown in Figure 6-1, realize that a modification to the code contained in auto will have no effect on the code (and data) contained in airplane, and vice versa.

CAUTION *A call to the constructor of a derived class does not imply that the constructor of the parent class is also called.*

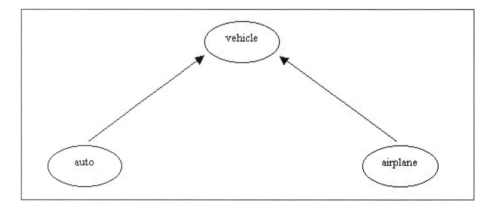

Figure 6-1. Relationship diagram of the various vehicle types

Let's use Listing 6-3 to build the code needed to accurately represent Figure 6-1.

Listing 6-3: Using inheritance to efficiently represent various vehicle types

```php
<?
class Vehicle {
    var $model;
    var $current_speed;

    function setSpeed($mph) {
        $this->current_speed = $mph;
    }

    function getSpeed() {
        return $this->current_speed;
    }
} // end class Vehicle

class Auto extends Vehicle {
    var $fuel_type;

    function setFuelType($fuel) {
        $this->fuel_type = $fuel;
    }

    function getFuelType() {
        return $this->fuel_type;
    }

} // end Auto extends Vehicle

class Airplane extends Vehicle {
    var $wingspan;

    function setWingSpan($wingspan) {
        $this->wingspan = $wingspan;
    }

    function getWingSpan() {
        return $this->wingspan;
    }
} // end Airplane extends Vehicle
```

We could then instantiate various objects as follows:

```
$tractor = new Vehicle;
$gulfstream = new Airplane;
?>
```

Two objects have been created. The first, `$tractor`, is a member of the Vehicle class. The second, `$gulfstream`, is a member of the Airplane class, possessing the characteristics of the Airplane and the Vehicle class.

> **CAUTION** *The idea of a class inheriting the properties of more than one parent class is known as* multiple inheritance. *Unfortunately, multiple inheritance is not possible in PHP. For example, you cannot do this in PHP:*
>
> ```
> Class Airplane extends Vehicle extends Building . . .
> ```

Multilevel Inheritance

As programs increase in size and complexity, you may need several levels of inheritance, or classes that inherit from other classes, which in turn inherit properties from other classes, and so on. Multilevel inheritance further modularizes the program, resulting in an increasingly maintainable and detailed program structure. Continuing along with the Vehicle example, a larger program may demand that an additional class be introduced between the Vehicle superclass to further categorize the class structure. For example, the class Vehicle may be divided into the classes land, sea, and air, and then specific instances of each of those subclasses can be based on the medium in which the vehicle in question travels. This is illustrated in Figure 6-2.

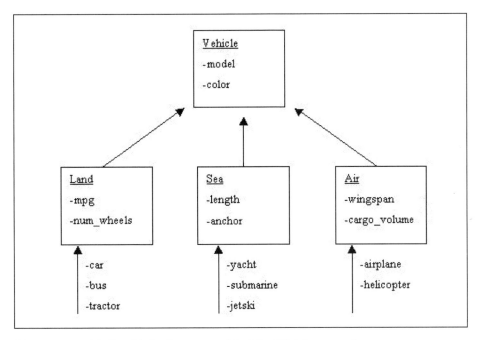

Figure 6-2. Multilevel inheritance model of the Vehicle superclass

Consider the brief example in Listing 6-4, which serves to highlight a few important aspects of multilevel inheritance in regard to PHP.

Listing 6-4: Making use of multilevel inheritance

```php
<?
class Vehicle {
    Attribute declarations. . .
    Method declarations. . .
}

class Land extends Vehicle {
    Attribute declarations. . .
    Method declarations. . .
}

class Car extends Land {
    Attribute declarations. . .
    Method declarations. . .
}
$nissan = new Car;
?>
```

Once instantiated, the object $nissan has at its disposal all of the attributes methods available in Car, Land, and Vehicle. As you can see, this is an extremely modular structure. For example, sometime throughout the lifecycle of the program, you may wish to add a new attribute to Land. No problem: just modify the Land class accordingly, and that attribute becomes immediately available to itself and Car, without affecting the functionality of any other class. This idea of code modularity and flexibility is indeed one of the great advantages of OOP.

> **NOTE** *Keep in mind that although a class can inherit characteristics from a chain of parents, the parents' constructors are not called automatically when you instantiate an object from the inheriting class. These constructors become methods for the child class.*

Class Abstraction

Sometimes it is useful to create a class that will never be instantiated and instead will just act as the base for a derived class. This kind of class is known as an *abstract class*. An abstract class is useful when a program designer wants to ensure that certain functionality is available in any subsequently derived classes based on that abstract class.

PHP does not offer explicit class abstraction, but there is an easy workaround. Just create a default constructor and place a call to die() in it. Referring to the classes in Listing 6-4, chances are you will never wish to instantiate the Land or Vehicle classes, because neither could represent a single entity. Instead, you would extend these classes into a real world object, such as the car class. Therefore, to ensure that Land or Vehicle is never directly instantiated, place the die() call in each, as seen in Listing 6-5.

Listing 6-5: Building abstract classes

```
<?
class Vehicle {
            Attribute declarations. . .
            function Vehicle() {
                        die("Cannot create Abstract Vehicle class!");
            }
            Other Method declarations. . .
}

class Land extends Vehicle {
            Attribute declarations. . .
            function Land() {
                        die("Cannot create Abstract Land class!");
            }
            Other Method declarations. . .
}

class car extends Land {
            Attribute declarations. . .
            Method declarations. . .
}
?>
```

Therefore, any attempt to instantiate these abstract classes results in an appropriate error message and program termination.

Method Overloading

Method overloading is the practice of defining multiple methods with the same name, but each having a different number or type of parameters. This too is not a feature supported by PHP, but an easy workaround exists, as shown in Listing 6-6.

Listing 6-6: Method overloading

```
<?
class Page {
    var $bgcolor;
    var $textcolor;

    function Page() {
        // Determine the number of arguments
        // passed in, and create correct method name
        $name = "Page".func_num_args();
        // Call $name with correct number of arguments passed in
        if ( func_num_args() == 0 ) :
            $this->$name();
        else :
            $this->$name(func_get_arg(0));
        endif;
    }

    function Page0() {
        $this->bgcolor = "white";
        $this->textcolor = "black";
        print "Created default page";
    }

    function Page1($bgcolor) {
        $this->bgcolor = $bgcolor;
        $this->textcolor = "black";
        print "Created custom page";
    }
}
$html_page = new Page("red");
?>
```

In this example, a new object entitled $html_page is created, with one argument passed in. Since a default constructor has been created (Page()), the instantiation begins there. However, this default constructor is simply used to determine exactly which of the other constructor methods (Page0() or Page1()) is called. This is determined by making use of the func_num_args() and func_get_arg() functions, which count the number of arguments and retrieve the arguments, respectively.

Obviously, this is not method overloading as it was intended to be implemented, but it does the job for those of you who cannot live without this important OOP feature.

Class and Object Functions

PHP offers a number of predefined class and object functions, which are discussed in the following sections. All can be useful, particularly for interface development, code administration, and error checking.

get_class_methods()

The get_class_methods() function returns an array of methods defined by the class specified by class_name. The syntax is:

```
array get_class_methods (string class_name)
```

A simple example of how get_class_methods() is used is in Listing 6-7.

Listing 6-7: Retrieving the set of methods available to a particular class

```
<?
. . .
class Airplane extends Vehicle {
    var $wingspan;

    function setWingSpan($wingspan) {
        $this->wingspan = $wingspan;
    }

    function getWingSpan() {
        return $this->wingspan;
    }
}

$cls_methods = get_class_methods(Airplane);
// $cls_methods will contain an array of all methods
// declared in the classes "Airplane" and "Vehicle".
?>
```

As you can see by following the code in Listing 6-7, get_class_methods() is an easy way to obtain a listing of all supported methods of a particular class.

get_class_vars()

The get_class_vars() function returns an array of attributes defined in the class specified by class_name. Its syntax is:

```
array get_class_vars (string class_name)
```

An example of how get_class_vars() is used is in Listing 6-8.

Listing 6-8: Using get_class_vars() to create $attribs

```
<?
class Vehicle {
    var $model;
    var $current_speed;
}
class Airplane extends Vehicle {
    var $wingspan;
}

$a_class = "Airplane";

$attribs = get_class_vars($a_class);
// $attribs = array ( "wingspan", "model", "current_speed")
?>
```

Therefore, the variable $attribs is created and becomes an array containing all available attributes of the class Airplane.

get_object_vars()

The get_object_vars() function returns an array containing the properties of the attributes assigned to the object specified by obj_name. Its syntax is:

```
array get_object_vars (object obj_name)
```

An example of how get_object_vars() is used is in Listing 6-9.

Listing 6-9: Obtaining object variables

```php
<?
class Vehicle {
    var $wheels;
}

class Land extends Vehicle {
    var $engine;
}

class car extends Land {
    var $doors;

    function car($doors, $eng, $wheels) {
        $this->doors = $doors;
        $this->engine = $eng;
        $this->wheels = $wheels;
    }

    function get_wheels() {
        return $this->wheels;
    }

}

$toyota = new car(2,400,4);

$vars = get_object_vars($toyota);

while (list($key, $value) = each($vars)) :

    print "$key ==> $value <br>";

endwhile;
// displays:
// doors ==> 2
// engine ==> 400
// wheels ==> 2
?>
```

Using get_object_vars() is a convenient way to quickly obtain all of the attribute/value mappings of a particular object.

method_exists()

The method_exists() function checks to see if a particular method (denoted by method_name), exists in the object specified by obj_name, returning true if it exists, or false if it does not. Its syntax is:

```
bool method_exists (object obj_name, string method_name)
```

An example of the usage of method_exists() is in Listing 6-10.

Listing 6-10: Using method_exists() to verify an object/method mapping.

```
<?
class Vehicle {
    . . .
    }

    class Land extends Vehicle {
        var $fourWheel;
        function setFourWheelDrive() {
            $this->fourWeel = 1;
        }
    }

    // create object named $car
    $car = new Land;

    // if method "fourWheelDrive" is a part of classes "Land" or "Vehicle",
    // then the call to method_exists() will return true;
    // Otherwise false will be returned.
    // Therefore, in this case, method_exists() will return true.

    if (method_exists($car, "setfourWheelDrive")) :
        print "This car is equipped with 4-wheel drive";
    else :
        print "This car is not equipped with 4-wheel drive";
    endif;
?>
```

In Listing 6-10, the function method_exists() is used to verify whether or not the object $car has access to the method setFourWheelDrive(). If it does, true is returned, and the appropriate message is displayed. Otherwise, false is returned, and a message stating that four-wheel drive is not available with that particular object.

get_class()

The get_class() function returns the name of the class from which the object specified by obj_name is instantiated. The syntax is:

```
string get_class(object obj_name);
```

An example of how get_class() is implemented is in Listing 6-11.

Listing 6-11: Using get_class()to return the name of an instantiation class

```
<?
class Vehicle {
    . . .
}

class Land extends Vehicle {
. . .
}

// create object named $car
$car = new Land;

// $class_a is assigned "Land"
$class_a = get_class($car);
?>
```

Simply enough, the variable $class_a is assigned the name of the class from which the object $car was derived.

get_parent_class()

The get_parent_class() function returns the name, if any, of the parent class of the object specified by objname. The syntax is:

```
string get_parent_class(object objname);
```

Listing 6-12 illustrates usage of get_parent_class().

Listing 6-12: Name of the class parent returned using get_parent_class()

```
<?
class Vehicle {

. . .
}

class Land extends Vehicle {

. . .
}

// create object named $car
$car = new Land;

// $parent is assigned "Vehicle"
$parent = get_parent_class($car);
?>
```

As you would expect, the call to get_parent_class() assigns the value "Vehicle" to the variable $parent.

is_subclass_of()

The is_subclass_of() function ensures whether or not an object was created from a class whose parent is specified by class_name, returning true if it was, and false otherwise. Its syntax is:

```
bool is_subclass_of (object obj, string class_name)
```

Listing 6-13 illustrates proper usage of is_subclass_of().

Listing 6-13: Using is_subclass_of() to determine whether an object was created from a class derived from a specific parent class

```
<?
class Vehicle {

. . .

}

class Land extends Vehicle {

. . .

}
$auto = new Land;
// $is_subclass receives the value "true"
$is_subclass = is_subclass_of($auto, "Vehicle");
?>
```

In Listing 6-13, the variable $is_subclass is used to determine whether the object $auto is derived from a subclass of the parent class Vehicle. In fact, $auto is derived from Land; therefore, $is_subclass will receive the boolean value true.

get_declared_classes()

The get_declared_classes() function returns an array of all defined classes, as shown in Listing 6-14. Its syntax is:

```
array get_declared_classes()
```

Listing 6-14: Retrieving all defined classes with get_declared_classes()

```
<?
class Vehicle {

. . .

}
class Land extends Vehicle {

. . .

}
// $declared_classes = array("Vehicle", "Land")
$declared_classes = get_declared_classes();
?>
```

What's Next?

This chapter introduced you to several of object-oriented programming's basic concepts, concentrating on how these concepts are applied to the PHP programming language. In particular, the following subjects were discussed in detail:

- Introduction to object-oriented programming

- Classes, objects, and methods

- Inheritance and multilevel inheritance

- Class abstraction

- Method overloading

- PHP's class and object functions

Although not overly complicated, the object-oriented programming strategy usually requires of the programmer an initial exploration period before all of the concepts are really understood. However, I guarantee that the extra time you take to understand these notions will add an entirely new level of efficiency and creativity to your programming repertoire.

File I/O
and the File System

This chapter introduces a particularly important aspect of PHP: file I/O (input/output). As you can imagine, data input and output flows are put to considerable use in the developing of Web applications. Not limited to simple reading and writing of files, PHP provides support for viewing and modifying server information, in addition to executing third-party programs. These features are the subject of this chapter.

Verifying a File's Existence and Size

It is useful to be able to determine the existence of a file before attempting to work with it. Two functions are particularly useful for accomplishing this: file_exists() and is_file().

file_exists()

The file_exists() function will ensure that file exists, returning true if it does, and false otherwise. Its syntax is:

```
bool file_exists (string file)
```

Here's how you can verify the existence of a file:

```
$filename = "userdata.txt";

if (! file_exists ($filename)) :
    print "File $filename does not exist!";
endif;
```

is_file()

The is_file() function will return true if file exists and is a readable/writable file. Essentially, is_file() is a bullet-proof version of file_exists(), verifying not only the file's existence but also whether it can be read from or written to:

```
bool is_file (string file)
```

This example shows how to verify the existence and validity of a file:

```
$file = "somefile.txt";
if (is_file($file)) :
    print "The file $file is valid and exists!";
else :
    print "Either $file does not exist or it is not a valid file!";
endif;
```

Once you have verified that the file of interest does exist and is capable of having various I/O operations performed on it, you can open it.

filesize()

The filesize() function will return the size, in bytes, of the file designated by filename, or false should an error occur. Its syntax is:

```
int filesize (string filename)
```

Assume that you want to know the size of a file named pastry.txt. You can use filesize() to retrieve this information:

```
$fs = filesize("pastry.txt");
print "Pastry.txt is $fs bytes.";
```

This will return:

```
Pastry.txt is 179 bytes.
```

Before files can be manipulated, they must be opened and assigned a file handle. Once you have finished working with a file, it should be closed. These subjects are the focus of the next section.

Opening and Closing I/O

Before you can perform any I/O operation on a file, you must open it using the fopen() function.

fopen()

The fopen() function opens a file, assuming that it exists, and returns an integer, better known as a file handle. Its syntax is:

```
int fopen (string file, string mode [, int use_include_path])
```

File may be a file contained in the local file system, an stdio stream, or a remote file obtained via HTTP or FTP.

The input file can be of several forms, denoted by the filename syntax. These forms are listed here:

- If file is perceived to be a local filename, the file will be opened, and a pointer to the file will be returned.

- If file is either php://stdin, php://stdout, or php://stderr, stdio will be opened accordingly.

- If file begins with http://, an HTTP connection will be opened to the file server in question and a file pointer will be returned to the file in question.

- If file begins with ftp://, an FTP connection to the server in question will be opened, and a file pointer will be returned to the specified file. Two particularities are worth noting regarding this option: If the server does not support passive mode FTP, fopen() will fail. Furthermore, FTP files can only be opened exclusively either for reading or writing.

> **NOTE** *When an FTP server is in passive mode, it is listening for a connection from a client. In contrast, when an FTP server is in active mode, the server makes the connection to the client. Active mode is generally the default.*

The mode specifies the read/write readiness of the file in question. Table 7-1 lists several possible modes pertaining to how a file can be opened.

Table 7-1. File modes

MODE	MEANING
r	Read only. The file pointer is placed at the beginning of the file.
r+	Reading and writing. The file pointer is placed at the beginning of the file.
w	Write only. The file pointer is placed at the beginning of the file, and the file contents are erased. If the file does not exist, an attempt will be made to create it.
w+	Reading and writing. The file pointer is placed at the beginning of the file, and the file contents are erased. If the file does not exist, an attempt will be made to create it.
a	Write only. The file pointer is placed at the end of the file. If the file does not exist, an attempt will be made to create it.
a+	Reading and writing. The file pointer is placed at the end of the file. If the file does not exist, an attempt will be made to create it.

The third input parameter, use_include_path, can be set to 1 if you would like the file path to be compared to the include path contained in the php.ini file (described in Chapter 1). The following listing illustrates the opening of a file with fopen(). It is a good idea to use the command die() in conjunction with fopen()to ensure display of an appropriate message should the function fail:

```
$file = "userdata.txt";                                 // some file
$fh = fopen($file, "a+") or die("File ($file) does not exist!");
```

The next listing will open a connection with the PHP site (http://www.php.net):

```
$site = "http://www.php.net";    // some server that can communicate via HTTP
$sh = fopen($site, "r");         // assigns PHP.net index page to a filehandle.
```

Once you have finished with a file, you should always close it. This is accomplished with the fclose() function.

fclose()

The fclose() function closes the file designated by filepointer, returning true on success and false otherwise:

```
int fclose (int filepointer)
```

The fclose() function will only successfully close those files opened by fopen() or fsockopen(). Here's how you can close a file:

```
$file = "userdata.txt";
if (file_exists($file)) :
     $fh = fopen($file, "r");
     // execute various file-related functions
     fclose($fh);
else:
     print "File $file does not exist!";
endif;
```

Writing to a File

Once a file has been opened, there are generally two operations that can be performed; writing and reading.

is_writeable()

The is_writeable() function will ensure that file exists and is writable. It is capable of checking the writability of both a file and a directory. Its syntax is:

```
bool is_writeable (string file)
```

It is important to note that PHP will likely be running under the user ID that the Web server is using (typically "nobody"). An example of is_writeable() is included in the next section, "fwrite()."

fwrite()

The fwrite() function will simply write the contents of string to the file specified by filepointer. Its syntax is:

```
int fwrite (int filepointer, string string [, int length])
```

If the optional input parameter length is provided, writing will stop either after length characters have been written or after the end of string has been reached. The following example shows how to check the writability of a file:

```
<?
// user site traffic Information
$data = "08:13:00|12:37:12|208.247.106.187|Win98";
$filename = "somefile.txt";
// If file exists and Is writable
if ( is_writeable($filename) ) :
    // open file and place file pointer at end of file
    $fh = fopen($filename, "a+");
    // write $data to file
    $success = fwrite($fh, $data);
    // close the file
    fclose($fh);
else :
    print "Could not open $filename for writing";
endif;
?>
```

> **NOTE** Fputs() *is an alias to* fwrite() *and can be used by substituting the function name* fwrite *with* fputs.

fputs()

The fputs() function is an alias to fwrite() and is implemented in exactly the same way. Its syntax is:

```
int fputs (int filepointer, string string [, int length])
```

As you have seen, I prefer fputs() to fwrite(). Keep in mind that this is just a stylistic preference and has nothing to do with any differences between the two functions.

Reading from a File

The ability to read from a file is of obvious importance. The following are a set of functions geared toward making file reading an efficient process. You will see that the syntax of many of the functions are almost replicas of those used for writing.

is_readable()

The is_readable() function will ensure that file exists and is readable. It is capable of checking the readability of both a file and a directory. Its syntax is:

```
bool is_readable (string filename)
```

It is important to note that PHP will likely be running under the user ID that the Web server is using (probably "nobody"), and therefore the file will have to be world readable for is_readable() to return a true value. Here's how you would ensure that a file exists and is readable:

```
if ( is_readable($filename) ) :
    // open file and place file pointer at end of file
    $fh = fopen($filename, "r");
else :
    print "$filename Is not readable!";
endif;
```

fread()

The fread() function reads up to length bytes from the file designated by filepointer, returning the file's contents. Its syntax is:

```
string fread (int filepointer, int length)
```

The file pointer must point to an opened file that is readable (see function is_readable()). Reading will stop either when length bytes have been read or when the end of the file has been reached. Consider the sample textfile pastry.txt, shown in Listing 7-1. It could be read in and displayed to the browser using this code:

```
$fh = fopen('pastry.txt', "r") or die("Can't open file!");
$file = fread($fh, filesize($fh));
print $file;
fclose($fh);
```

By using filesize() to retrieve the byte size of pastry.txt, you ensure that fread() will read in the entire contents of the file.

Listing 7-1: A sample file, pastry.txt

```
Recipe: Pastry Dough
1 1/4 cups all-purpose flour
3/4 stick (6 tablespoons) unsalted butter, chopped
2 tablespoons vegetable shortening
1/4 teaspoon salt
3 tablespoons water
```

fgetc()

The fgetc() function returns a string containing one character from the file pointed to by filepointer or returns false on reaching the end of file. Its syntax is:

```
string fgetc (int filepointer)
```

The file pointer must point to an opened file that is readable. (To ensure that a file is readable, see "is_readable()," earlier in this chapter.) Here is an example of outputting a file, character by character:

```
$fh = fopen("pastry.txt", "r");
while (! feof($fh)) :
    $char = fgetc($fh);
    print $char;
endwhile;

fclose($fh);
```

fgets()

The fgets() function returns a string read from a file pointed to by the file pointer. The file pointer must point to an opened file that is readable (see "is_readable()," earlier in this chapter). Its syntax is:

```
string fgets (int filepointer, int length)
```

Reading will stop when one of the following conditions has been met:

- Length: 1 byte is read.

- A newline is read (returned with the string).

- An end of file (EOF) is read.

If you are interested in reading in a file line by line, you should just set the length parameter to a value higher than the number of bytes on a line. Here's an example of outputting a file, line by line:

```
$fh = fopen("pastry.txt", "r");
while (! feof($fh)) :
    $line = fgets($fh, 4096);
    print $line."<br>";
endwhile;
fclose($fh);
```

fgetss()

The fgetss() function operates exactly like fgets(), except that it will attempt to strip all HTML and PHP tags from the file designated by filepointer as its text is read:

```
string fgetss (int filepointer, int length [, string allowable_tags])
```

Before proceeding with an example, take a moment to read through Listing 7-2, as it is the file used in Listings 7-3 and 7-4.

Listing 7-2: The science.html sample program

```
<html>
<head>
<title>Breaking News - Science</title>
<body>
<h1>Alien lifeform discovered</h1><br>
<b>August 20, 2000</b><br>
Early this morning, a strange new form of fungus was found growing in the closet
of an old apartment refrigerator. It is not known if powerful radiation emanating
from the tenant's computer monitor aided in this evolution.
</body>
</html>
```

Listing 7-3: Stripping all tags from an HTML file before browser display

```
<?
$fh = fopen("science.html", "r");
while (!feof($fh)) :
   print fgetss($fh, 2048);
endwhile;
fclose($fh);
?>
```

As you can see from the resulting output, all HTML tags are stripped from science.html, eliminating all formatting:

Breaking News - Science Alien lifeform discovered August 20, 2000. Early this morning, a strange new form of fungus was found growing in the closet of an old apartment refrigerator. It is not known if powerful radiation emanating from the tenant's computer monitor aided in this evolution.

Of course, you might be interested in stripping all but a select few tags from the file, for example line breaks (<br>). This is illustrated in Listing 7-4.

Listing 7-4: Stripping all but a select few tags from an HTML file

```
<?
$fh = fopen("science.html", "r");
$allowable = "<br>";
while (!feof($fh)) :
    print fgetss($fh, 2048, $allowable);
endwhile;
fclose($fh);
?>
```

Breaking News - Science Alien lifeform discovered August 20, 2000
Early this morning, a strange new form of fungus was found growing in the closet of an old apartment refrigerator. It is not known if powerful radiation emanating from the tenant's computer monitor aided in this evolution.

As you can see, fgetss() can be rather useful for file conversion, particularly when you have a large group of HTML files similarly formatted.

Reading a File into an Array

The file() function will read the entire contents of a file into an indexed array. Each element in the array corresponds to a line in the file. Its syntax is:

```
array file (string file [, int use_include_path])
```

If the optional input parameter use_include_path is set to 1, then the file is searched along the include path in the php.ini file (See Chapter 1 for more information about the php.ini file.) Listing 7-5 shows how to use file() to read pastry.txt, first shown in Listing 7-1.

Listing 7-5: Reading pastry.txt using file()

```
<?
$file_array = file( 'pastry.txt' );

while ( list( $line_num, $line ) = each( $file_array ) ) :
    print "<b>Line $line_num:</b> " . htmlspecialchars( $line ) . "<br>\n";
endwhile;
?>
```

Cycling through the array, each line is output along with the corresponding line number:

```
Line 0: Recipe: Pastry Dough
Line 1: 1 1/4 cups all-purpose flour
Line 2: 3/4 stick (6 tablespoons) unsalted butter, chopped
Line 3: 2 tablespoons vegetable shortening
Line 4: 1/4 teaspoon salt
Line 5: 3 tablespoons water
```

Redirecting a File Directly to Output

The readfile() function reads in a file and outputs it to standard output (in most cases the browser). Its syntax is:

```
int readfile (string file [, int use_include_path])
```

The number of bytes read in is returned to the caller. File may be a file contained in the local file system, an stdio stream, or a remote file obtained via HTTP or FTP. Its specifications for the file input parameter mimic those of the fopen() function.

Suppose you had a restaurant review that you wanted to display online. This review, entitled "latorre.txt", follows:

Restaurant "La Torre," located in Nettuno, Italy, offers an eclectic blend of style, history, and fine seafood cuisine. Within the walls of the medieval borgo surrounding the city, one can dine while watching the passersby shop in the village boutiques. Comfort coupled with only the freshest seafare make La Torre one of Italy's finest restaurants.

Executing the following code will result in the entire contents of "latorre.txt" being displayed to standard output:

```
<?
$restaurant_file = "latorre.txt";
// display entire file to standard output
readfile($restaurant_file);
?>
```

Opening a Process File Pointer with popen()

Just as a file can be opened, so can a file pointer to a server process. This is accomplished with the function popen(). Its syntax is:

```
int popen (string command, string mode)
```

The input parameter command refers to the system command that will be executed, and *mode* refers to how you would use the popen() function to search a file:

```
<?
// open file "spices.txt" for writing purposes
$fh = fopen("spices.txt","w");
// Add a few lines of text
fputs($fh, "Parsley, sage, rosemary\n");
fputs($fh,"Paprika, salt, pepper\n");
fputs($fh,"Basil, sage, ginger\n");
// close the file handle
fclose($fh);
// Open UNIX grep process, searching for "Basil" in spices.txt
$fh =popen("grep Basil < spices.txt", "r");
// output the result of the grep
fpassthru($fh);
?>
```

The resulting output:

```
Basil, sage, ginger
```

The fpassthru() function is covered later this chapter in "External Program Execution."

pclose()

After you're done with a file or process, you should close it. The pclose() function simply closes the connection to a process designated by filepointer, just as fclose() closes a file opened by fopen(). Its syntax is:

```
int pclose (int filepointer)
```

The input parameter *filepointer* refers to a previously opened file pointer.

Opening a Socket Connection

PHP does not limit you to working solely with files and processes. You can also manipulate socket connections. A *socket* is a software tool that allows you to make connections with various services offered by some machine.

fsockopen()

The fsockopen() function establishes a socket connection to an Internet server via either TCP or UDP. Its syntax is:

```
int fsockopen (string host, int port [, int errnumber [, string errstring [, int
timeout]]])
```

The optional input parameters errnumber and errstring return error information specific to the attempt to connect to the host. Both of these parameters must be specified as reference variables. The other optional input parameter, timeout, can be used to specify the number of seconds the call should wait before the host to respond. Listing 7-6 shows how you might use fsockopen() to retrieve information about a server. However, before Listing 7-6, I need to introduce another function, set_socket_blocking().

> **NOTE** *UDP, short for User Datagram Protocol, is a connectionless protocol similar to TCP/IP.*

set_socket_blocking()

The set_socket_blocking() function, when the mode is set to false, allows you to obtain control of the timeout setting specified by the server pointed to by filepointer:

```
set_socket_blocking(int filepointer, boolean mode)
```

The input parameter *filepointer* refers to a previously opened socket pointer, and *mode* refers to the mode that the socket file pointer will be switched to; false for nonblocking mode, true for blocking mode. An example of fsockopen() and set_socket_blocking() in shown in Listing 7-6.

Listing 7-6: Using fsockopen() to retrieve information about a server
```
<?
function get_the_host($host,$path) {
    // open the host
    $fp = fsockopen($host, 80, &$errno, &$errstr, 30);
    // take control of server timeout
    socket_set_blocking($fp, 1);
    // send the appropriate headers
    fputs($fp,"GET $path HTTP/1.1\r\n");
    fputs($fp,"Host: $host\r\n\r\n");
    $x = 1;
    // grab a bunch of headers
    while($x < 10) :
        $headers = fgets($fp, 4096);
      print $headers;
        $x++;
    endwhile;
    // close the filepointer.
    fclose($fp);
}

get_the_host("www.apress.com", "/");
?>
```

Execution of Listing 7-6 results in the following output:

```
HTTP/1.1 200 OK Server: Microsoft-IIS/4.0 Content-Location:
http://www.apress.com/Default.htm Date: Sat, 19 Aug 2000 23:03:25 GMT Content-
Type: text/html Accept-Ranges: bytes Last-Modified: Wed, 19 Jul 2000 20:25:06
GMT ETag: "f0a6166dbff1bf1:34a5" Content-Length: 1311
```

pfsockopen()

The pfsockopen() function is just a persistent version of fsockopen() This means that it will not automatically close the connection once the script making use of the command has terminated. Its syntax is:

```
int pfsockopen (string hostname, int port [, int errno [, string errstr [, int
timeout]]])
```

Depending on the exact purpose of your application, it may be more convenient to choose pfsockopen() over fsockopen().

External Program Execution

It is also possible to execute programs residing on a server. These functions can be particularly useful when administrating various aspects of the system via a Web browser, in addition to creating more user-friendly system summaries.

exec()

The exec() function will execute the program specified by command and return the last line of the command output. Its syntax is:

```
string exec (string command [, string array [, int return_variable]])
```

Note that it will not display the command output, just execute it. It is possible to store all of the command output in the optional input parameter array. Furthermore, if the optional input parameter return_variable is provided in conjunction with array, it will be assigned the status of the executed command.

Listing 7-7 shows how exec can be used to execute the UNIX system function ping.

Listing 7-7: Using exec() to ping a server

```
<?
exec("ping -c 5  www.php.net", $ping);
// For Windows, do exec("ping -n 5 www.php.net", $ping);
for ($i=0; $i < count($ping); $i++) :
    print "<br>$ping[$i]";
endfor;
?>
```

```
PING www.php.net (208.247.106.187): 56 data bytes
64 bytes from 208.247.106.187: icmp_seq=0 ttl=243 time=66.602 ms
64 bytes from 208.247.106.187: icmp_seq=1 ttl=243 time=55.723 ms
64 bytes from 208.247.106.187: icmp_seq=2 ttl=243 time=70.779 ms
64 bytes from 208.247.106.187: icmp_seq=3 ttl=243 time=55.339 ms
64 bytes from 208.247.106.187: icmp_seq=4 ttl=243 time=69.865 ms

-- www.php.net ping statistics --
5 packets transmitted, 5 packets received, 0% packet loss
round-trip min/avg/max/stddev = 55.339/63.662/70.779/6.783 ms
```

Backticks

An alternative method exists for execution of a system command, in which no predefined function is required. The command can be executed if it is enclosed within backticks (``), and its output subsequently displayed to the browser. An example follows:

```
$output = `ls`;
print "<pre>$output</pre>";
```

This would result in the directory contents from which the script executing these commands resides being output to the browser.

> **NOTE** *The -c 5 (-n 5 for Windows) is a parameter internal to ping that tells it to ping the server x times. The -c means count, and the -n means number.*

If you are interested in simply returning unformatted command output, check out passthru( ), described next.

passthru()

The passthru() function works almost exactly like exec(), except that the command output is automatically output. Its syntax is:

```
void passthru (string command [, int return_variable])
```

    If the optional input parameter *return_variable* is provided, it will be assigned the command return status.
    You can use passthru() to view the uptime of the server, for example:

```
passthru("uptime");
1:21PM up 4 days, 23:16, 1 user, load averages: 0.02, 0.01, 0.00
```

fpassthru()

The fpassthru() function behaves exactly like passthru(), except that it works with file pointers pointing to files or processes opened by popen(), fopen(), or fsockopen(). Its syntax is:

```
int fpassthru (int fp)
```

    It will read the entire file or process pointed to by the file pointer and forward it directly to standard output.

system()

You can think of the system() function as a hybrid of exec() and passthru(), executing command and automatically outputting the results and returning the last line of command, the input parameter command being a call to some system command that the server recognizes. Its syntax is:

```
string system (string command [, int return_variable])
```

    If the optional input parameter return_variable is provided, it will be assigned the command return status.

The escapeshellcmd() Security Feature

The escapeshellcmd() function will escape any potentially dangerous characters that may be supplied by a user (via an HTML form, for example) for reason of executing the exec(), passthru(), system() or popen() commands. Its syntax is:

```
string escapeshellcmd (string command)
```

User input should always be treated with some degree of caution, and even more so when users can input commands that may be executed with functions capable of executing system commands. Consider the following:

```
$user_input = 'rm -rf *'; // Input means erase the parent directory and _all_ of
                                Its children.
exec( $user_input);        // execute $user_input!!!
```

Left uncontrolled, such commands could cause disaster. However, if you use escapeshellcmd() to escape user input:

```
$user_input = `rm -rf *`;                    // Input means erase the parent
                                                directory and _all_ of Its children.
exec( escapeshellcmd($user_input));          // escapes dangerous characters.
```

Keep in mind that the function escapeshellcmd() will escape the *, preventing the command from being executed as intended.

> **NOTE** *Because security is such an important issue in the Web environment, I have devoted an entire chapter to it and how it relates to PHP programming. See Chapter 16, "Security," for more information.*

Working with the File System

PHP provides a number of functions geared toward viewing and manipulating server files. Obtaining numerous facts about server files, such as location, owner, and privileges, can be useful.

basename()

The basename() function returns the file pointed to by path. Its syntax is:

```
string basename (string path)
```

Here's how you would parse out the base name of a path:

```
$path = "/usr/local/phppower/htdocs/index.php";
$file = basename($path);      // $file = "index.php"
```

This effectively parses the path, returning just the filename.

getlastmod()

The getlastmod() function returns the most recent modification date and time of the page in which the function is placed. The syntax:

```
int getlastmod (void)
```

The return value is in the form of a UNIX timestamp and can be formatted using the date() function. Here's how you could display the last modified time of a page:

```
echo "Last modified: ".date( "H:i:s a", getlastmod() );
```

stat()

The stat() function returns a comprehensive indexed array of information concerning the file designated by filename:

```
array stat (string filename)
```

The indexed values correspond to the following pieces of information:

0	Device
1	Inode
2	Inode protection mode
3	Number of links
4	Owner user ID
5	Owner group ID
6	Inode device type
7	Byte size
8	Last access time
9	Last modification time
10	Last change time
11	File system I/O block size
12	Block allocation

Therefore, if you wanted the last access time of the filename in question, you would call element 8 of the returned array. Consider this example:

```
$file = "datafile.txt";
list ($dev, $inode, $inodep, $nlink, $uid, $gid, $inodev, $size, $atime, $mtime,
$ctime, $bsize) = stat($file);

print "$file is $size bytes. <br>";
print "Last access time: $atime <br>";
print "Last modification time: $mtime <br>";
```

```
popen.php is 289 bytes.
Last access time: August 15 2000 12:00:00
Last modification time: August 15 2000 10:07:18
```

In this example, I used list() to explicitly name each piece of returned information. Of course, you could also just return an array and then use an iterative loop to display each piece of information as necessary. As you can see, stat() can be particularly useful when you need to retrieve various information about a file.

Displaying and Modifying File Characteristics

All files on UNIX-based systems have three basic characteristics:

- Group membership

- Ownership

- Permissions

Each of these characteristics can be changed through its respective PHP functions. The functions described in this section will not work on Windows-based systems.

> **NOTE** *If you are new to the UNIX operating system, a great resource for learning about the UNIX file system characteristics is at http://sunsite.auc.dk/linux-newbie/FAQ2.htm. Section 3.2.6 in particular addresses group, ownership, and permission issues.*

chgrp()

The chgrp() function will attempt to change the group of the file denoted by file-name to group. Its syntax is:

```
int chgrp (string filename, mixed group)
```

filegroup()

The filegroup() function returns the group ID of the owner of a file specified by filename, or false should some error occur. Its syntax is:

```
int filegroup (string filename)
```

chmod()

The chmod() function changes the mode of filename to permissions. Its syntax is:

```
int chmod (string filename, int permissions)
```

The permissions must be specified in octal mode. The following example shows that chmod() is particular about the permissions input parameter:

```
chmod ("data_file.txt", g+r); // This will not work
chmod ("data_file.txt", 766); // This will not work
chmod ("data_file.txt", 0766); // This will work
```

fileperms()

The fileperms() function returns the permissions of a file specified by filename, or false should some error occur. Its syntax is:

```
int fileperms (string filename)
```

chown()

The chown() function attempts to change the ownership of a filename to user. Only the superuser can change the ownership of a file. Its syntax is:

```
int chown (string filename, mixed user)
```

fileowner()

The fileowner() function returns the user ID of the owner of the file specified by filename. Its syntax is:

```
int fileowner (string filename)
```

Copying and Renaming Files

Other useful system functions that can be performed via a PHP script are copying and renaming files on the server. The two functions capable of doing so are copy() and rename().

copy()

You can easily make a copy of a file much in the same way as you would with the UNIX cp command. This is done with PHP's copy() function. Its syntax is:

```
int copy (string source, string destination)
```

The copy() function will attempt to copy a file by the name of source to a file named destination, returning true on success and false otherwise. If destination does not exist, copy() will create it. Here's how to back up a file with copy():

```
$data_file = "data1.txt";
copy($data_file, $data_file'.bak') or die("Could not copy $data_file");
```

rename()

A file can be renamed with the rename() function, returning true on success and false otherwise. Its syntax is:

```
bool rename (string oldname, string newname)
```

Here's how you would use the rename() function for renaming a file:

```
$data_file = "data1.txt";
rename($data_file, $data_file'.old') or die("Could not rename $data_file");
```

Deleting Files

unlink()

You can delete a file with the unlink() function. Its syntax is:

```
int unlink (string file)
```

If you are using PHP on a Windows system, you may have problems with this function. If so, you can use the previously discussed system() function, deleting a file with a call to the DOS del function:

```
system ("del filename.txt");
```

Working with Directories

You can modify and traverse directories just as you are able to modify and traverse files. A typical non-Windows directory structure might look similar to the one displayed in Listing 7-8.

Listing 7-8: A typical directory structure

```
drwxr-xr-x  4 root  wheel   512 Aug 13  13:51   book/
drwxr-xr-x  4 root  wheel   512 Aug 13  13:51   code/
-rw-r-r-    1 root  wheel   115 Aug  4  09:53   index.html
drwxr-xr-x  7 root  wheel  1024 Jun 29  13:03   manual/
-rw-r-r-    1 root  wheel    19 Aug 12  12:15   test.php
```

dirname()

The dirname() function operates as the counterpart to basename(), returning the directory element of path. Its syntax is:

```
string dirname (string path)
```

Here's an example of using basename() to parse the base name of a path:

```
$path = "/usr/local/phppower/htdocs/index.php";
$file = basename($path);      // $file = "/usr/local/phppower/htdocs"
```

You can also use dirname() in conjunction with the predefined variable *$SCRIPT_FILENAME* to obtain the complete path of the script executing the command:

```
$dir = dirname($SCRIPT_FILENAME);
```

is_dir()

The is_dir() function verifies that the file designated by filename is a directory:

```
bool is_dir (string filename)
```

Refer to Listing 7-8 to understand the following example:

```
$isdir = is_dir("index.html"); // returns false
```

```
$isdir = is_dir("book"); // returns true
```

mkdir()

The mkdir() function has the same purpose as the UNIX command mkdir(), creating a new directory. Its syntax is:

```
int mkdir (string pathname, int mode)
```

The pathname specifies the path in which the directory is to be created. Don't forget to include the directory name at the end of this path! The mode is the file permission setting to which the newly created directory should be set.

opendir()

Just as fopen() opens a file pointer to a given file, opendir() will open a directory stream specified by directory_path. Its syntax is:

```
int opendir (string directory_path)
```

closedir()

The closedir() function will close the directory stream pointed to by directory_handle. Its syntax is:

```
void closedir (int directory_handle)
```

readdir()

The readdir() function returns each element in a given directory. Its syntax is:

```
string readdir (int directory_handle)
```

Using it, we can easily list all files and child directories in a given directory:

```
$dh = openddir('.');
while ($file = readdir($dh)) :
    print "$file <br>";
endwhile;
closedir($dh);
```

chdir()

The chdir() function operates just like the UNIX cd function, changing to the file directory specified by directory. Its syntax is:

```
int chdir (string directory)
```

Assume that you were currently sitting at the directory. You could change to and subsequently output the contents of the book/directory as follows:

```
$newdir = "book";
chdir($newdir) or die("Could not change to directory ($newdir)");
$dh = opendir('.');
print "Files:";
while ($file = readdir($dh)) :
    print "$file <br>";
endwhile;
closedir($dh);
```

rewinddir()

The rewinddir() function will reset the directory pointer pointed to by directory_handle. Its syntax is:

```
void rewinddir (int directory_handle)
```

Project 1: A Simple Access Counter

This simple access counter will keep count of the number of visits to the page in which the script is inserted. Before checking out the code in Listing 7-9, take a moment to review the pseudocode:

1. Assign $access the name of the file in which you would like to store the counter.

2. Use file() to read the contents of $access into the $visits array. The @ preceding the function acts to suppress any potential errors (such as a nonexistent file).

3. Assign the first (and only) element of the $visits array to $current_visitors.

4. Increment $current_visitors by 1.

5. Open the $access file for writing, placing the file pointer at the beginning of the file.

6. Write $current_visitors to the $access file.

7. Close the file handle pointing to the $access file.

Listing 7-9: A simple access counter

```
<?
// script: simple access counter
// purpose: uses a file to keep track of visitor count.
$access = "hits.txt";              // name this file whatever you want
$visits = @file($access);          // feed file into array
$current_visitors = $visits[0];    // extract first (and only) element from array
++$current_visitors;               // increment visitor count
$fh = fopen($access, "w");         // open "hits.txt" and place file pointer at
                                   //     beginning of file

@fwrite($fp, $current_visitors);   // write new visitor count to "hits.txt"
fclose($fh);                       // close filepointer to "hits.txt"
?>
```

Project 2: A Site Map Generator

The script in Listing 7-10 produces a site map of all folders and files on a server, starting from a specified directory. The site map is staggered through the calculation of indentation values through several functions defined in this and previous chapters. Before checking out the code, take a moment to review the pseudocode:

1. Declare a few necessary variables: parent directory, folder graphic location, page title, and server OS flag (Windows or non-Windows).

2. Declaration of `display_directory()` function, which parses and formats a directory for display in the browser.

3. Concatenate the directory passed in as `$dir1` to `$dir`, producing the correct directory path.

4. Open the directory and read its contents. Format the directory name and files and display them to the browser.

5. If the file in question is a directory, recursively call `display_directory()` with the file passed in as the new directory to parse. Also calculate specific indentation value for formatting purposes.

If the file in question is a file, format it as a link to itself, in addition to calculating a specific indentation value for formatting purposes.

Listing 7-10: The sitemap.php sample program

```
<?
// file: sitemap.php
// purpose: display a map of entire site structure

// From which parent directory should the sitemap begin?
$beg_path = "C:\Program Files\Apache Group\Apache\htdocs\phprecipes";

// What Is the location of the folder graphic?
// This path should be *relative* to the Apache server root directory
$folder_location = "C:\My Documents\PHP for Programmers\FINAL
CHPS\graphics\folder.gif";

// What should be displayed in the sitemap title bar?
$page_name = "PHPRecipes SiteMap";
```

```
// Will this script be used on a Windows or non-Windows server?
// (0 for Windows; 1 for non-Windows)
$using_linux = 0;
// function: display_directory
// purpose: Parses a directory specified by $dir1 and formats directory and file
structure.
// This function is recursively called.

function display_directory($dir1, $folder_location, $using_linux, $init_depth) {

// update the directory path
$dir .= $dir1;
$dh = opendir($dir);

while ($file = readdir($dh)) :
    // do not display the "." and ".."in each directory.
    if ( ($file != ".") && ($file != "..") ) :

        if ( $using_linux == 0 ) :
            $depth = explode("\\", $dir);
        else :
            $depth = explode("/", $dir);
        endif;
        $current_depth = sizeof($depth);

        // Build path In accordance with what OS Is being used.
        if ($using_linux == 0) :
            $tab_depth = $current_depth - $init_depth;
            $file = $dir."\\".$file;
        else :
            $file = $dir."/".$file;
        endif;

        // Is $file a directory?
        if ( is_dir($file) ) :
            $x = 0;
            // calculate tab depth
            while ( $x < ($tab_depth * 2) ) :
                print " ";
                $x++;
            endwhile;

            print "<img src=\"$folder_location\" alt=\"[dir]\">
".basename($file)."<br>";
```

```
                // Increment the   count

                // Recursive call to display_directory() function
                display_directory($file, $folder_location, $using_linux,
                // $init_depth);

          // Not dealing with a directory
          else :
                // Build path In accordance with what OS Is being used.
                if ($using_linux == 0) :
                    $tab_depth = ($current_depth - $init_depth) - 2;

                    $x = 0;
                    // calculate tab depth
                    while ( $x < (($tab_depth * 2) + 5) ) :
                        print " ";
                        $x++;
                    endwhile;
                    print "<a href =
\"".$dir."\\".basename($file)."\">".basename($file)."</a> <br>";
                else :
                    print "<a href =
\"".$dir."/".basename($file)."\">".basename($file)."</a> <br>";
                endif;

          endif; // Is_dir(file)
      endif; // If ! "." or ".."

endwhile;

// close the directory
closedir($dh);
}
?>
<html>
<head>
<title> <? print "$page_name"; ?> </title>
</head>
<body bgcolor="#ffffff" text="#000000" link="#000000" vlink="#000000"
alink="#000000">
<?
// calculate Initial tab depth
if ($using_linux == 0) :
        $depth = explode("\\", $beg_path);
```

```
else :
    $depth = explode("/", $beg_path);
endif;
$init_depth = sizeof($depth);
display_directory($beg_path, $folder_location, $using_linux, $init_depth);
?>
</body>
</html>
```

Executing this script on the directory pointing to the folder I am using to organize a few of the chapters of this book displays the output shown in Figure 7-1.

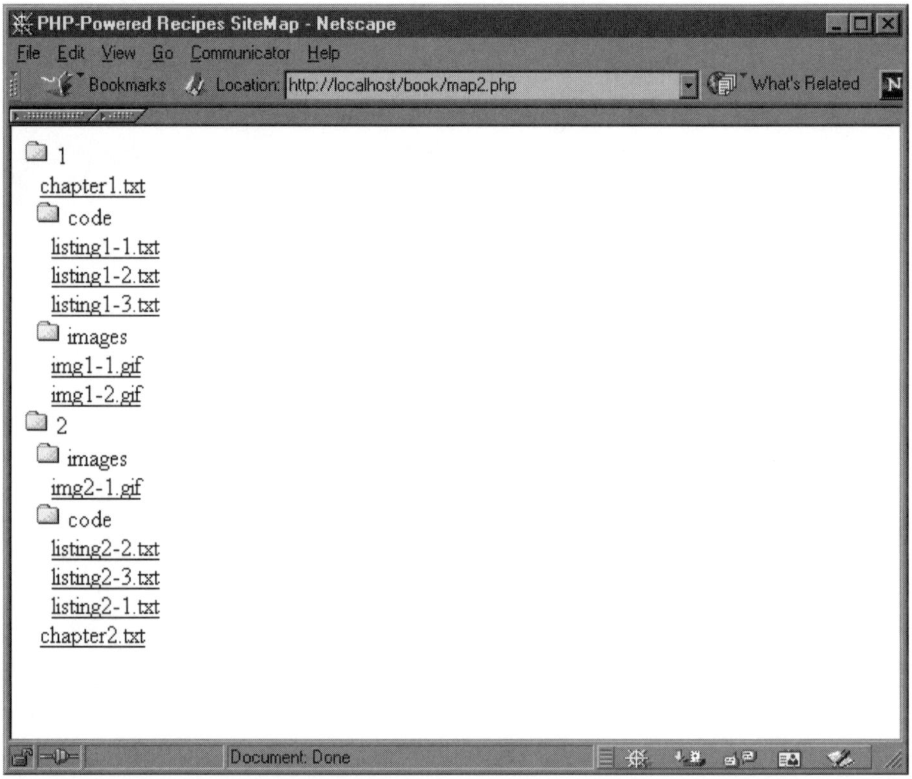

Figure 7-1. Using sitemap.php to display the structure of a server directory

What's Next?

This chapter introduced many aspects of PHP's file-handling functionality, in particular:

- Verifying a File's Existence

- Opening I/O and closing I/O

- Writing to and reading from a file

- Redirecting a file directly to output

- External program execution

- Working with the file system

These topics set the stage for the next chapter, "Strings and Regular Expressions," as string manipulation and I/O manipulation go hand in hand when you are developing PHP-enabled Web applications. With that said, let's forge ahead!

Strings and Regular Expressions

The ability to efficiently organize, search, and disseminate information has long been a topic of great interest for computer scientists. Because most of this information is text based as alphanumeric characters, a good deal of research has been invested in developing techniques to search and organize information based on an analysis of the patterns (known as *pattern matching*) in the text itself.

Pattern matching makes it possible not only to locate specific string instances but also to replace these instances with alternative strings. Common use of pattern matching is made in the find/replace functionality in word processors such as MS Word, Emacs, and my personal favorite, vi. UNIX users are undoubtedly familiar with programs such as sed, awk, and grep, all of which use pattern-matching techniques to provide the powerful functionality in each. Summarizing, pattern matching provides four useful functions:

- Locating strings exactly matching a specified pattern

- Searching strings for substrings matching a specified pattern

- Replacing strings and substrings matching a specified pattern

- Finding strings where the specified pattern does *not* match

The advent of the Web has caused a surge in research in faster, more efficient data-mining techniques, providing users worldwide with the capability to sift through the billions of pages of information. Search engines, online financial services, and ecommerce sites would all be rendered useless without the ability to analyze the mammoth quantities of data in these sectors. Indeed, string-manipulation capabilities are a vital part of almost any sector involving itself with information technology today.

This chapter concentrates on PHP's adept string-handling functionality. I will focus on a number of the more than 60 predefined string functions, providing definitions and practical examples that will give you the knowledge you need to begin coding powerful Web applications. However, before presenting the PHP-specific content of this chapter, I would like to provide a brief introduction to the underlying mechanics that make pattern matching possible: regular expressions.

Regular Expressions

Regular expressions, or regexps, as they are so affectionately called by programmers, provide the foundation for pattern-matching functionality. A regular expression is nothing more than a sequence or pattern of characters itself, matched against the text in which a search has been requested. This sequence may be a pattern with which you are already familiar, such as the word "dog," or it may be a pattern having specific meaning in the context of the world of pattern-matching, such as <(?)>.*<\/.?>.

PHP offers functions specific to two sets of regular expression functions, each corresponding to a certain type of regular expression: POSIX and Perl style. Each has its own unique style of syntax and is discussed accordingly in later sections. Keep in mind that innumerable tutorials have been written regarding this matter; you can find them both on the Web and in various books. Therefore, I will provide you with a basic introduction to both and leave it to you to search out further information should you be so inclined.

If you are not already familiar with the mechanics of general expressions, please take some time to read through the short tutorial comprising the remainder of this section. If you are already a regexp pro, feel free to skip past the tutorial to subsequent sections.

Regular Expression Syntax (POSIX)

The structure of a POSIX regular expression is not dissimilar to that of a typical arithmetic expression: various elements (operators) are combined to form more complex expressions. However, it is the meaning of the combined regexp elements that makes them so powerful. It is possible not only to locate literal expressions, such as a specific word or number, but also to locate a multitude of semantically different but syntactically similar strings, for instance, all HTML tags in a file.

The simplest regular expression is one that matches a single character, such as *g,* matching strings such as *g, haggle,* and *bag.* You could combine several letters together to form larger expressions, such as *gan,* which logically would match any string containing *gan; gang, organize,* or *Reagan,* for example.

It is possible to simultaneously test for several different expressions by using the pipe (|) operator. For example, you could test for *php or zend* via the regular expression php|zend.

Bracketing

Brackets ([ ]) have a special meaning when used in the context of regular expressions, used to find a *range* of characters. Contrary to the regexp *php*, which will find strings containing the explicit string *php*, the regexp [*php*] will find any string containing the character *p* or *h*. Bracketing plays a significant role in regular expressions, since many times you may be interested in finding strings containing any of a range of characters. Several commonly used character ranges follow:

- [0–9] matches any decimal digit from 0 through 9.

- [a–z] matches any character from lowercase *a* through lowercase *z*.

- [A–Z] matches any character from uppercase *A* through uppercase *Z*.

- [a–Z] matches any character from lowercase *a* through uppercase *Z*.

   Of course, the ranges shown above are general; you could also use the range [0–3] to match any decimal digit ranging from 0 through 3, or the range [b–v] to match any lowercase character ranging from *b* through *v*. In short, you are free to specify whatever range you wish.

Quantifiers

The frequency or position of bracketed character sequences and single characters can be denoted by a special character, each special character having a specific connotation. The +, *, ?, {int. range}, and $ flags all follow a character sequence:

- p+ matches any string containing at least one *p*.

- p* matches any string containing zero or more *p*'s.

- p? matches any string containing zero or more *p*'s. This is just an alternative way to use p*.

- p{2} matches any string containing a sequence of two *p*'s.

- p{2,3} matches any string containing a sequence of two or three *p*'s.

- p{2, } matches any string containing a sequence of at least two *p*'s.

- p$ matches any string with *p* at the end of it.

Still other flags can precede and be inserted before and within a character sequence:

- ^p matches any string with *p* at the beginning of it.

- [^a–zA-Z] matches any string *not* containing any of the characters ranging from *a* through *z* and *A* through *Z*.

- p.p matches any string containing *p*, followed by any character, in turn followed by another *p*.

You can also combine special characters to form more complex expressions. Consider the following examples:

- ^.{2}$ matches any string containing *exactly* two characters.

- <b>(.*)</b> matches any string enclosed within <b> and </b> (presumably HTML bold tags).

- p(hp)* matches any string containing a *p* followed by zero or more instances of the sequence *hp*.

You may wish to search for these special characters in strings instead of using them in the special context just described. For you to do so, the characters must be escaped with a backslash (\). For example, if you wanted to search for a dollar amount, a plausible regular expression would be as follows: ([^\$])([0-9]+), that is, a dollar sign followed by one or more integers. Notice the backslash preceding the dollar sign. Potential matches of this regular expression include $42, $560, and $3.

Predefined Character Ranges (Character Classes)

For your programming convenience several predefined character ranges, also known as *character classes*, are available. Character classes specify an entire range of characters, for example, the alphabet or an integer set:

[[:alpha:]] matches any string containing alphabetic characters *aA* through *zZ*.

[[:digit:]] matches any string containing numerical digits 0 through 9.

[[:alnum:]] matches any string containing alphanumeric characters *aA* through *zZ* and 0 through 9.

[[:space:]] matches any string containing a space.

PHP's Regexp Functions (POSIX Extended)

PHP currently offers seven functions for searching strings using POSIX-style regular expressions:

ereg()

ereg_replace()

eregi()

eregi_replace()

split()

spliti()

sql_regcase()

These functions are discussed in the following sections.

ereg()

The ereg() function searches a string specified by *string* for a string specified by *pattern*, returning true if the pattern is found, and false otherwise. Its syntax is:

```
int ereg(string pattern, string string, [array regs])
```

The search is case sensitive in regard to alphabetical characters. Here's how you could use ereg() to search strings for .com domains:

```
$is_com = ereg("(\.)(com$)", $email);
// returns true if $email ends with ".com".
// "www.wjgilmore.com" and "someemail@apress.com" would both return true values.
```

Note that since the $ concludes the regular expression, this will match only strings that end in com. For example, while this would match www.apress.com, it would *not* match www.apress.com/catalog.

The optional input parameter *regs* contains an array of all matched expressions that were grouped by parentheses in the regular expression. Making use of this array, we could segment a URL into several pieces, as shown in Listing 8-1.

Listing 8-1: Displaying elements of $regs array

```
<?
$url = "http://www.apress.com";

// break $url down into three distinct pieces: "http://www", "apress", and "com"
$www_url = ereg("^(http://www)\.([[:alnum:]]+)\.([[:alnum:]]+)", $url, $regs);

if ($www_url) :          // if $www_url is a valid URL
    echo $regs[0];       // outputs the entire string "http://www.apress.com"
    print "<br>";
    echo $regs[1];       // outputs "http://www"
    print "<br>";
    echo $regs[2];       // outputs "apress"
    print "<br>";
    echo $regs[3];       // outputs "com"
endif;
?>
```

Executing Listing 8-1 results in:

```
http://www.apress.com
http://www
apress
com
```

ereg_replace()

The ereg_replace() function searches for *string* specified by *pattern* and replaces *pattern* with *replacement* if found. The syntax is:

```
string ereg_replace (string pattern, string replacement, string string)
```

The ereg_replace() function operates under the same premises as ereg(), except that the functionality is extended to finding and replacing *pattern* instead of simply locating it. After the replacement has occurred, the modified string will be returned. If no matches are found, the string will remain unchanged. Like ereg(), ereg_replace() is case sensitive. Here is a simple string replacement example that uses the function:

```
$copy_date = "Copyright 1999";
$copy_date = ereg_replace("([0-9]+)", "2000", $copy_date);
print $copy_date;     // displays "Copyright 2000"
```

A rather interesting feature of PHP's string-replacement capability is the ability to back-reference parenthesized substrings. This works much like the optional input parameter *regs* in the function ereg(), except that the substrings are referenced using backslashes, such as \0, \1, \2, and so on, where \0 refers to the entire string, \1 the first successful match, and so on. Up to nine back references can be used. This example shows how to replace all references to a URL with a working hyperlink:

```
$url = "Apress (http://www.apress.com)";
$url = ereg_replace("http://(([A-Za-z0-9.\-])*)", "<a href=\"\\0\">\\0</a>",$url);
print $url;
// Displays Apress (<a href="http://www.apress.com">http://www.apress.com</a>)
```

> **NOTE** *Although* ereg_replace() *works just fine, another predefined function named* str_replace() *is actually much faster when complex regular expressions are not required.* Str_replace() *is discussed later in this chapter.*

eregi()

The eregi() function searches throughout a string specified by *pattern* for a string specified by *string*. Its syntax is:

```
int eregi(string pattern, string string, [array regs])
```

The search is *not* case sensitive. Eregi() can be particularly useful when checking the validity of strings, such as passwords. This concept is illustrated in the following sample:

```
$password = "abc";

if (! eregi ("[[:alnum:]]{8,10}", $password)) :
    print "Invalid password! Passwords must be from 8 through 10 characters in
length.";
endif;

// execution of the above code would produce the error message
// since "abc" is not of length ranging from 8 through 10 characters.
```

eregi_replace()

The eregi_replace() function operates exactly like ereg_replace(), except that the search for *pattern* in *string* is not case sensitive. Its syntax is:

```
string eregi_replace (string pattern, string replacement, string string)
```

split()

The split() function will divide a string into various elements, the boundaries of each element based on the occurrence of *pattern* in *string*. Its syntax is:

```
array split (string pattern, string string [, int limit])
```

   The optional input parameter *limit* is used to signify the number of elements into which the string should be divided, starting from the left end of the string and working rightward. In cases where the pattern is an alphabetical character, split() is case sensitive. Here's how you would use split() to partition an IP address:

```
$ip = "123.456.789.000";      // some IP address
$iparr = split ("\.", $ip);    // Note that since "." is a special character, it
                                     must be escaped.
print "$iparr[0] <br>";       // outputs "123"
print "$iparr[1] <br>";       // outputs "456"
print "$iparr[2] <br>";       // outputs "789"
print "$iparr[3] <br>";       // outputs "000"
```

You could also use split() to limit a parameter to restrict division of $ip:

```
$ip = "123.456.789.000";         // some IP address
$iparr = split ("\.", $ip, 2);    // Note that since "." is a special character,
                                      it must be escaped.
print "$iparr[0] <br>";          // outputs "123"
print "$iparr[1] <br>";          // outputs "456.789.000"
```

spliti()

The spliti() function operates exactly in the same manner as its sibling split(), except that it is *not* case sensitive. Its syntax is:

```
array split (string pattern, string string [, int limit])
```

Of course, case-sensitive characters are an issue only when the pattern is alphabetical. For all other characters, `spliti()` operates exactly as `split()` does.

sql_regcase()

The `sql_regcase()` function can be thought of as a utility function, converting each character in the input parameter *string* into a bracketed expression containing two characters. Its syntax is:

```
string sql_regcase (string string)
```

If the alphabetical character has both an uppercase and a lowercase format, the bracket will contain both forms; otherwise the original character will be repeated twice. This function is particularly useful when PHP is used in conjunction with products that support solely case-sensitive regular expressions. Here's how you would use `sql_regcase()` to convert a string:

```
$version = "php 4.0";

print sql_regcase($version);
// outputs [Pp] [Hh] [Pp] [ ] [44] [..] [00]
```

Regular Expression Syntax (Perl Style)

Perl (http://www.perl.com), long considered one of the greatest parsing languages ever written, provides a comprehensive regular expression language that can be used to search and replace even the most complicated of string patterns. The developers of PHP felt that instead of reinventing the regular expression wheel, so to speak, they should make the famed Perl regular expression syntax available to PHP users, thus the Perl-style functions.

Perl-style regular expressions are similar to their POSIX counterparts. In fact, Perl's regular expression syntax is a distant derivation of the POSIX implementation, resulting in the fact that the POSIX syntax can be used almost interchangeably with the Perl-style regular expression functions.

I devote the remainder of this section to a brief introduction of Perl regexp syntax. This is a simple example of a Perl regexp:

```
/food/
```

Notice that the string 'food' is enclosed between two forward slashes. Just like with POSIX regexps, you can build a more complex string through the use of quantifiers:

```
/fo+/
```

This will match 'fo' followed by one or more characters. Some potential matches include 'food', 'fool', and 'fo4'. Here is another example of using a quantifier:

```
/fo{2,4}/
```

This matches ''f'' followed by two to four occurrences of 'o.' Some potential matches include 'fool', 'fooool', and 'foosball'.

In fact, you can use any of the quantifiers introduced in the previous POSIX section.

Metacharacters

Another cool thing you can do with Perl regexps is use various metacharacters to search for matches. A *metacharacter* is simply an alphabetical character preceded by a backslash that acts to give the combination a special meaning. For instance, you can search for large money sums using the '\d' metacharacter:

```
/([\d]+)000/
```

'\d' will search for any string of numerical character. Of course, searching for alphabetical characters is important, thus the '\w' metacharacter:

```
/<([\w]+)>/
```

This will match things like HTML tags. (By contrast, the '\W' metacharacter searches for nonalphabetical characters.)

Another useful metacharacter is '\b', which searches for word boundaries:

```
/sa\b/
```

Because the word boundary is designated to be on the right-side of the strings, this will match strings like 'pisa' and 'lisa' but not 'sand'. The opposite of the word boundary metacharacter is '\B'. This matches on anything *but* a word boundary:

```
/sa\B/
```

This will match strings like 'sand' and 'Sally' but not 'Alessia'.

Modifiers

Several modifiers are available that can make your work with regexps much easier. There are many of these; however, I will introduce just a few of the more interesting ones in Table 8-1. These modifiers are placed directly after the regexp, for example, /string/i.

Table 8-1. Three Sample Modifiers

MODIFIER	DESCRIPTION
m	Treats a string as several ('m' for multiple) lines. By default, the '^' and '$' special characters match at the very start and very end of the string in question. Using the 'm' modifier will allow for '^' and '$' to match at the beginning of *any line* in a string.
s	Accomplishes just the opposite of the 'm' modifier, treating a string as a single line, ignoring any newline characters found within.
i	Implies a case-insensitive search.

This introduction has been brief, as attempting to document regular expressions in their entirety is surely out of the scope of this book and could easily fill many chapters rather than just a few pages. For more information regarding regular expression syntax, check out these great online resources:

- http://www.php.net/manual/pcre.pattern.modifiers.php

- http://www.php.net/manual/pcre.pattern.syntax.php

- http://www.perl.com/pub/doc/manual/html/pod/perlre.html

- http://www.codebits.com/p5be/

- http://www.metronet.com/1/perlinfo/doc/FMTEYEWTK/regexps.html

PHP's Regexp Functions (Perl Compatible)

PHP offers five functions for searching strings using Perl-compatible regular expressions:

- preg_match()

- preg_match_all()

- preg_replace()

- preg_split()

- preg_grep()

These functions are discussed in the following sections.

preg_match()

The preg_match() function searches *string* for *pattern*, returning true if *pattern* exists, and false otherwise. Its syntax follows:

```
int preg_match (string pattern, string string [, array pattern_array])
```

If the optional input parameter *pattern_array* is provided, then *pattern_array* will contain various sections of the subpatterns contained in the search pattern, if applicable. Here's an example that uses preg_match() to perform a case-sensitive search:

```
$line = "Vi is the greatest word processor ever created!";
// perform a case-Insensitive search for the word "Vi"
if (preg_match("/\bVi\b/i", $line, $match)) :
    print "Match found!";
endif;
// The if statement will evaluate to true in this example.
```

preg_match_all()

The preg_match_all() function matches all occurrences of *pattern* in *string*. Its syntax is:

```
int preg_match_all (string pattern, string string, array pattern_array [, int
order])
```

It will place these matches in the array *pattern_array* in the order you specify using the optional input parameter *order*. There are two possible types of *order*:

- PREG_PATTERN_ORDER is the default if the optional order parameter is not included. PREG_PATTERN_ORDER specifies the order in the way that you might think most logical; $pattern_array[0] is an array of all complete pattern matches, $pattern_array[1] is an array of all strings matching the first parenthesized regexp, and so on.

- PREG_SET_ORDER will order the array a bit differently than the default set-ting. $pattern_array[0] will contain elements matched by the first paren-thesized regexp, $pattern_array[1] will contain elements matched by the second parenthesized regexp, and so on.

Here's how you would use preg_match_all to find all strings enclosed in bold HTML tags:

```
$userinfo = "Name: <b>Rasmus Lerdorf</b> <br> Title: <b>PHP Guru</b>";
preg_match_all ("/<b>(.*)<\/b>/U", $userinfo, $pat_array);
print $pat_array[0][0]." <br> ".$pat_array[0][1]."\n";
```

```
Rasmus Lerdorf
PHP Guru
```

preg_replace()

The preg_replace() function operates just like ereg_replace(), except that regu-lar expressions can be used in the *pattern* and *replacement* input parameters. Its syntax is:

```
mixed preg_replace (mixed pattern, mixed replacement, mixed string [, int limit])
```

The optional input parameter *limit* specifies how many matches should take place. Interestingly, the *pattern* and *replacement* input parameters can be arrays. Preg_replace() will cycle through each element of each array, making replace-ments as they are found.

preg_split()

The preg_split() function operates exactly like split(), except that regular ex-pressions are accepted as input parameters for *pattern*. Its syntax is:

```
array preg_split (string pattern, string string [, int limit [, int flags]])
```

If the optional input parameter *limit* is specified, then only *limit* number of substrings are returned. This example uses preg_split() to parse a variable.

```
$user_info = "+WJ+++Gilmore+++++wjgilmore@hotmail.com++++++++Columbus+++OH";
$fields = preg_split("/\+{1,}/", $user_info);
while ($x < sizeof($fields)) :
   print $fields[$x]. "<br>";
   $x++;
endwhile;
```

```
WJ
Gilmore
wjgilmore@hotmail.com
Columbus
OH
```

preg_grep()

The preg_grep() function searches all elements of *input_array,* returning all elements matching the regexp *pattern.* Its syntax is:

```
array preg_grep (string pattern, array input_array)
```

Here's how you would use preg_grep() to search an array for foods beginning with *p:*

```
$foods = array("pasta", "steak", "fish", potatoes");
// find elements beginning with "p", followed by one or more letters.
$p_foods = preg_grep("/p(\w+)/", $foods);

$x = 0;

while ($x < sizeof($p_foods)) :
   print $p_foods[$x]. "<br>";
   $x++;
endwhile;
```

```
pasta
potatoes
```

Other String-Specific Functions

In addition to the regular expression–based functions discussed in the first half of this chapter, PHP provides 70+ functions geared toward manipulating practically every aspect of a string that you can think of. To list and explain each function would be out of the scope of this book and would not accomplish much more than repeat much of the information in the PHP documentation. Therefore, I have devoted the remainder of this chapter to a FAQ of sorts, the questions being those that seem to be the most widely posed in the many PHP discussion groups and related sites. Hopefully, this will be a much more efficient means for covering the generalities of the immense PHP string-handling library.

Padding and Compacting a String

For formatting reasons, it is necessary to modify the string length via either padding or stripping characters. PHP provides a number of functions for doing so.

chop()

The chop() function returns a string minus any ending whitespace and newlines. Its syntax is:

```
string chop (string str)
```

This example uses chop() to remove unnecessary newlines:

```
$header = "Table of Contents:\n\n";
$header = chop($header);
// $header = "Table of Contents"
```

str_pad()

The str_pad() function will pad *string* to length *pad_length* with a specified set of characters, returning the newly formatted string. Its syntax is:

```
string str_pad (string input, int pad_length [, string pad_string [, int
pad_type]])
```

If the optional parameter *pad_string* is not specified, *string* will be padded with blank spaces; otherwise it will be padded with the character pattern specified in *pad_string*. By default, the *string* will be padded to the right; however, the optional *pad_type* may be assigned STR_PAD_RIGHT, STR_PAD_LEFT, or STR_PAD_BOTH, padding the string accordingly. This example shows how to pad a string using str_pad() defaults:

```
$food = "salad";
print str_pad ($food, 5);      // prints "salad     "
```

This sample makes use of str_pad()'s optional parameters:

```
$header = "Table of Contents";
print str_pad ($header, 5, "=+=+=", STR_PAD_BOTH);
// "=+=+=Table of Contents=+=+=" will be displayed to the browser.
```

trim()

The trim() function will remove all whitespace from both the left and right sides of *string*, returning the resulting string. Its syntax is:

```
string trim (string string)
```

It will also remove the special characters "\n", "\r", "\t", "\v" and "\0".

ltrim()

The ltrim() function will remove the whitespace and special characters from the left side of *string*, returning the remaining string. Its syntax follows:

```
string ltrim (string str)
```

The special characters that will be removed are the same as those removed by trim().

Finding Out the Length of a String

You can determine the length of a string through use of the strlen() function. This function returns the length of a string, each character in the string being equivalent to one unit. Its syntax is:

```
int strlen (string str)
```

This example uses `strlen()` to determine the length of a string:

```
$string = "hello";
$length = strlen($string);
// $length = 5
```

Comparing Two Strings

String comparison is arguably one of the most important features of the string-handling capabilities of any language. Although there are many ways in which two strings can be compared for equality, PHP provides four functions for performing this task:

- strcmp()

- strcasecmp()

- strspn()

- strcspn()

These functions are discussed in the following sections.

strcmp()

The `strcmp()` function performs a case-sensitive comparison of two strings. Its syntax follows:

```
int strcmp (string string1, string string2)
```

On completion of the comparison, `strcmp()` will return one of three possible values:

- 0 if *string1* and *string2* are equal

- < 0 if *string1* is less than *string2*

- > 0 if *string2* is less than *string1*

This listing compares two equivalent string values:

```
$string1 = "butter";
$string2 = "butter";

if ((strcmp($string1, $string2)) == 0) :
    print "Strings are equivalent!";
endif;
// If statement will evaluate to true
```

strcasecmp()

The strcasecmp() function operates exactly like strcmp(), except that its comparison is case *insensitive*. Its syntax is:

```
int strcasecmp (string string1, string string2)
```

The following example compares two equivalent string values:

```
$string1 = "butter";
$string2 = "Butter";

if ((strcasecmp($string1, $string2)) == 0) :
    print "Strings are equivalent!";
endif;
// If statement will evaluate to true
```

strspn()

The strspn() function returns the length of the first segment in *string1* containing characters also in *string2*. Its syntax is:

```
int strspn (string string1, string string2)
```

Here's how you would use strspn() to validate a password:

```
$password = "12345";
if (strspn($password, "1234567890") != strlen($password)) :
    print "Password cannot consist solely of numbers!";
endif;
```

strcspn()

The strcspn() function returns the length of the first segment in *string1* containing characters *not* in *string2*. Its syntax is:

```
int strcspn (string str1, string str2)
```

Here's an example of password validation using strcspn():

```
$password = "12345";
if (strcspn($password, "1234567890") == 0) :
    print "Password cannot consist solely of numbers!";
endif;
```

Alternatives for Regular Expression Functions

When processing large amounts of information, the regular expression functions can slow matters dramatically. You should use these functions only when you are interested in parsing relatively complicated strings that require the use of regular expressions. If you are instead interested in parsing for simple expressions, there are a variety of predefined functions that will speed up the process considerably. Each of these functions is described below.

strtok()

The strtok() function will tokenize *string*, using the characters specified in *tokens*. Its syntax is:

```
string strtok (string string, string tokens)
```

One oddity about strtok() is that it must be continually called in order to completely tokenize a string; Each call to strtok() only tokenizes the next piece of the string. However, the *string* parameter only needs to be specified once, as the function will keep track of its position in *string* until it either completely tokenizes *string* or a new *string* parameter is specified. This example tokenizes a string with several delimiters:

```
$info = "WJ Gilmore:wjgilmore@hotmail.com|Columbus, Ohio";

// delimiters include colon (:), vertical bar (|), and comma (,)
$tokens = ":|,";

$tokenized = strtok($info, $tokens);
// print out each element in the $tokenized array
while ($tokenized) :
    echo "Element = $tokenized<br>";
    // Note how strtok does not take the first argument on subsequent executions
    $tokenized = strtok ($tokens);
endwhile;
```

```
Element =WJ Gilmore
Element = wjgilmore@hotmail.com
Element = Columbus
Element = Ohio
```

parse_str()

The parse_str() function parses *string* into various variables, setting the variables in the current scope. The syntax is:

void parse_str (string string)

This function is particularly useful when handling URLs that contain HTML form or otherwise extended information. The following example parses information passed via a URL. This string is the common form for a grouping of data that is passed from one page to another, compiled either directly in a hyperlink or in an HTML form:

```
$url = "fname=wj&lname=gilmore&zip=43210";
parse_str($url);
// after execution of parse_str(), the following variables are available:
// $fname = "wj"
// $lname = "gilmore"
// $zip = "43210"
```

Because this function was created to work with URLs, it ignores the ampersand (&) symbol.

> **NOTE** *The subject of PHP and HTML forms is introduced in Chapter 10, "Forms."*

explode()

The explode() function will divide *string* into various elements, returning these elements in an array. The syntax is:

```
array explode (string separator, string string [, int limit])
```

The division takes place at each occurrence of *separator*, and the number of divisions can be regulated with the optional inclusion of the input parameter *limit*. This example divides a string using the explode() function:

```
$info = "wilson|baseball|indians";
$user = explode("|", $info);
// $user[0] = "wilson";
// $user[1] = "baseball";
// $user[2] = "indians";
```

> **NOTE** *The* explode() *function is virtually identical to the POSIX regular expression function* split(), *described earlier in this chapter. The main difference is that split() should only be used when you need to employ regular expressions in the input parameters.*

implode()

Just as you can use the explode() function to project a string into various elements of an array, you can implode an array to form a string. This is accomplished with the implode() function. Its syntax is:

```
string implode (string delimiter, array pieces)
```

This example forms a string out of the elements of an array:

```
$ohio_cities = array("Columbus", "Youngstown", "Cleveland", "Cincinnati");
$city_string = implode("|", $ohio_cities);
// $city_string = "Columbus|Youngstown|Cleveland|Cincinnati";
```

> **NOTE** Join() *is an alias for* implode.

strpos()

The strpos() function finds the position of the first *occurrence* in *string*. Its syntax is:

```
int strpos (string string, string occurrence [, int offset])
```

The optional input parameter *offset* specifies the position at which to begin the search. If *occurrence* is not in *string*, strpos() will return false (0).

The following example determines the location of the first date entry in an abbreviated log:

```
$log = "
206.169.23.11:/www/:2000-08-10
206.169.23.11:/www/logs/:2000-02-04
206.169.23.11:/www/img/:1999-01-31";
// what is first occurrence of year 1999 in log?
$pos = strpos($log, "1999");
// $pos = 95, because first occurrence of "1999" is
// at position 95 of the string contained in $log,
```

strrpos()

The strrpos() function locates the last occurrence of *character* in *string*. Its syntax is:

```
int strrpos (string string, char character)
```

This function is less powerful than its counterpart, strpos(), because the search can only be performed on one character rather than a string. If a string is passed as the second input parameter into strrpos(), only the first character of that string will be used in the search.

str_replace()

The str_replace() function searches for *occurrence* in *string*, replacing all instances with *replacement*. Its syntax is:

```
string str_replace (string occurrence, string replacement, string string)
```

If *occurrence* is not in *string*, the string is not modified.

> **TIP**   substr_replace(), *described later in this section, allows you to re-place just a portion of a string. This example shows how* str_replace() *can replace several instances of an element in a string:*
>
> ```
> $favorite_food = "My favorite foods are ice cream and chicken wings";
> $favorite_food = str_replace("chicken wings", "pizza", $favorite_food);
> // $favorite_food = "My favorite foods are ice cream and pizza"
> ```

strstr()

The strstr() function returns the remainder of *string* beginning at the first *occurrence*. Its syntax is:

```
string strstr (string string, string occurrence)
```

This example uses strstr() to return the domain name of a URL:

```
$url = "http://www.apress.com";
$domain = strstr($url, ".");
// $domain = ".apress.com"
```

substr()

The substr() function returns the part of the string between the *start* and *start+length* parameters. Its syntax is:

```
string substr (string string, int start [, int length])
```

If the optional *length* parameter is not specified, the substring is considered to be the string starting at *start* and ending at the end of *string*. There are four points to keep in mind when using this function:

- If *start* is positive, the returned substring will begin at the *start*'th position of the string.

- If *start* is negative, the returned substring will begin at the string (*length* – *start*'th position of the string.

- If *length* is provided and is positive, the returned substring will consist of the characters between *start* and (*start* + *length*). If this distance is greater than the distance between *start* and the end of *string*, then only the substring between *start* and the string's end will be returned.

- If *length* is provided and is negative, the returned substring will end *length* characters from the end of *string*.

> **TIP** *Keep in mind that start is the offset from the first character of the string; therefore the returned string will actually start at character position (start + 1).*

This sample returns a portion of a string using `substr()`:

```
$car = "1944 Ford";
$model = substr($car, 6);
// $model = "Ford"
```

The following code is an example of a positive `substr()` *length* parameter:

```
$car = "1944 Ford";
$yr = substr($car, 0, 4);
// $yr = "1944"
```

Here is an example of a negative `substr()` *length* parameter:

```
$car = "1944 Ford";
$yr = substr($car, 2, -5);
// $yr = "44"
```

substr_count()

The `substr_count()` function returns the number of times *substring* occurs in *string*. Its syntax is:

```
int substr_count (string string, string substring)
```

This example counts the frequency of occurrence of a substring in a string:

```
$tng_twist = "The rain falls mainly on the plains of Spain";
$count = substr_count($tng_twist, "ain");
// $count = 4
```

substr_replace()

The substr_replace() function will replace a portion of *string* with *replacement*, beginning the replacement at *start* position of the string, and ending at *start* + *length* (assuming that the optional input parameter *length* is included). Its syntax is:

```
string substr_replace (string string, string replacement, int start [, int length])
```

Alternatively, the replacement will stop on the complete placement of *replacement* in *string*. There are several subtleties regarding the values of *start* and *length*:

- If *start* is positive, *replacement* will begin at character *start*.

- If *start* is negative, *replacement* will begin at (string length – *start*).

- If *length* is provided and is positive, *replacement* will be *length* characters long.

- If *length* is provided and is negative, *replacement* will end at (string length – *length*) characters.

This example shows a simple replacement of the remainder of a string using substr_replace():

```
$favs = "'s favorite links";
$name = "Alessia";
// The "0, 0" means that the replacement should begin at
// string's first position, and end at the original first position.
$favs = substr_replace($favs, $name, 0, 0);
print $favs;
```

Resulting in:

```
Alessia's favorite links
```

Converting Strings and Files to HTML and Vice Versa

Converting a string or an entire file into one suitable for viewing on the Web (and vice versa) is easier than you would think. Several functions are suited for this task.

Plain Text to HTML

It is often useful to be able to quickly convert plain text into a format that is readable in a Web browser. Several functions can aid you in doing so. These functions are the subject of this section.

nl2br()

The nl2br() function will convert all newline (\n) characters in a string to their HTML equivalent, that is, <br>. Its syntax is:

```
string nl2br (string string)
```

The newline characters could be invisible, created via hard returns, or visible, explicitly written in the string. The following example translates a text string (having newline characters '\n' to break lines) to HTML format:

```
// text string as it may be seen in a word processor.
$text_recipe = "
Party Sauce recipe:
1 can stewed tomatoes
3 tablespoons fresh lemon juice
Stir together, Serve cold.";
// convert the newlines to <br>'s.
$html_recipe = nl2br ($text_recipe);
```

Subsequently printing $html_recipe to the browser would result in the following HTML content being output:

```
Party Sauce recipe:<br>
1 can stewed tomatoes<br>
3 tablespoons fresh lemon juice<br>
Stir together, Serve cold.<br>
```

htmlentities()

The htmlentities() function will convert all characters into their equivalent
HTML entities. The syntax is:

```
string htmlentities (string string)
```

The following example converts necessary characters for Web display:

```
$user_input = "The cookbook, entitled 'Cafè Française' costs < $42.25.";
$converted_input = htmlentities($user_input);
// $converted_input = "The cookbook, entitled 'Caf&egrave;
// Fran&ccedil;aise' costs &lt; 42.24.";
```

> **NOTE** *The* htmlentities() *function currently only works in conjunction
> with the ISO-8859-1 (ISO-Latin-1) character set. Also,* htmlentities() *does
> not convert spaces to   as you may expect.*

htmlspecialchars()

The htmlspecialchars() function converts a select few characters having special
meaning in the context of HTML into their equivalent HTML entities. Its syntax is:

```
string htmlspecialchars (string string)
```

The htmlspecialchars() function currently only converts the following characters:

- & becomes &amp

- "" becomes &quot

- < becomes <

- > becomes &gt

This function is particularly useful in preventing users from entering HTML
markup into an interactive Web application, such as a message board. Improperly
coded HTML markup can cause an entire page to be formed incorrectly. However,
perhaps a more efficient way to do this is to use strip_tags(), which deletes the
tags from the string altogether.

The following example converts potentially harmful characters using htmlspecialchars():

```
$user_input = "I just can't get <<enough>> of PHP & those fabulous cooking recipes!";
$conv_input = htmlspecialchars($user_input);
// $conv_input = "I just can't get &lt;&lt;enough&gt;&gt; of PHP &amp those fabulous cooking recipes!"
```

> **TIP** *If you are using* gethtmlspecialchars() *in conjunction with* nl2br(), *you should execute* nl2br() *after* gethtmlspecialchars(); *otherwise the
's generated with* nl2br() *will be converted to visible characters.*

get_html_translation_table()

Using get_html_translation_table() is a convenient way to translate text to its HTML equivalent. Its syntax is:

```
string get_html_translation_table (int table)
```

Basically, get_html_translation_table() returns one of the two translation tables (specified by the input parameter *table*) used for the predefined htmlspecialchars() and htmlentities() functions. This returned value can then be used in conjunction with another predefined function, strtr() (defined later in this chapter), to essentially translate the text into HTML code.

The two tables that can be specified as input parameters to this function are:

- HTML_ENTITIES

- HTML_SPECIALCHARS

The following sample uses get_html_translation_table() to convert text to HTML:

```
$string = "La pasta é il piatto piú amato in Italia";
$translate = get_html_translation_table(HTML _ENTITIES);
print strtr($string, $translate);
// the special characters are converted to HTML entities and properly
// displayed in the browser.
```

Interestingly, `array_flip()` is capable of reversing the text-to-HTML translation and vice versa. Assume that instead of printing the result of `strtr()` in the preceding code sample, we assigned it to the variable $translated_string.

The next example uses `array_flip()` to return a string back to its original value:

```
$translate = array_flip($translate);
$translated_string = "La pasta &eacute; il piatto pi&uacute; amato in Italia"
$original_string = array_flip($translated_string, $translate);
// $original_string = "La pasta é il piatto piú amato in Italia";
```

strtr()

The `strtr()` function will convert all characters contained in *destination* to their corresponding character matches in *source*. Its syntax:

```
string strtr (string string, string source, string destination)
```

If the *source* and *destination* strings are of different length, any characters in the longer of the two will be truncated.

Essentially, you can think of `strtr()` as inversely comparing the values of two sets of arrays and making the replacements from *source* to *destination* as necessary. This example converts HTML characters to XML-like format:

```
$source = array("<title>" => "<h1>", "</title>" => "</h1>");
$string = "<h1>Today In PHP-Powered News</h1>";
print strtr($string, $source);
// prints "<title>Today In PHP-Powered News</title>"
```

HTML to Plain Text

You may sometimes need to convert an HTML file to plain text. The following functions can help you to do so.

strip_tags()

The `strip_tags()` function will remove all HTML and PHP tags from *string*, leaving only the text entities. Its syntax is:

```
string strip_tags (string string [, string allowable_tags])
```

The optional *allowable_tags* parameter allows you to specify which tags you would like to be skipped during this process.

This example uses strip_tags() to delete all HTML tags from a string:

```
$user_input = "i just <b>love</b> PHP and <i>gourmet</i> recipes!";
$stripped_input = strip_tags($user_input);
// $stripped_input = "I just love PHP and gourmet recipes!";
```

The following sample strips all except a few tags:

```
$input = "I <b>love</b> to <a href = \"http://www.eating.com\">eat<a>!";
$strip_input = strip_tags($user_input, "<a>");
// $strip_input = "I love to <a href = \"http://www.eating.com\">eat</a>!";
```

> **NOTE**   *Another function that performs similarly to* strip_tags() *is* fgetss(). *This function is described in Chapter 7, "File I/O and the File System."*

get_meta_tags()

Although perhaps not relating directly to the question of conversion, get_meta_tags() can be such a useful function that I did not want to leave it out. Its syntax is:

```
array get_meta_tags (string filename/URL [, int use_include_path])
```

The get_meta_tags() function will search an HTML file for what are known as META tags.

META tags are special descriptive tags that provide information, primarily to search engines, about a particular page. These tags are contained in the <head>...</head> HTML tags of a page. An example set of some available META tags might look like the following (we'll call this example.html, as it will be used in Listing 8-1):

```
<html>
<head>
<title>PHP Recipes</title>
<META NAME="keywords" CONTENT="gourmet, PHP, food, code, recipes, chef,
programming, Web">
```

```
<META NAME="description" CONTENT="PHP Recipes provides savvy readers with the
latest in PHP programming and gourmet cuisine!">
<META NAME="author" CONTENT="WJ Gilmore">
</head>
```

Get_meta_tags() will search for tags beginning with the word META in the head of a document and will place all tag names and their content in an associative array. Considering the previous META tag example, take a look at Listing 8-1.

Listing 8-1: Using get_meta_tags() to parse META tags in an HTML file

```
$meta_tags = get_meta_tags("example.html");
// $meta_tags will return an array containing the following information:
// $meta_tags["keywords"] = "gourmet, PHP, food, code, recipes, chef, programming,
Web";
// $meta_tags["description"] = "PHP-Powered Recipes provides savvy readers with
the latest in PHP
// programming and gourmet cuisine!";
// $meta_tags["author"] = "WJ Gilmore";
```

Interestingly, it is possible to extract META tags not only from a file residing on the server from which the script resides but also from other URLs.

> **TIP** *For a great tutorial describing what META tags are and how to use them, I suggest checking out Joe Burn's tutorial, "So, You Want a Meta Command, Huh?" on the HTML Goodies site at http://htmlgoodies .earthweb.com/tutors/meta.html.*

Converting a String into Uppercase and Lowercase Letters

Four functions are available to aid you in accomplishing this task:

- strtolower()

- strtoupper()

- ucfirst()

- ucwords()

These functions are discussed in the following sections.

strtolower()

The strtolower() function does exactly what you would expect it to: it converts a string to all lowercase letters. Its syntax is:

```
string strtolower (string string)
```

Nonalphabetical characters are not affected. The following example uses strtolower() to convert a string to all lowercase letters:

```
$sentence = "COOKING and PROGRAMMING PHP are my TWO favorite pastimes!";
$sentence = strtolower($sentence);
// $sentence is now
// "cooking and programming php are my two favorite pastimes!"
```

strtoupper()

Just as you can convert a string to lowercase, so can you convert one to uppercase. This is accomplished with the function strtoupper(), and its syntax is:

```
string strtoupper (string string)
```

Nonalphabetical characters are not affected. This example uses strtoupper() to convert a string to all uppercase letters:

```
$sentence = "cooking and programming PHP are my two favorite pastimes!";
$sentence = strtoupper($sentence);
// $sentence is now
// "COOKING AND PROGRAMMING PHP ARE MY TWO FAVORITE PASTIMES!"
```

ucfirst()

The ucfirst() function capitalizes the first letter of a string, provided that it is alphabetical. Its syntax is:

```
string ucfirst (string string)
```

Nonalphabetical characters will not be affected. The following example uses ucfirst() to capitalize the first letter of a string:

```
$sentence = "cooking and programming PHP are my two favorite pastimes!";
$sentence = ucfirst($sentence);
// $sentence is now
// "Cooking and programming PHP are my two favorite pastimes!"
```

ucwords()

The ucwords() function capitalizes the first letter of each word in a string. Its syntax is:

```
string ucwords (string string)
```

Nonalphabetical characters are not affected. A *word* is defined as a string of characters separated from other entities in the string by a blank space on each side. This example uses ucwords() to capitalize each word in a string:

```
$sentence = "cooking and programming PHP are my two favorite pastimes!";
$sentence = ucwords($sentence);
// $sentence is now
// "Cooking And Programming PHP Are My Two Favorite Pastimes!"
```

Project: Browser Detection

Anyone who attempts to develop a user-friendly Web site must take into account the differences of page formatting when the site is viewed using the various Web browsers and operating systems. Even though the W3 (http://www.w3.org) organization continues to offer standards that Internet application developers should adhere to, the various browser developers just love to add their own little "improvements" to these standards, essentially causing havoc and confusion for content developers worldwide. Developers have largely resolved this problem by actually creating different pages for each type of browser and operating system, a process that at times can be painful but results in sites that conform perfectly for any user, building the reputability and confidence that user has in returning to that site.

For users to view the page format that is intended for their browser and operating system, the incoming page request is "sniffed" for browser and platform information. Once the necessary information has been determined, users are then redirected to the correct page.

The purpose of this project is to show you how PHP's regular expression functionality can be used to build a "browser sniffer," sniffer.php. This sniffer will determine the operating system and browser type and version, displaying the information to the browser window. However, before delving into the code, I would like to take a moment to review one of the primary pieces of the sniffer, the pre-defined PHP variable $HTTP_USER_AGENT. This variable basically stores various information in string format about the requesting user's browser and operating system, which is exactly what we are looking for. We could easily display this information to the screen with just one line of code:

```
<?
echo $HTTP_USER_AGENT;
?>
```

If you are using Internet Explorer 5.0 on a Windows 98 machine, you will see the following output:

```
Mozilla/4.0 (compatible; MSIE 5.0; Windows 98; DigExt)
```

In contrast, Netscape Navigator 4.75 would display the following:

```
Mozilla/4.75 [en] (Win98; U)
```

Finally, the Opera browser displays:

```
Mozilla/4.73 (Windows 98; U) Opera 4.02  [en]
```

Sniffer.php will make use of the information returned by $HTTP_USER_AGENT, parsing out the relevant pieces using various regular expression and string-handling functions. Before reviewing the code, take a moment to read through the following pseudocode:

- Two functions are used to determine the browser and operating system information: browser_info() and opsys_info(). Let's start with the browser_info() pseudocode.

- Determine the browser type using the ereg() function. Although it is slower than using another non-Perl-style function such as strstr(), it comes in handy because a regular expression can be used to determine the browser version.

- Use a compound *if* statement to test for the following browsers and their versions: Internet Explorer, Opera, Netscape, and unknown. Simple enough.

- The resulting browser and version is returned in an array.

- The opsys_info() function determines the operating system type. This time, the strstr() function is used because there is no need to use a regular expression to determine the OS.

- A compound *if* statement is used to test for the following operating systems: Windows, Linux, UNIX, Macintosh, and unknown.

The resulting operating system is returned.

Listing 8-3: Determining client operating system and browser

```php
<?
/*
File: sniffer.php
Purpose: Determines browser type / version and platform information
Date: August 24, 2000
*/


// Function: browser_info
// Purpose: Returns browser type and version

function browser_info ($agent) {
    // Determine browser type
    //   Search for Internet Explorer signature.
    if (ereg( 'MSIE ([0-9].[0-9]{1,2})', $agent, $version)) :
        $browse_type = "IE";
        $browse_version = $version[1];


    //   Search for Opera signature.
    elseif (ereg( 'Opera ([0-9].[0-9]{1,2})', $agent, $version)) :
        $browse_type = "Opera";
        $browse_version = $version[1];


    //   Search for Netscape signature. The search for the Netscape browser
    //   *must* take place after the search for the Internet Explorer and Opera
    //   browsers, because each likes to call itself
    //   Mozilla as well as by its actual name.
    elseif (ereg( 'Mozilla/([0-9].[0-9]{1,2})', $agent, $version)) :
        $browse_type = "Netscape";
        $browse_version = $version[1];
```

```
                    // If not Internet Explorer, Opera, or Netscape, then call it unknown.
                    else :
                        $browse_type = "Unknown";
                        $browse_version = "Unknown";
                    endif;

                    // return the browser type and version as array
                    return array($browse_type, $browse_version);

        } // end browser_info

        // Function: opsys_info
        // Purpose: Returns the user operating system

        function opsys_info($agent) {
            // Determine operating system
            // Search for Windows platform
            if ( strstr ($agent, 'Win') ) :
                $opsys = "Windows";

            // Search for Linux platform
            elseif ( strstr($agent, 'Linux') ) :
                $opsys = "Linux";

            // Search for UNIX platform
            elseif ( strstr ($agent, 'Unix') ) :
                $opsys = "Unix";

            // Search for Macintosh platform
            elseif ( strstr ($agent,'Mac') ) :
                $opsys = "Macintosh";

            // Platform is unknown
            else :
                $opsys = "Unknown";
            endif;

            // return the operating system
            return $opsys;

        } // end opsys_info

        // receive returned array as a list
```

```
list ($browse_type, $browse_version) = browser_info ($HTTP_USER_AGENT);
$operating_sys = opsys_info ($HTTP_USER_AGENT);

print "Browser Type: $browse_type <br>";
print "Browser Version: $browse_version <br>";
print "Operating System: $operating_sys <br>";

?>
```

Easy as that! For example, if the user is using Netscape 4.75 on a Windows machine, the following will be displayed:

```
Browser Type: Netscape
Browser Version: 4.75
Operating System: Windows
```

Next chapter, you'll learn how to perform page redirects and even create style sheets based on the operating system and browser.

What's Next?

This chapter covered quite a bit of ground. After all, what good would a programming language be to you if you couldn't work with text? In particular, the following subjects were covered:

- A general introduction to regular expressions, both POSIX and Perl style

- PHP's predefined regular expression functionality

- Manipulating string length

- Determining string length

- Faster alternatives to PHP's regular expression functionality

- Converting plain text to HTML and vice versa

- Manipulating character case of strings

Next chapter begins Part II of this book, which also happens to be my favorite. Here we begin a survey of PHP's Web capabilities, covering dynamic content creation, file inclusion, and basic template generation. Subsequent chapters in Part II delve into HTML forms usage, databasing, session tracking, and advanced templates. So hold on to your hat; things are about to get really interesting!

The Web PART TWO

CHAPTER 9

PHP and Dynamic Site Development

If you're anything like myself, chances are you typically flip through the chapters of any computer textbook that do not apply immediately to what you're interested in learning, instead skipping directly to those chapters that apply to what you *do* want to know. Chances are, that's just fine; computer textbooks usually aren't meant to be read from cover to cover anyway. You are probably smiling as you read this paragraph, because you indeed did just this, skipping past the first eight chapters, settling on this one because it has the most interesting title. After all, no time to read the details when the big bossman is screaming in your ear, right?

Luckily, your eagerness won't inhibit you too much in regard to your comprehension of much of the material covered in Part II of this book, which turns our attention directly toward how PHP is used to build and interact with the Web. This chapter introduces how PHP's dynamic properties can easily change the content and navigability of Web pages through the use of links and various predefined functions. The next chapter will build on what you've learned here, delving into how PHP perpetuates user interaction via HTML forms. Chapter 11 then turns to PHP's database-interfacing capabilities. And onward we march toward the conclusion of Part II, covering several of the more advanced subjects of PHP's Web development capability.

However, keep in mind that the material covered in Part I is *indispensable* to the language. I will make use of many of the concepts covered in my code examples and will assume that you have read Part I. So if you have skipped ahead, be prepared to occasionally refer to previous chapters to bring yourself up to speed regarding a few topics.

Simple Linking

Just as a link can be used to direct a user to an HTML page, it can be used to lead to a PHP-enabled page, as shown here:

```
<a href = "date.php">View today's date</a>
```

Clicking the link will transport you to the page entitled "date.php". Simple enough, right? Building on this example, you can use a variable to construct a dynamic link:

```
<?
$link = "date.php";
print "<a href = \"$link\">View today's date</a> <br>\n";
?>
```

You're probably wondering why the double quotation marks ("") are preceded by backslashes (\). This is because double quotation marks are special characters in PHP, since they are also used to enclose print statements. Thus, they must be escaped with the backslash.

> **TIP** *If you find escaping double quotation marks annoying, just enable magic_quotes_gpc in the php.ini file. Once this is enabled, all single quotation marks, double quotation marks, backslashes, and NULL characters will be automatically escaped!*

Building on this example, you can use an array to quickly display a list of links to the browser:

```
<?
// create array of content titles
$contents = array("tutorials", "articles", "scripts", "contact");
// loop through and display each element of the array.
for ($i = 0; $i < sizeof($contents); $i++)
    print " &#149; <a href = \"".$contents[$i].".php\">".$contents[$i]."</a>
<br>\n";
    // The &149; is the special character for a bullet.
endfor;
?>
```

The result:

```
&#149; <a href = "tutorials.php">tutorials</a> <br>
&#149; <a href = "articles.php">articles</a> <br>
&#149; <a href = "scripts.php">scripts</a> <br>
&#149; <a href = "contact.php">contact</a> <br>
```

File Components (Basic Templates)

At this point, I turn to one of my favorite capabilities of PHP: templates. A template as it pertains to Web building is essentially a particular part of the Web document that you would like to use in more than one page. A template, just like a PHP function, saves you from needing to redundantly type or cut and paste sections of page content and code. This concept will become particularly important as your site grows in size, as use of templates will allow you to quickly and easily perform sitewide modifications quickly. In the next few pages, I will introduce the advantages of building basic templates.

Typically, these code/content sections (or templates) are placed in one or more separate files. As you build your Web document, you simply "include" these pages into their respective position on the page. Two PHP functions provide for doing just this: include() and require().

include() and require()

One of the powerful aspects of PHP is the ability to build templates and code libraries that can be easily inserted into new scripts. In the long run, using code libraries can drastically minimize time and tears when you need to reuse common functionality across Web sites. Those of you with backgrounds in other languages (such as C, C++, or Java) are familiar with this concept of code libraries (hereafter code libraries and templates will be singly referred to as templates) and including them in your program to extend functionality.

You can build basic templates easily by including one or a series of files via two of PHP's predefined functions, require() and include(). Each has its specific application, as you will learn in the next section.

The Functions

There are four functions that can be used to include files in a PHP script:

- include()

- include_once()

- require()

- require_once()

Although some of these seem equivalent in function due to the similarity of their names, be forewarned that each has a distinct purpose.

include()

The include() function does exactly what its name implies; it includes a file. This is its syntax:

```
include (file insertion_file)
```

An interesting characteristic of include() is that you can execute it condition-ally. For example, if an include is placed in an *if* statement, *insertion_file* will be included only if the *if* statement in which it is enclosed evaluates to true. Keep in mind that if you decide to use include() in a conditional, the include() construct *must* be enclosed in statement block curly brackets or in the alternative statement enclosure. Consider the difference in syntax between Listings 9-1 and 9-2.

Listing 9-1: Incorrect usage of include()

```
...
if (some_conditional)
    include ('some_file');
else
    include ('some_other_file');
...
```

Listing 9-2: Correct usage of include()

```
. . .
if (some_conditional) :
    include ('some_file');
else :
    include ('some_other_file');
endif;
. . .
```

One misleading aspect of the include() statement is that any PHP code in the included file *must* be escaped with valid PHP enclosure tags. Therefore, you could not just place a PHP command in a file and expect it to parse correctly, such as the one found here:

```
print "this is an invalid include file";
```

Instead, any PHP statements must be enclosed with the correct escape tags, as shown here:

```
<?
print "this is an invalid include file";
?>
```

include_once()

The include_once() function has the same purpose as include(), except that it first verifies whether or not the file has already been included. If it has been, include_once() will not execute. Otherwise, it will include the file as necessary. Other than this difference, include_once() operates in exactly the same way as include(). Its syntax follows:

```
include_once (file insertion_file)
```

require()

For the most part, require() operates like include(), including a template into the file in which the require() call is located. It has this syntax:

```
require(file insertion_file)
```

However, there is one important difference between require() and include(). The *insertion_file* will be included in the script in which the require() construct appears regardless of where require() is located. For instance, if require() were placed in an if statement that evaluated to false, *insertion_file* would be included anyway!

> **TIP** *A URL can be used with* require() *only if "URL fopen wrappers" has been enabled, which by default it is.*

It is often useful to create a file containing variables and other information that may be used throughout the site and then require it where necessary. Although you can name this file anything you like, I like to call mine "init.tpl" (short for "*init*ialization.*template*"). Listing 9-3 shows what a very simple init.tpl file would look like. Listing 9-4 subsequently uses require() to include the init.tpl information into its script.

Listing 9-3: A sample file to be inserted (init.tpl)

```
<?
$site_title = "PHP Recipes";
$contact_email = "wjgilmore@hotmail.com";
$contact_name = "WJ Gilmore";
?>
```

Listing 9-4 inserts the init.tpl information into its script and then uses the variables in it to dynamically change the page contents.

Listing 9-4: Making use of init.tpl

```
<? require ('init.tpl'); ?>
<html>
<head>
<title><?=$site_title;?></title>
</head>
<body>
<?
print "Welcome to $site_title. For questions, contact <a href =
\"mailto:$contact_email\">$contact_name</a>."; ?>
</body>
</html>
```

As your site grows in size, you may find yourself redundantly including particular files. While this might not always be a problem, sometimes you will not want modified variables in the included file to be overwritten by a later inclusion of the same file. Another problem that arises is the clashing of function names should they exist in the inclusion file. And thus I introduce the next function, require_once().

require_once()

The require_once() function ensures that the insertion file is included only once in your script. After require_once() is encountered, any subsequent attempts to include the same file will be ignored. Its syntax follows:

```
require_once(file insertion_file)
```

Other than the verification procedure of require_once(), all other aspects of the function are the same as for require().

You will probably use these functions extensively as your Web applications grow in size. You will regularly see these functions in my examples throughout the remainder of this book in order to eliminate code redundancies. The first practical use of these functions occurs in the next section, where I introduce basic template construction strategies.

Building Components

When referring to the structure of a typical Web page, I generally like to break it up into three distinct parts: header, footer, and body. Usually, most well-organized Web sites have a top section that remains largely unchanged; a middle section that displays the requested content, thus changing regularly; and finally a bottom section containing copyright and general link information that, like the header, generally does not change. Don't get me wrong; I'm not trying to stifle creativity. I've seen many fantastic sites that do not follow this structure. I'm just attempting to set up a framework from which we can begin.

The Header

One thing I like to use in almost all of my PHP-enabled Web sites is a header file, such as the one shown in Listing 9-5. This file holds several pieces of information that will be applied sitewide, such as the title, contact information, and actual initial HTML components of the page.

Listing 9-5: A sample header file

```
<?
// filename: header.tpl
// purpose: site header file for PhpRecipes site
// date: August 22, 2000

$site_name = "PHPRecipes";
$site_email = "wjgilmore@hotmail.com";
$site_path = "http://localhost/phprecipes";
?>
<html>
<head>
<title> <?=$site_name;?> </title>
</head>
<body bgcolor="#7b8079" text="#ffffff" link="#e7d387" alink="#e7d387"
vlink="#e7f0e4">
<table width = "95%" cellpadding="0" cellspacing="0" border="1">
    <tr>
    <td valign = "top">
    PHPRecipes
    </td>
```

```
      <td valign = "top" align="right">
      <?
      // output current date and time
      print date ("F d, h:i a");
      ?>
      </td>
      </tr>
</table>
```

You may often want to ensure that unwanted visitors do not view your included files, particularly if they hold information such as access passwords. In Apache, you can wholly deny the viewing of certain files by modifying your http.conf or htaccess file. This is an example of how you can prevent the viewing of any file with a .tpl extension:

```
<Files "*.tpl">
  Order allow,deny
  Allow from 127.0.0.1
  Deny from all
</Files>
```

NOTE *PHP and site security are discussed in more detail in Chapter 16.*

The Footer

What is typically deemed the "footer" of a site is the information at the bottom of site pages, generally the contact, linking, and copyright information. This information can be placed in a single file and included as a template just as easily as the header information can. Consider the need to change the copyright information to read "Copyright © 2000-2001" You have two choices: spend your New Year's Eve frantically changing hundreds of static pages *or* use a footer template like the one in Listing 9-6. Make one simple change and voilà! Back to the festivities.

Listing 9-6: A sample footer file (footer.tpl)

```
<table width="95%" cellspacing="0" cellpadding="0" border="1">
<tr><td valign="top" align="middle">
Copyright &copy; 2000 PHPRecipes. All rights reserved.<br>
<a href = "mailto:<?=$site_email;?>">contact</a> | <a href =
"<?=$site_path;?>/privacy.php">your privacy</a>
</td></tr>
</table>
</body>
</html>
```

Take note that I am using one of the global variables ($site_email) within the footer file. This is because that variable will propagate throughout the entire page, since it is assumed that the header.tpl and footer.tpl files will be assimilated into one cohesive page. Also, notice that I output $site_path in the "privacy" link. I always want to use a complete path to any link in a template file because if I use this footer in any child directories, the path would not be correct if I were only to use privacy.php as the link URL.

The Body

The page body connects the header to the footer. The body section of a Web document is basically the "meat-and-bones" section of the page—that is, the page that the readers care about. Sure, the header is cool, the footer is helpful, but it is the body that keeps readers returning. Although I can't provide any pointers as to the content of your page structure, I can help in terms of your ease of page administration by providing Listing 9-7.

Listing 9-7: A simple body section (index_body.tpl)

```
<table width="95%" cellspacing="0" cellpadding="0" border="1">
<tr>
<td valign="top" width="25%">
<a href = "<?=$site_path;?>/tutorials.php">tutorials</a> <br>
<a href = "<?=$site_path;?>/articles.php">articles</a> <br>
<a href = "<?=$site_path;?>/scripts.php">scripts</a> <br>
<a href = "<?=$site_path;?>/contact.php">contact</a> <br>
</td>
<td valign="top" width="75%">
Welcome to PHPRecipes, the starting place for PHP scripts, tutorials, and
information about gourmet cooking!
</td>
</tr>
</table>
```

Putting It Together: Incorporating the Header, Footer, and Body

My feelings are perhaps best phrased as Colonel "Hannibal" Smith (George Peppard) put it on the famous *A-Team* television show, "I love it when a good plan comes together." In my nerdy way, I feel the same when I see several template files come together to form a complete Web document. Combining the three document sections, header.tpl, index_body.tpl, footer.tpl, you can quickly build a basic page like the one in Listing 9-8.

Listing 9-8: Various includes compiled together to produce index.php

```
<?
// file: index.php
// purpose: Home page of PHPRecipes
// date: August 23, 2000
// Include the header
include ("header.tpl");
// Include the index body
include ("index_body.tpl");
// Include the footer
include ("footer.tpl");
?>
```

How about that? Three simple commands, and the page is built. Check out the resulting page in Listing 9-9.

Listing 9-9: Resulting HTML constructed from Listing 9-8 (index.php)

```
<html>
<head>
<title> PHPRecipes </title>
</head>
<body bgcolor="#7b8079" text="#ffffff" link="#e7d387" alink="#e7d387"
vlink="#e7f0e4">
<table width = "95%" cellpadding="0" cellspacing="0" border="1">
   <tr>
   <td valign = "top">
   PHP Recipes
   </td>
   <td valign = "top" align="right">
```

```
   August 23, 03:17 pm
   </td>
   </tr>
</table>
<table width="95%" cellspacing="0" cellpadding="0" border="1">
<tr>
<td valign="top" width="25%">
<a href = "http://localhost/phprecipes/tutorials.php">tutorials</a> <br>
<a href = "http://localhost/phprecipes/articles.php">articles</a> <br>
<a href = "http://localhost/phprecipes/scripts.php">scripts</a> <br>
<a href = "http://localhost/phprecipes/contact.php">contact</a> <br>
</td>
<td valign="top" width="75%">
Welcome to PHPRecipes, the starting place for PHP scripts, tutorials, and gourmet
cooking tips and recipes!
</td>
</tr>
</table><table width="95%" cellspacing="0" cellpadding="0" border="1">
<tr><td valign="top" align="middle">
Copyright &copy; 2000 PHPRecipes. All rights reserved.<br>
<a href = "mailto:wjgilmore@hotmail.com">contact</a> | <a href =
"http://localhost/phprecipes/privacy.php">your privacy</a>
</td></tr>
</table>
</body>
</html>
```

Figure 9-1 shows you the resulting page as viewed in the browser. Although I detest table borders, I set them to 1 so that you can more easily differentiate the three sections of the page.

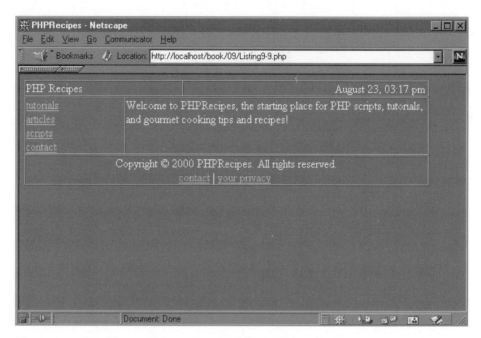

Figure 9-1. Resulting page as constructed from Listing 9-8

Optimizing Your Site's Templates

A second, and arguably preferred, method of using your templates is to store them in functions, placed in a single file. This further organizes your template, making a "template of templates." I also call this my initialization file, as I tend to store other useful information in it. Since you already have been exposed to a relatively lengthy header and footer example, I'll abbreviate the ones in Listings 9-10 and 9-11 for the sake of illustrating this new idea.

Listing 9-10: Optimized site template (site_init.tpl)

```
<?
// filename: site_init.tpl
// purpose: PhpRecipes Initialization file.
// date: August 22, 2000

$site_name = "PHPRecipes";
$site_email = "wjgilmore@hotmail.com";
$site_path = "http://localhost/phprecipes";

function show_header($site_name) {
?>
<html>
```

```
<head>
<title> <? print $site_name; ?> </title>
</head>
<body bgcolor="#7b8079" text="#ffffff" link="#e7d387" alink="#e7d387"
vlink="#e7f0e4">
This is the header
<hr>
<?
}
function show_footer() {
?>
<hr>
This Is the footer
</body>
</html>
<?
}
?>
```

Listing 9-11: Using the initialization file

```
<?
// Include site Initialization Information
include("site_init.tpl");
// display the header
show_header($site_name);
?>
This is some body information
<?
// display the footer
show_footer();
?>
```

Using functions further condenses the code and number of templates needed, ultimately allowing you to more efficiently administer your site. This strategy also makes it easier to reuse your code to build other sites without having to keep track of a number of involved files.

Project: Build a Page Generator

Although large parts of the Web sites I build make use of database information to display content, there are always a few pages that aren't going to change much.

Some of these pages may contain information about the development team, contact information, advertising information, and so on. You get the picture. I generally store this "static" information in its own folder and use a PHP script to pull it to the Web page on request. Of course, since this information is static, you may be asking yourself why you should even employ the use of a PHP script. Why not just use plain old HTML pages? The advantage of using PHP is that you can take advantage of the templates, just inserting the static part as necessary.

The link used to call the various static files is dynamic. Its general form is:

```
<a href = "<?=$site_path;?>/static.php?content=$content">Static Page Name</a>
```

To begin, create your various static pages. For sake of simplicity, I'll create three of them: About This Site (Listing 9-12), Advertising Information (Listing 9-13), and Contact Us (Listing 9-14).

Listing 9-12: About This Site (about.html)

```
<h3>About PHPRecipes</h3>
What programmer doesn't mix all night programming with gourmet cookies? Here at
PHPRecipes, hardly a night goes by without one of our coders mixing a little bit
of HTML with a tasty plate of Portobello Mushrooms or even Fondue. So we decided
to bring you the best of what we love most: PHP and food!
<p>
That's right, readers. Tutorials, scripts, souffles and more. <i>Only</i> at
PHPRecipes.
```

Listing 9-13: Advertising Information (advert_info.html)

```
<h3>Advertising Information</h3>
Regardless of whether they come to learn the latest PHP techniques or for brushing
up on how to bake chicken, you can bet our readers are decision makers. They are
the Industry professionals who make decisions about what their company purchases.
For advertising information, contact <a href = "mailto:ads@phprecipes.com
">ads@phprecipes.com</a>.
```

Listing 9-14 Contact Us (contact.html)

```
<h3>Contact Us</h3>
Have a coding tip? <br>
Know the perfect topping for candied yams?<br>
 Let us know! Contact the team at <a href =
"mailto:theteam@phprecipes.com">team@phprecipes.com</a>.
```

Now you will design the page that will house the requested information, entitled "static.php". This file acts as the aggregator of the various components of a page on our site and makes use of the site_init.tpl file, shown in Listing 9-15.

Listing 9-15: Page aggregator (static.php)

```
<?
// file: static.php
// purpose: display various requested static pages.
// IMPORTANT: It Is assumed that "site_init.tpl" and all of the static files are
located in the same directory.
// load functions and site variables
include("site_init.tpl");
// display the page header
show_header($site_name);
// display the requested content
include("$content.html");
// display the page footer
show_footer();
?>
```

OK, now you're ready to implement this script. Simply place the correct link reference relative to the page, as shown here:

```
<a href = "static.php?content=about">About This Site</a><br>
<a href = "static.php?content=advert_info">Advertising Information</a><br>
<a href = "static.php?content=contact">Contact Us</a><br>
```

Clicking any of the links will take you to the respective static page, embedded in static.php!

What's Next?

This chapter introduced you to the heart of what PHP was intended to do in the first place: dynamic Web page generation. In this chapter, you learned how to do the following:

- Manipulate URLs

- Generate dynamic content

- Include and build basic templates

The project concluding the chapter illustrated how you could build a page generator that would pull static pages into a larger template structure, making it ever so easy for you to maintain large numbers of static HTML pages.

The next chapter builds on this foundation significantly, introducing how PHP can be used in conjunction with HTML forms, adding a whole new degree of user interactivity into your site. Then, it's onward to databasing! What an exciting few chapters these are going to be!

CHAPTER 10

Forms

The ability to retrieve and process user-provided information has become an integral part of most successful Web sites. The ability to collect statistics, poll users, store preferential information, and offer document searches certainly adds a whole new dimension to what would be an otherwise only minimally interactive medium.

Information retrieval is largely implemented through the use of HTML forms. Certainly you are already familiar with the look and feel of an HTML form. General practice is that you enter one or more pieces of data (for example, your name and email address), press a submit button of sorts, and are then greeted with a response message.

You may be thinking that the process of collecting user data via HTML forms is a complicated and tedious process. If so, you will be surprised to learn that it is actually quite easy.

An Introduction to Forms

There are a number of different forms you can use to input information. Some require users to enter information using their keyboard, while others require the users to select one or more choices by clicking with a mouse. Yet others simply involve a hidden form value that is embedded in the form itself and is not intended to be modified by the user.

It is possible to have multiple forms on the same page, so there must be some way to distinguish one form from the other. Furthermore, there must be a way to tell the form where to go once the user initiates the form action (usually by clicking a button). Both of these needs are taken care of by enclosing the form entities in the following HTML tags:

```
<form action="some_action" method="post">
    … form entities …
</form>
```

As you can see, two important elements make up this enclosure: the action and the method. The *action* specifies what script should process the form, while the *method* specifies how the form data will be sent to the script. There are two possible methods:

- The get method sends all of the form information at the end of the URL. This method is rarely used, due to various language and length restrictions.

- The post method sends all of the form information in the request body. This method is usually preferred over get.

> **NOTE** *This introduction is intended to be a brief primer regarding the basic syntax of HTML forms. For a more complete introduction, I suggest checking out* Special Edition Using HTML 4 *by Molly E. Holzschlag (QUE; ISBN* 0789722674, December 1999*).*

Keyboard-Oriented Form Entities

Now you're ready to begin building forms. The first step is to learn the keyboard-oriented form entities. There are only two: the text box and the text area box.

The Text Box

The text box is typically used for short text entries, such as an email address, postal address, or name. Its syntax is:

```
<input type="text" name="variable_name" size="N" maxlength="N" value="">
```

There are five text box components:

- type: Type of form input, in this case text.

- name: Variable name used to store the data.

- size: Total size of the text box as it will display in the browser.

- maxlength: Total number of characters that can be input into the text box.

- value: Default value that will display in the text box.

A sample text box is shown in Figure 10-1.

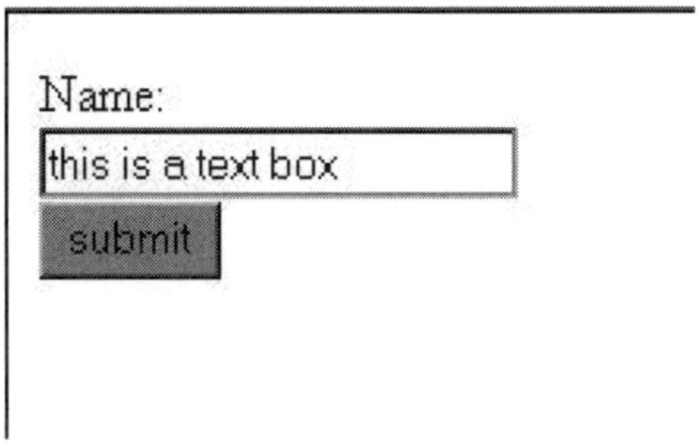

Figure 10-1. A text box

A variation on the text box is the password text box, which operates exactly like the text box, except that the data is hidden with asterisks as it is entered in the text field. To change the text box to a password text box, just use type = "password" instead of type = "text".

The Text Area Box

The text area box is useful when you would like the reader to be a bit more verbose than just entering a name or email address. Its syntax is:

```
<textarea name="variable_name" rows="N" cols="N"></textarea>
```

There are three textarea components:

- name: Variable name used to store the data.

- rows: Number of rows comprising textarea.

- cols: Number of columns comprising textarea.

A sample text area box is shown in Figure 10-2.

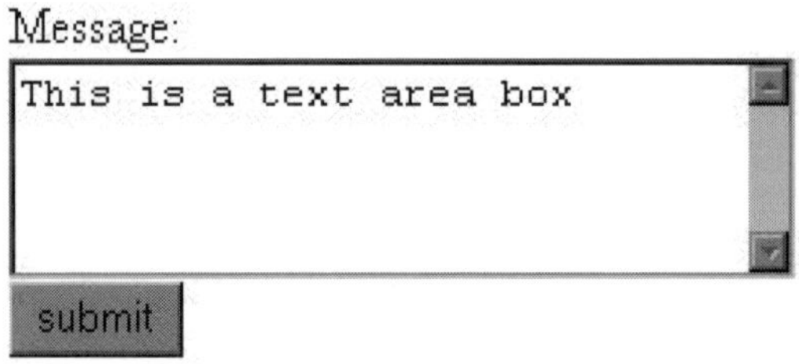

Message:

```
This is a text area box
```

submit

Figure 10-2. A text area box

Mouse-Oriented Form Entities

There are several other form entities that are controlled by the user selecting a predefined value with a mouse. I will limit the introduction to checkboxes, radio buttons, and pull-down menus.

The Checkbox

Checkboxes are convenient when you would like to present users with one or more choices to check, much like making a checkmark on some form with a pencil. The syntax is:

```
<input type="checkbox" name="variable_name" value="variable_value">
```

There are three checkbox components:

- type: Type of form input, in this case a checkbox.

- name: Variable name used to store the data, in this case the entity value.

- value: Default value that will be assigned to the variable name. Note that if the checkbox is checked, *this* is the value that is assigned to variable name. If it is not checked, then this variable will *not* be passed.

A sample checkbox is shown in Figure 10-3.

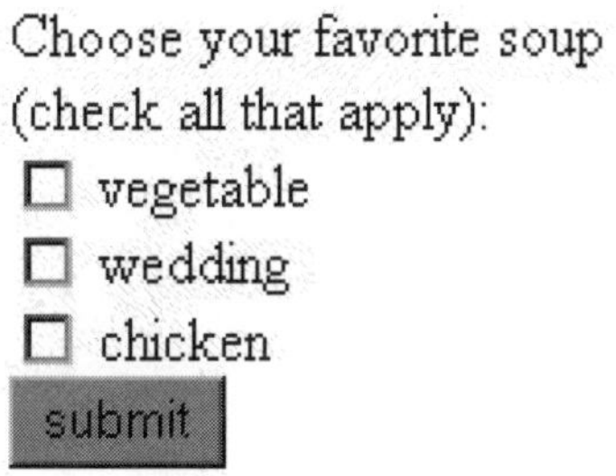

Choose your favorite soup
(check all that apply):
☐ vegetable
☐ wedding
☐ chicken
[submit]

Figure 10-3. Checkboxes

The Radio Button

The radio button is a variation of the checkbox, similar in all aspects except that only one button can be checked. The syntax is:

```
<input type="radio" name="variable_name" value="variable_value">
```

As you can see, its syntax is exactly like that of the checkbox. There are three radio button components:

- type: Type of form input, in this case a radio.

- name: Variable name used to store the data, in this case the entity value.

- value: Default value that will display in the text box. Note that if the radio button is selected, *this* is the value that is assigned to variable name. If it is not selected, then this variable will *not* be passed.

Sample radio buttons are shown in Figure 10-4.

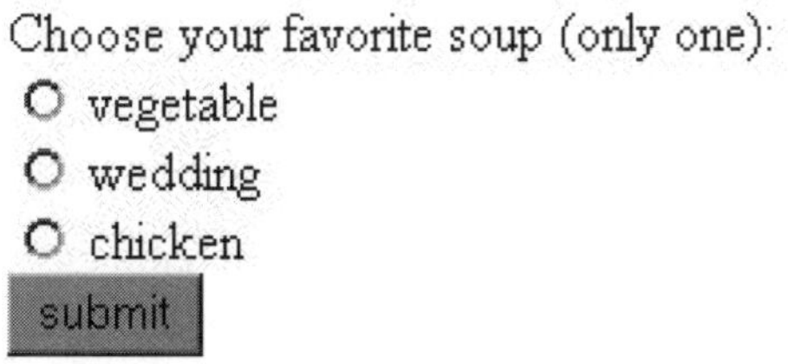

Choose your favorite soup (only one):
○ vegetable
○ wedding
○ chicken
[submit]

Figure 10-4. Radio buttons

The Pull-Down Menu

Pull-down menus are particularly convenient when you have a long list of data from which you would like users to select a value. Pull-down menus are commonly used for large data sets, a list of American states or countries, for example. The syntax is:

```
<select name="variable_name">
<option value="variable_value1">
<option value="variable_value2">
<option value="variable_value3">
. . .
<option value="variable_valueN">
</select>
```

There are two pull-down menu components:

- name: Variable name used to store the data, in this case the variable name that will store the chosen value.

- value: Default value that will display in the text box. Note that if the checkbox is checked, *this* is the value that is assigned to variable name.

A sample pull-down menu is shown in Figure 10-5.

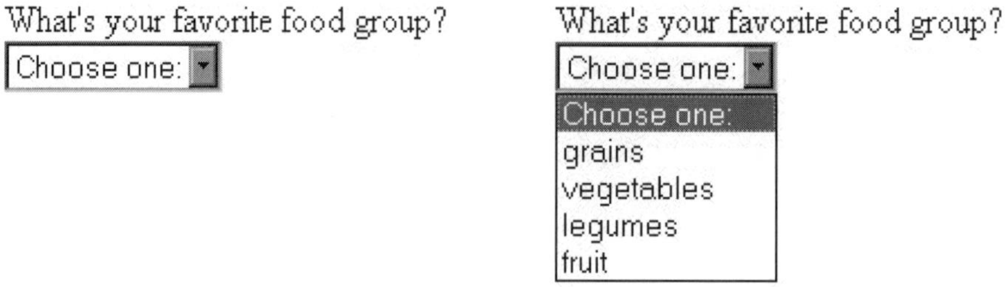

Figure 10-5. A pull-down menu

Hidden Values

Hidden form values are embedded in the form itself and are generally used as a means to persist data from one script to the other. While there is nothing wrong with doing so, PHP offers a much more convenient method for keeping persistent data: session tracking, which is the subject of Chapter 13. Regardless, hidden values have their uses, so I will proceed with the introduction.

The syntax of the hidden form value is exactly like that of the text box, save for the differing type value. Since the hidden value is hidden from the user, there is no way to show a sample. The syntax is:

```
<input type="hidden" name="variable_name" value="variable_value">
```

There are three hidden value components:

- type: Type of form input. In this case it's hidden.

- name: Variable name used to store the hidden data.

- value: Default value that will display in the text box.

Keep in mind that perhaps the title of this form entity is a misnomer. While the hidden value does not display to the browser, the user could simply perform a View Source and view whatever hidden values are in the form.

The Submit Button

The submit button actuates the action specified in the *action* component of the *form* enclosure. Its syntax is:

```
<input type="submit" value="button_name">
```

There are two submit button components:

- type: Type of form input, in this case submit.

- value: Default value that will display in the text box.

A sample submit button is shown in Figure 10-6.

Figure 10-6. A submit button

The Reset Button

The reset button will erase all information entered into the form. This is generally a pretty useless feature, but has become so commonly used in forms on the Web that I thought I should include it. The syntax is:

```
<input type="reset" name="reset" value="button_name">
```

There are two reset button components:

- type: Type of form input, in this case reset.

- value: Name shown on top of the button.

A reset button looks exactly like a submit button (illustrated in Figure 10-6), except that its type and value are set to "reset".

NOTE *Jakob Nielsen, a noted Web-usability expert, recently wrote a rather interesting article about the drawbacks to the reset button. It is at http://www.useit.com/alertbox/20000416.html.*

Putting It Together: A Sample Form

Now that you have been introduced to the basic form components, you can create one that will accept user information. Suppose you wanted to create a form that would pose various questions to users about what they think about your new site. I'll create this form in Listing 10-1.

Listing 10-1: Sample user feedback form

```
<form action = "process.php" method = "post">
<b>Please take a moment to tell us what you think about our site:</b><p>
<b>Name:</b><br>
<input type="text" name="name" size="15" maxlength="25" value=""><br>
<b>Email:</b><br>
<input type="text" name="email" size="15" maxlength="45" value=""><br>
<b>How frequently do you visit our site?:</b><br>
<select name="frequency">
<option value="">Site frequency:
<option value="0">This is my first time
<option value="1">&lt; 1 time a month
<option value="2">Roughly once a month
<option value="3">Several times a week
```

```
<option value="4">Every day
<option value="5">I'm addicted
</select><br>
<b>I frequently purchase the following products from our site:</b><br>
<input type="checkbox" name="software" value="software">Software<br>
<input type="checkbox" name="cookware" value="cookware">Cookware<br>
<input type="checkbox" name="hats" value="hats">Chef's Hats<br>
<b>Our site's greatest asset is:</b><br>
<input type="radio" name="asset" value="products">Product selection<br>
<input type="radio" name="asset" value="design">Cool design<br>
<input type="radio" name="asset" value="service">Customer Service<br>
<b>Comments:</b><br>
<textarea name="comments" rows="3" cols="40"></textarea><br>
<input type="submit" value="Submit!">
</form>
```

The form as displayed in the browser is illustrated in Figure 10-7.

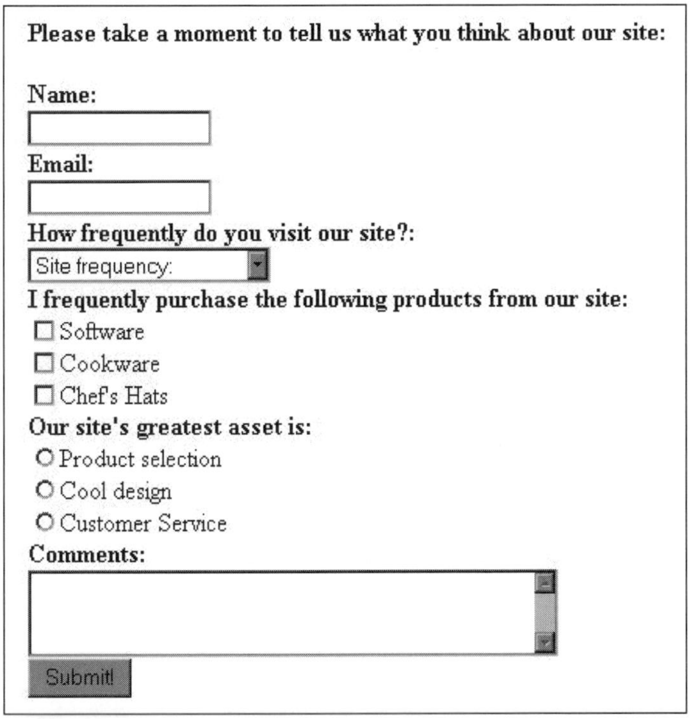

Figure 10-7. A sample user input form

Pretty straightforward, right? But the question now arises of how you take the user input and do something useful with it. That is the subject of the next section, "Forms and PHP."

Keep in mind that this introduction to forms should be considered just that; an introduction. It is by no means a comprehensive summary of all options offered to the various form components. Check out any of the many forms-related tutorials on the Web and recently released HTML books for further information.

Having completed this introduction to HTML forms, I now proceed to the really interesting part of this chapter; that is, how PHP can be used to process and interact with user information input via these forms.

Forms and PHP

How PHP handles form information is really not all that different from how PHP handles variable data passed along with the URL, a subject I discussed in detail in the previous chapter.

Introductory Examples

To facilitate rapid learning of the various ways you can use PHP to manipulate form information, I present a series of scenarios. Each scenario illustrates a different way you can take advantage of this technology to add interactivity to your site.

Scenario 1: Passing Form Information from One Script to Another

This is perhaps the most basic of examples, in which user input is simply gathered on one page and displayed on another. Listing 10-2 contains the form that will prompt a user for a name and email address. When the user clicks the submit button, entitled "go!" the form will request listing10-3.php. Listing 10-3 will in turn display the $name and $email variables that were passed along with the page request.

Listing 10-2: A simple form

```
<html>
<head>
<title>Listing 10-2</title>
</head>
```

```
<body bgcolor="#ffffff" text="#000000" link="#cbda74" vlink="#808040"
alink="#808040">


<form action="listing10-3.php" method="post">
<b>Give us some information!</b><br>
Your Name:<br>
<input type="text" name="name" size="20" maxlength="20" value=""><br>
Your Email:<br>
<input type="text" name="email" size="20" maxlength="40" value=""><br>
<input type="submit" value="go!">
</form>

</body>
</html>
```

Listing 10-3: Displaying the data collected in Listing 10-1
```
<html>
<head>
<title>Listing 10-3</title>
</head>
<body bgcolor="#ffffff" text="#000000" link="#cbda74" vlink="#808040"
alink="#808040">
<?
// output the user's name and email address.
print "Hi, $name!. Your email address is $email";
?>
</body>
</html>
```

In summary, the user fills out the form fields, clicks the submit button, and is directed to Listing 10-3, which then formats and displays the data. Simple as that.

An alternative method to carry out form processing uses just one script. The disadvantage of this method is that the script becomes longer and therefore relatively more difficult to view and understand; the advantage is that you minimize the total number of files to handle. Furthermore, you eliminate code redundancy when error checking, a subject I discuss later in this chapter. Of course, there will be times when one script is not advantageous, but it's always nice to keep in mind that it's easily done. In Scenario 2, I reconsider Scenario 1, this time using just one script.

Scenario 2: Alternative (One-Script) Form Processing

Processing forms using one script is fairly simple, making use of an if conditional statement to tell us whether or not the form variables have been set. If they have been set, then they will be processed (in this example, displayed). Otherwise, the form will be displayed. Verifying whether or not the variables have been set is accomplished with the strcmp() function, described in Chapter 8, "Strings and Regular Expressions." Listing 10-4 provides an example of one-script processing. Notice how the form action calls the page in which it resides. A conditional *if* statement is used to check for the transmission of a hidden variable named *seen-form*. If *seenform* doesn't exist, the form will be displayed. If *seenform* does exist, this implies that the form has been filled out by the user, and the information is processed, in this case output to the browser.

Listing 10-4: One-script form processing

```
<html>
<head>
<title>Listing 10-4</title>
</head>
<body bgcolor="#ffffff" text="#000000" link="#cbda74" vlink="#808040"
alink="#808040">
<?
// all double quotations in $form must be escaped,
// otherwise a parse error will occur
$form = "
<form action=\"listing10-4.php\" method=\"post\">
<input type=\"hidden\" name=\"seenform\" value=\"y\">
<b>Give us some information!</b><br>
Your Name:<br>
<input type=\"text\" name=\"name\" size=\"20\" maxlength=\"20\" value=\"\"><br>
Your Email:<br>
<input type=\"text\" name=\"email\" size=\"20\" maxlength=\"40\" value=\"\"><br>
<input type=\"submit\" value=\"subscribe!\">
</form>";
// If we haven't already seen the form ($seenform passed by hidden
// form value), show the form.
if ($seenform != "y"):
    print "$form";
else :
    print "Hi, $name!. Your email address is $email";
endif;
?>
</body>
</html>
```

Keep in mind that this is not the most user-friendly format, as it does not specifically inform readers that they have not correctly filled in the form on subsequent reloads of the page. The issue of error verification is discussed later in this chapter. For the moment, it's just important to realize how one script can be used to perform these operations.

Now that you're getting an idea just how easy it is to process form information, I'll proceed with an interesting example that will automatically mail the user information to an address that you specify. This is illustrated in Scenario 3.

Scenario 3: Sending the Information to an Email Address

While the idea of simply displaying the entered user information to the browser is appealing, it doesn't do too much for us in the sense of actually processing the user input in a meaningful way. One way to process this information could be to send it to a particular email address, for example, the site administrator's. While the mailto: hyperlink can spurn an email message from the browser, keep in mind that not all computers are configured with an external email application. Therefore, using a Web-based form to send email is one foolproof way to make sure the user's message gets to you.

In the next section, "mail()," I create a short form that prompts the user to enter some information and comments about the site. This data is then formatted accordingly and fed to PHP's predefined mail() function. Before delving into this sample form, take a moment to brush up on the mail() syntax.

mail()

The mail() function, as you may have surmised, is used to mail information to a given recipient. Its syntax is:

```
boolean mail(string recipient, string subject, string message [, string
addl_headers])
```

The *subject* is, of course, the subject of the email. The *message* is the textual body of the email, and the optional input parameter *addl_headers* is used to supply any additional header information (such as HTML formatting) that is sent along with the email.

> **NOTE** *The function* mail() *uses sendmail on UNIX-based machines. For Windows, this function will not work unless you have a mail server installed or you point* mail() *to a working SMTP server. This is accomplished by modifying the SMTP variable, in the php.ini file.*

Assuming you have heeded the preceding note, and your mail() function is operating properly, go ahead and execute the following code (of course first changing *youraddress@yourserver.com* to your valid email address):

```
$email = "youraddress@yourserver.com";
$subject = "This is the subject";
$message = "This is the message";
$headers = "From: somebody@somesite.com ";

mail($email, $subject, $message, $headers);
```

Although for large volumes of email you are definitely better off going with a robust mailer application such as majordomo (http://www.greatcircle.com /majordomo/), PHP's mail() function works great when the need arises.

Now that you've been brought up to speed regarding the mail() function, you are ready to implement it. Check out Listing 10-5, which gathers user information and sends it to an address specified by the script administrator.

Listing 10-5: Using mail() to redirect user information

```
<html>
<head>
<title>Listing 10-5</title>
</head>
<body bgcolor="#ffffff" text="#000000" link="#cbda74" vlink="#808040"
alink="#808040">

<?
$form = "
<form action=\"listing10-5.php\" method=\"post\">
<input type=\"hidden\" name=\"seenform\" value=\"y\">
<b>Send us your comments!</b><br>
Your Name:<br>
<input type=\"text\" name=\"name\" size=\"20\" maxlength=\"20\" value=\"\"><br>
```

```
Your Email:<br>
<input type=\"text\" name=\"email\" size=\"20\" maxlength=\"40\" value=\"\"><br>
Your Comments:<br>
<textarea name=\"comments\" rows=\"3\" cols=\"30\"></textarea><br>
<input type=\"submit\" value=\"submit!\">
</form>
";


// If we haven't already seen the form ($seenform passed by hidden
// form value), show the form.
if ($seenform != "y") :
    print "$form";
else :
    // change $recipient to be the recipient of the form information
    $recipient = "yourname@youremail.com";
    // email subject
    $subject = "User Comments ($name)";
    // extra email headers
    $headers = "From: $email";
    // send the email or produce an error
    mail($recipient, $subject, $comments, $headers) or die("Could not send
    email!");
    // send the user an appropriate message
    print "Thank you $name for taking a moment to send us your comments!";

endif;
?>
</body>
</html>
```

Pretty slick, isn't it? Listing 10-5 works like Listing 10-4, first checking whether or not the form has already been viewed by the user. Assuming that it has, the `mail()` function is invoked, and the user information is sent to the recipient address as designated by `$recipient` The user is then greeted with a thank you message, displayed to the browser.

An easy add-on to this example is a second `mail()` call that formats a short thank you that is subsequently sent to the user. The next example builds on this premise, providing the user with a choice of newsletters. The user will be sent the corresponding newsletters based on the selections made.

Scenario 4: Sending the User Information via Email

In this scenario, I use a series of checkboxes, each specifying a different informational brochure. Users can click one, two, or three of these checkboxes, enter their email address, and they will be sent the selected brochures. Note the usage of an array in the checkboxes. This will facilitate the verification of which checkboxes have been selected, in addition to improving the code organization.

Each informational email should be kept in a separate file. For purposes of this scenario, there are three text files:

- Site architecture: site.txt is the information about the site.

- Development team: team.txt is the information about our talented team.

- Upcoming events: events.txt invites you to join a wild event.

Now check out Listing 10-6.

Listing 10-6: Sending user-requested information

```
<html>
<head>
<title>Listing 10-6</title>
</head>
<body bgcolor="#ffffff" text="#000000" link="#cbda74" vlink="#808040"
alink="#808040">
<?

$form = "
<form action=\"listing10-6.php\" method=\"post\">
<input type=\"hidden\" name=\"seenform\" value=\"y\">
<b>Receive information about our site!</b><br>
Your Email:<br>
<input type=\"text\" name=\"email\" size=\"20\" maxlength=\"40\" value=\"\"><br>
<input type=\"checkbox\" name=\"information[site]\" value=\"y\">Site
Architecture<br>
<input type=\"checkbox\" name=\"information[team]\" value=\"y\">Development
Team<br>
<input type=\"checkbox\" name=\"information[events]\" value=\"y\">Upcoming
Events<br>
<input type=\"submit\" value=\"send it to me!\">
</form>";
```

```
if ($seenform != "y") :
     print "$form";
else :
     $headers = "From: devteam@yoursite.com";
     // cycle through each array key/value element
     while ( list($key, $val) = each ($information) ) :
          // verify if the current value is "y"
          if ($val == "y") :

                // create filename that corresponds with current key
                $filename = "$key.txt";
                $subject = "Requested $key information";

                // open the filename
                $fd = fopen ($filename, "r");
                // read the entire file into a variable
                $contents = fread ($fd, filesize ($filename));

                // send email.
                mail($email, $subject, $contents, $headers) or die("Can't send
                // email!");
                fclose($fd);
          endif;
     endwhile;
     // Notify user of success
     print sizeof($information)." informational newsletters have been sent to
$email!";
endif;
?>
</body>
</html>
```

Listing 10-6 uses a convenient while loop to cycle through each array key/value pair, sending out only those informational newsletters that correspond to those key/value pairs in which the value has been set to y. It is important to remember that the text files *must* be named in accordance with each key in the array (site.txt, team.txt, and events.txt). I dynamically create the filename using each key and then open that filename, in turn reading the file contents to a variable (*$contents*). The *$contents* variable is then used as the message parameter of the mail() function.

The next scenario deals with storing the user information in a more organized format, using a text file to do so.

Scenario 5: Adding the User Information to a Text File

This text file information can later be analyzed for statistical meaning, searched, or whatever your heart desires. Listing 10-7 is a one-script form processor like those in the previous scenarios. The user is prompted to complete four items: name, email address, preferred language, and occupation. This information is then appended to a text file aptly named user_information.txt. Information elements are separated by a vertical bar (|) to distinguish them from each other.

Listing 10-7: Storing user information in a text file

```
<html>
<head>
<title>Listing 10-7</title>
</head>
<body bgcolor="#ffffff" text="#000000" link="#cbda74" vlink="#808040"
alink="#808040">
<?
// create the form
$form = "
<form action=\"listing10-7.php\" method=\"post\">
<input type=\"hidden\" name=\"seenform\" value=\"y\">
<b>Give us your personal info!</b><br>
Your Name:<br>
<input type=\"text\" name=\"name\" size=\"20\" maxlength=\"20\" value=\"\"><br>
Your Email:<br>
<input type=\"text\" name=\"email\" size=\"20\" maxlength=\"20\" value=\"\"><br>
Your Preferred Language:<br>
<select name=\"language\">
<option value=\"\">Choose a language:
<option value=\"English\">English
<option value=\"Spanish\">Spanish
<option value=\"Italian\">Italian
<option value=\"French\">French
<option value=\"Japanese\">Japanese
<option value=\"newyork\">NewYork-ese
</select><br>
Your Occupation:<br>
<select name=\"job\">
<option value=\"\">What do you do?:
<option value=\"student\">Student
<option value=\"programmer\">Programmer
<option value=\"manager\">Project Manager
```

```
<option value=\"slacker\">Slacker
<option value=\"chef\">Gourmet Chef
</select><br>
<input type=\"submit\" value=\"submit!\">
</form>";

// has the form already been filled in?
if ($seenform != "y") :
    print "$form";
else :
    $fd = fopen("user_information.txt", "a");

    // make sure user has not entered a vertical bar in the input
    $name = str_replace("|", "", $name);
    $email = str_replace("|", "", $email);

    // assemble user information
    $user_row = $name."|".$email."|".$language."|".$job."\n";
    fwrite($fd, $user_row) or die("Could not write to file!");
    fclose($fd);
    print "Thank you for taking a moment to fill out our brief questionnaire!";

endif;
?>
</body>
</html>
```

One important item is the section of code that ensures that the user did not insert any vertical bars (|) in the name or email data. The function str_replace() strips those out, replacing them with nothing. If this were not done, any user-inserted vertical bars would act to corrupt the data file, making it difficult, if not impossible, to correctly parse that file.

Keep in mind that when dealing with relatively large amounts of information, a text file works just fine. However, when you are dealing with many users, or large amounts of information, you may wish to make use of a database to store and manipulate forms-entered data. This matter is covered in detail in Chapter 11.

Up to this point, the forms that I have covered have generally assumed that the user will enter correct and nonmalicious data. This is a very unwise assumption! In the next section I complement the scenarios discussed in this section, showing how you can verify the integrity of the forms information. In addition to weeding out any information that may be malicious or insufficient, error checking ultimately results in a more efficient and user-friendly interface.

Error Checking

Processing user information could be rather useless if it were constantly filled with misleading data. While there is no way to ensure that users are not lying, you can verify the information's integrity (for example, you can verify whether or not an email address is valid). While JavaScript is a popular technology for form verification, browser incompatibilities can render this useless. Since PHP executes on the server side, you can rest assured that the form data will always be correctly verified (provided that your code is correct).

When you find errors in user data, you need to inform users what errors were found and suggest how they could fix these errors. Some possible methods of informing users include simply displaying proper error messages and suggesting alternative variations of the entered information (as may be the case when the user enters a username that is already taken). In this section, I cover verification and message display, saving input information for a larger example in the project at the end of this chapter.

Scenario 6: Displaying Missing or Erred Form Fields

The last thing you want as a site developer is for users to become frustrated due to lack of feedback as to what they are doing wrong when filling out a form, particularly when requesting further product information or even making a purchase! One efficient way to ensure that users understand which form fields are missing or not being accepted is to display explicit error messages.

The idea behind this form of error checking is to check each field separately, ensuring that it is not empty and that illegal data has not been entered. If the field is OK, move on to the next field. Otherwise, display an appropriate error message, set a flag that will later be used as a means for triggering the form redisplay, and move on to the next field, repeating this process until you've checked the entire form. This method is illustrated in Listing 10-8.

Listing 10-8: Verifying form information and displaying appropriate messages

```
<html>
<head>
<title>Listing 10-8</title>
</head>
<body bgcolor="#ffffff" text="#000000" link="#cbda74" vlink="#808040"
alink="#808040">
<?
// create the form
$form = "
```

```
<form action=\"listing10-8.php\" method=\"post\">
<input type=\"hidden\" name=\"seenform\" value=\"y\">
<b>Give us some information!</b><br>
Your Name:<br>
<input type=\"text\" name=\"name\" size=\"20\" maxlength=\"20\"
value=\"$name\"><br>
Your Email:<br>
<input type=\"text\" name=\"email\" size=\"20\" maxlength=\"40\"
value=\"$email\"><br>
<input type=\"submit\" value=\"subscribe!\">
</form>";

// has the form already been filled in?
if ($seenform != "y"):
    print "$form";

// The user has filled out the form. Now verify the information
else :
    $error_flag = "n";
    // ensure that the name variable is not empty
    if ($name == "") :
        print "<font color=\"red\">* You forgot to enter your name!</font>
        // <br>";
        $error_flag = "y";
    endif;
    // ensure that the email variable is not empty
    if ($email == "") :

        print "<font color=\"red\">* You forgot to enter your email!</font>
        <br>";
        $error_flag = "y";

    else :
        // convert all email alphabetical characters to lowercase
        $email = strtolower(trim($email));
        // ensure the email address is of valid syntax
        if (! @eregi('^[0-9a-z]+'.
                        '@'.
                        '([0-9a-z-]+\.)+'.
                        '([0-9a-z]){2,4}$', $email)) :
```

```
            print "<font color=\"red\">* You entered an invalid email
            address!</font> <br>";
            $error_flag = "y";
        endif;
    endif;

    // If the $error_flag has been set, redisplay the form
    if ($error_flag == "y") :
        print "$form";
    else :
        // do something with that user information
        print "You entered valid form information!";
    endif;
endif;
?>
</body>
</html>
```

Listing 10-8 ensures that the form fields, in this case name and email address, is not empty and verifies that the supplied email address is valid. If any of the data checks out as invalid, the appropriate error messages are displayed, and the form is again displayed, with all of the previously entered data *already* filled in The fact that the information is already filled in will make users more willing to attempt to correct the incorrect information. An empty form invites users to go elsewhere for the services they need.

Dynamic Forms Construction

To this point, I have been coding each form manually, toiling away as I bask in the irradiated glow of my computer screen. In the programming world, we all know that doing anything manually is bad, as it introduces the chance for errors, not to mention that it cuts into our game-playing time.

Therefore, in this section, I provide a scenario in which you use array data to dynamically build a pull-down menu. It's a rather simple process, but can cut quite a bit of time from the initial coding and later code maintenance.

Scenario 7: Generating a Pull-Down Menu

Assume that you have a list of your favorite sites that you would like to provide to your site readers as examples of cool design. Rather than hard coding each, you could build an array and then use that array to populate your form.

Listing 10-9 makes use of the one-script processor, first checking whether or not the *$site* variable has been assigned a value. If it has, the header() function is called, and the *$site* variable is appended to the string "Location: http://". This command tells the header() function to redirect the browser to whatever URL is specified in that command. If *$site* has not been assigned a value, then the form is displayed. The pull-down menu is created by looping *x* times based on the size of the *$favsites* array. This array contains five of my favorite sites. Of course, you can add as many sites as you wish.

> **CAUTION**   *It is extremely important that you understand that the* header() *function must be called before any output is displayed to the browser. You cannot just call* header() *whenever you wish in a PHP script. Calling* header() *at the wrong time has caused such grief among novice PHP developers that I suggest you repeat this rule five times.*

Listing 10-9: Generating a dynamic pull-down menu

```
<?
if ($site != "") :
    header("Location: http://$site");
    exit;
else :
?>

<html>
<head>
<title>Listing 10-9</title>
</head>
<body bgcolor="#ffffff" text="#000000" link="#cbda74" vlink="#808040"
alink="#808040">
<?
$favsites = array ("www.k10k.com",
                    "www.yahoo.com",
                    "www.drudgereport.com",
                    "www.phprecipes.com",
                    "www.frogdesign.com");

// now build the form
?>
<form action = "listing10-9.php" method="post">
<select name="site">
<option value = "">Choose a site:
<?
```

```
$x = 0;

while ( $x < sizeof ($favsites) ) :
        print "<option value='$favsites[$x]'>$favsites[$x]";
        $x++;
endwhile;
?>
</select>
<input type="submit" value="go!">
</form>
<?
endif;
?>
```

Generating dynamic forms is particularly useful when you are dealing with a large amount of data that could change at a given time, thus causing any hard-coded form information to become outdated. However, I do recommend hard coding any information that you would deem to be static (for example, a listing of the U.S. states), as this could result in a slight gain in performance.

Project: Create a Guestbook

Ever since the dawn of the World Wide Web, site builders have been interested in providing ways for visitors to post comments and thoughts onsite. Typically, this feature is known as a *guestbook*. Using HTML forms, PHP's form-processing capabilities, and a text file, I'll show you just how easily you can create a customizable guestbook.

First, you want to create an initialization file that holds certain global variables and application functions. This file, entitled "init.inc", is shown in Listing 10-10.

Listing 10-10: The init.inc file used to create your guestbook

```
<?
// file: init.inc
// purpose: provides global variables and functions for use in guestbook project

// Default page title
$title = "My Guestbook";

// Background color
$bg_color = "white";
```

```php
// Font face
$font_face = "Arial, Verdana, Times New Roman";

// Font color
$font_color = "black";

// Posting date
$post_date = date("M d y");

// Guestbook data
$guest_file = "comments.txt";

// This function retrieves the guestbook information
// and displays it to the browser.
function view_guest($guest_file) {

    GLOBAL $font_face, $font_color;

    print "Return to <a href=\"index.php\">index</a>.<br><br>";

    // If there is data in the guestbook data file…

    if (filesize($guest_file) > 0) :

        // open the guestbook data file
        $fh = fopen($guest_file, "r") or die("Couldn't open $guest_file");

        print "<table border=1 cellpadding=2 cellspacing=0 width=\"600\">";

        // while not the end of the file
        while (! feof($fh)) :

            // get the next line
            $line = fgets($fh, 4096);

            // split the line apart, and assign each component to a variable
            list($date, $name, $email, $comments) = explode("|", $line);

            // If there is a name, print it
            if ($name != "") :

                print "<tr>";
                print "<td><font color=\"$font_color\"
                face=\"$font_face\">Date:</font></td>";
```

```
                        print "<td><font color=\"$font_color\"
                        // face=\"$font_face\">$date</font></td>";
                        print "</tr>";

                        print "<tr>";
                        print "<td><font color=\"$font_color\"
                        // face=\"$font_face\">Name:</font></td>";
                        print "<td><font color=\"$font_color\"
                        // face=\"$font_face\">$name</font></td>";
                        print "</tr>";

                        print "<tr>";
                        print "<td><font color=\"$font_color\"
                        // face=\"$font_face\">Email:</font></td>";
                        print "<td><font color=\"$font_color\"
                        // face=\"$font_face\">$email</font></td>";
                        print "</tr>";

                        print "<tr>";
                        print "<td valign=\"top\"><font color=\"$font_color\"
                        // face=\"$font_face\">Message:</font></td>";
                        print "<td><font color=\"$font_color\"
                        // face=\"$font_face\">$comments</font></td>";
                        print "</tr>";

                        print "<tr><td colspan=\"2\"> </td></tr>";
                endif;

            endwhile;

            print "</table>";

            // close the file
            fclose($fh);

        else :

            print "Currently there are no entries in the guestbook!";

        endif;

    } // view_guest
```

```
// This function adds new information to the datafile.
function add_guest($name, $email, $comments) {

    GLOBAL $post_date, $guest_file;

    // format the data for file input
    $contents = "$post_date|$name|$email|$comments\n";

    // open the data file
    $fh = fopen($guest_file, "a") or die("Could not open $guest_file!");

    // write the data contents to the file
    $wr = fwrite($fh, $contents) or die("Could not write to $guest_file!");

    // close the file
    fclose($fh);

} // add_guest
?>
```

Next, you want to create three files: an index file containing the "add" and "view" links for the guestbook, a file that will display the guestbook information, and a file that will prompt users for new guestbook information. The index file in Listing 10-11 simply displays two links to the functions of the guestbook: adding and viewing data. You could easily incorporate these links into a more comprehensive site.

Listing 10-11: An index file containing add and view links for your guestbook

```
<html>
<?
INCLUDE("init.inc");
?>
<head>
<title><?=$page_title;?></title>
</head>
<body bgcolor="<?=$bg_color;?>" text="#000000" link="#808040" vlink="#808040"
alink="#808040">
<a href="view_guest.php">View the guestbook!</a><br>
<a href="add_guest.php">Sign the guestbook!</a><br>
</body>
</html>
```

The view_guest.php file in Listing 10-12 displays all guestbook information in the data file.

Listing 10-12: The view_guest.php file

```
<html>
<?
INCLUDE("init.inc");
?>
<head>
<title><?=$page_title;?></title>
</head>
<body bgcolor="<?=$bg_color;?>" text="#000000" link="#808040" vlink="#808040"
alink="#808040">
<?
view_guest($guest_file);
?>
```

The add_guest.php file in Listing 10-13 prompts users for new guestbook data. Subsequently, it is used to add the information to the data file.

Listing 10-13: The add_guest.php file

```
<html>
<?
INCLUDE("init.inc");
?>
<head>
<title><?=$page_title;?></title>
</head>
<body bgcolor="#ffffff" text="#000000" link="#808040" vlink="#808040"
alink="#808040">

<?
// If the form data has not yet been passed, display the form.
if (! $seenform) :
?>

<form action="add_guest.php" method="post">
<input type="hidden" name="seenform" value="y">

Name:<br>
<input type="text" name="name" size="15" maxlength="30" value=""><br>
```

```
Email:<br>
<input type="text" name="email" size="15" maxlength="35" value=""><br>

Comment:<br>
<textarea name="comment" rows="3" cols="40"></textarea><br>
<input type="submit" value="submit">
</form>
<?
// The form data has been passed. Therefore, add it to the text file
else :

    add_guest($name, $email, $comment);

    print "Your comments have been added to the guestbook. <a
    href=\"index.php\">Click here</a> to return to the index.";

endif;

?>
```

One of the greatest advantages of developing an application using well-defined functions is ease of portability. For example, you may be interested in storing guestbook data in a database instead of a text file. No problem: just change the contents of the add_guest() and view_guest() files for database operation, and you've successfully ported the guestbook application for database use.

Figure 10-8 illustrates how the guestbook would be viewed after a few entries have been inserted:

Return to index.

Date:	Oct 29 00
Name:	Michele
Email:	michelle@latorre.com
Message:	I love cheese!
Date:	Oct 29 00
Name:	Nino
Email:	nino@latorre.com
Message:	Great site!

Figure 10-8. view_guest.php

The datafile would store the same information shown in Figure 10-8 as follows:

```
Oct 29 00|Michele|michelle@latorre.com|I love cheese!
Oct 29 00|Nino|nino@latorre.com|Great site!
```

What's Next?

Processing form information is arguably one of PHP's greatest features, as it introduces ease and reliability to an already extremely valuable site feature, that is, user interactivity. In this chapter we covered quite a bit of material regarding forms and PHP's role in forms processing, namely:

- An introduction to form syntax

- Passing form info from one PHP script to another

- One-script forms processing

- The `mail()` function

- Sending forms information to an email address

- Automating user information requests via email

- Adding user information to a text file

- Error checking

- Dynamic forms construction

Incorporating a database into your site infrastructure is one of the first steps you should consider taking if you intend to provide any substantial amount of information over the Web. This is the subject of the next chapter.

CHAPTER 11

Databases

The ability to efficiently store and retrieve large amounts of information has contributed enormously to the success of the Internet. Usually this information storage is implemented through the use of a database (db). Sites such as Yahoo, Amazon, and Ebay depend heavily on the reliability of their databases for storing enormous amounts of information. However, db support is certainly not limited to the behemoth corporations of the Web, as several powerful database implementations are available at relatively low cost (or even free) to Web developers.

When a database is properly implemented, using it to store data results in faster and more flexible retrieval of data. Adding searching and sorting features to your site is greatly simplified, and control over viewing permissions becomes a nonissue by way of the privilege control features in many database systems. Data replication and backup are also simplified.

This chapter begins with an in-depth discussion of how PHP is used to mine and update information in what is arguably PHP's most popular database counterpart, MySQL (http://www.mysql.com). I use MySQL to illustrate how PHP can display and update data in a database, with examples of a basic search engine and sorting mechanism, both of which prove useful in many Web applications. I continue the database discussion with a look into PHP's ODBC (Open Data Base Connectivity) features, which provide a single interface that can be used for simultaneously connecting to several different databases. PHP's ODBC support is demonstrated by an illustration of the process of connecting and retrieving data from a Microsoft Access database. The chapter concludes with a project showing you how to use PHP and a MySQL database to create a categorized online bookmark repository. Users will be able to add information about their favorite sites, placing each site under a predefined set of categories specified by the administrator.

Before commencing the discussion of MySQL, I would like to brief those users unfamiliar with what has become the worldwide standard database language, Structured Query Language (SQL). SQL forms the foundation of practically every popular database implementation; therefore it is imperative that you understand at least the basic underlying ideas of SQL before proceeding to the many database examples throughout the remainder of this book.

What Is SQL?

SQL could be defined as the standard language used to interact with relational databases, discussed shortly. However, SQL is not a computer language like C, C++, or PHP. Instead, it is an interfacing tool for performing various database management tasks, offering a predefined set of commands to the user. Much more than just a query language, as its name implies, SQL offers an array of tools for interacting with a database, including the following:

- **Data structure definition**: SQL can define the various constructs that the database uses to store the data.

- **Data querying**: SQL can retrieve data in the database and present it in an easily readable format.

- **Data manipulation**: SQL can insert, update, and delete database data.

- **Data access control**: SQL makes it possible to coordinate user-specific control over who is capable of viewing, inserting, updating, and deleting data.

- **Data integrity**: SQL prevents data corruption that could be caused by such problems as concurrent updates or system failures.

Note from the SQL definition that SQL's use is specific to *relational* databases. A *relational database* is essentially a database implementation where all data is organized into related table structures. It is possible to create tables that "relate" to one another through the use of data inferences from one table to another. You can think of a *table* as a gridlike arrangement of data values, the position of each determined by a row/column position, which is generally how they're displayed. A sample relational database is illustrated in Figure 11-1.

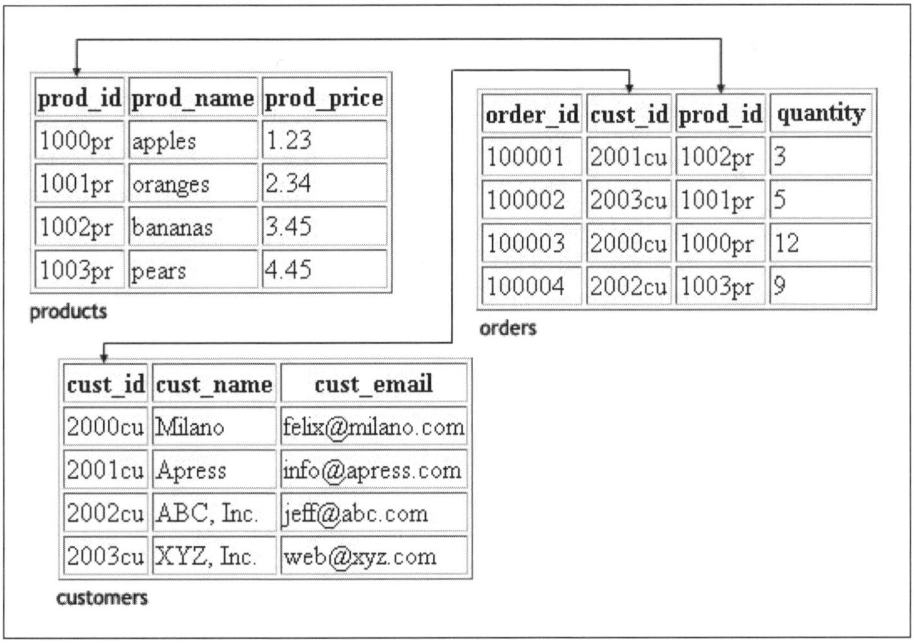

products

prod_id	prod_name	prod_price
1000pr	apples	1.23
1001pr	oranges	2.34
1002pr	bananas	3.45
1003pr	pears	4.45

orders

order_id	cust_id	prod_id	quantity
100001	2001cu	1002pr	3
100002	2003cu	1001pr	5
100003	2000cu	1000pr	12
100004	2002cu	1003pr	9

customers

cust_id	cust_name	cust_email
2000cu	Milano	felix@milano.com
2001cu	Apress	info@apress.com
2002cu	ABC, Inc.	jeff@abc.com
2003cu	XYZ, Inc.	web@xyz.com

Figure 11-1. A sample relational database (entitled "company")

As you can see in Figure 11-1, each table is arranged in a row/column structure, with each column given a unique title (the scope of the uniqueness limited to the table itself). Notice how a relation is drawn between the customer and orders table, using the cust_id to correctly identify a customer without having to redundantly include the customer's name and other information. There also exists another relation, this one between the orders and products tables. This relation is drawn using the prod_id, which identifies the product that the customer (specified by cust_id) has ordered. Using these relations, you can easily make inferences to both the customer and product information, simply by using these unique identification numbers. As you can now surmise, when used properly relational databases are a powerful tool for organizing and efficiently storing data with a minimum of redundancy. Keep the company database in mind, as I will refer to it frequently in later examples.

So how does SQL communicate with the relational database? This is accomplished through the tailored use of generally defined commands. These commands are clearly descendant from our own spoken language, using easily understood English verbs such as *select, insert, update,* and *delete.* For example, referring to Figure 11-1, if you wanted to retrieve the email of the customer having the identification number 2001cu, you could execute this SQL command:

```
SELECT cust_email FROM customers WHERE cust_id = '2001cu'
```

Logical enough, right? This command could be generalized as follows:

```
SELECT column name FROM table name [ WHERE some condition]
```

The square brackets around the concluding part of the generalized command mean that it is optional. For example, if you wanted to retrieve all of the customer emails from the *customers* table, you could query the database using the following command:

```
SELECT cust_email FROM customers
```

Moving onward, assume that you wanted to insert a new row of data into the products table (thus a new product, since it is assumed that each product is unique). A sample insertion command is:

```
INSERT into products VALUES ('1009pr', 'Red Tomatoes', '1.43');
```

Suppose that you later wanted to delete that data. A sample deletion command is:

```
DELETE FROM products WHERE prod_id = '1009pr';
```

There are many SQL command variations, a complete introduction of them certainly out of the scope of this book. Entire books are devoted to just this subject! However, I will attempt to keep the SQL commands throughout the remainder of this book relatively simple, while at the same time attaining a certain level of practicality in the examples. I suggest searching the Web for several of the many SQL resources and primers. I have included a few of my personal favorites at the conclusion of this section.

NOTE *It is not required that you capitalize the SQL commands in a query. This is my personal preference, done so as to more easily distinguish the query's various components.*

Given the fact that you are reading this book, you are likely already wondering how a database is accessed from the Web environment. Typically, some interfacing language such as PHP, Java, or Perl is used to initiate a connection with the database, and then through the use of predefined functionality the database is queried as necessary. You can think of this interface language as the "glue" that melds the database and the Web together. With that said, I turn my attention to my favorite glue language, PHP.

Additional Resources

Here are a few online resources that the SQL novice and expert alike may find useful.

- Various SQL tutorials:
  `http://perl.about.com/compute/perl/cs/beginningsql/index.htm`

- SQLCourse.com (also offers an onsite practice database):
  `http://www.sqlcourse.com/`

- SQL for Web nerds:
  `http://www.arsdigita.com/books/sql/`

- SQL introduction (focus on MySQL):
  `http://www.devshed.com/Server_Side/MySQL/Intro/`

PHP's Extensive Database Support

If I could name any single most important feature of PHP, it would likely be its database support. PHP offers vast support for practically every prominent db server available today, including those listed below:

Adabas D	Informix	PostgreSQL
Dbase	Ingres	Solid
Direct MS-SQL	InterBase	Sybase
Empress	mSQL	UNIX dbm
FilePro (read-only)	MySQL	Velocis
FrontBase	ODBC	
IBM DB2	Oracle (OCI7 and OC18)	

As you can see from the preceding list, PHP's database support options are extensive, including compatibility with many databases that you have certainly heard of (Oracle, for example) and likely several that you haven't. The bottom line is, if you plan on using a competent database to store your Web information, chances are it will be one that PHP supports. PHP supports a database by offering a set of predefined functions capable of connecting to, querying, and closing the connection to a database.

Discussing the features of each supported database is certainly out of the scope of this book. However, the MySQL database server sufficiently summarizes the general capabilities of many of PHP's supported database servers and serves as a base for any SQL-based server. For this reason, MySQL syntax is used throughout the remainder of this chapter and in any database-related examples in the concluding chapters of this book. Regardless of the database server you decide to implement, you should be able to translate the examples from here on with relative ease.

MySQL

MySQL (http://www.mysql.com) is a robust SQL database server developed and maintained by T.c.X DataKonsultAB of Stockholm, Sweden. Publically available since 1995, MySQL has risen to become one of the most popular database servers in the world, this popularity due in part to the server's speed, robustness, and flexible licensing policy. (See note for more information regarding MySQL's licensing strategy.)

Given the merits of MySQL's characteristics, coupled with a vast and extremely easy-to-use set of predefined interfacing functions, MySQL has arguably become PHP's most-popular database counterpart.

> **NOTE** *MySQL is licensed under the GNU General Public License (GPL). Please read the MySQL license information on the MySQL site (http://www.mysql.com) for a full accounting of the current MySQL licensing policy.*

Installation

MySQL is so popular among PHP users that support for the db server is automatically built into the PHP distribution. Therefore, the only task that you are left to deal with is the proper installation of the MySQL package. MySQL is compatible with practically every major operating system, including, among others, FreeBSD, Solaris, UNIX, Linux, and the various Windows versions. While the licensing policy is considerably more flexible than that of other database servers, I strongly suggest taking some time to read through the licensing information found at the MySQL site (http://www.mysql.com).

You can download the latest version of MySQL from one of the many world-wide mirrors. A complete listing of these mirrors is at `http://www.mysql.com/downloads/mirrors.html`. At the time of this writing the latest stable version of MySQL was 3.22.32, with version 3.23 in beta. It is in your best interest to always download the latest stable version. Go to the mirror closest to you and download the version that corresponds with your operating system platform. You'll see links at the top of the page pointing to the most recent versions. Be sure to read through the entire page, as several OS-specific downloads are at the conclusion.

The MySQL development team has done a great job putting together extensive documentation regarding the installation process. I recommend taking some time to thoroughly read through all general installation issues in addition to the information that applies to your operating system.

Configuring MySQL

After a successful installation, it is time to configure the MySQL server. This process largely consists of creating new databases and configuring the MySQL *privilege tables*. The privilege tables control the MySQL database access permissions. Correct configuration of these tables is pivotal to securing your database system, and therefore it is imperative that you fully understand the details of the privilege system before launching your site into a production environment.

Although a chore to learn at first, the MySQL privilege tables are extremely easy to maintain once you understand them. A complete introduction to these tables is certainly out of the scope of this book. However, a number of resources available on the Web are geared toward bringing MySQL users up to speed. Check out the MySQL site (http://www.mysql.com) for further information.

Once you have correctly installed and configured the MySQL distribution, it's time to begin experimenting with Web-based databasing! The next section turns our attention towards exactly this matter, starting with an introduction of PHP's MySQL functionality.

PHP's Predefined MySQL Functions

Once you have created and successfully tested the necessary permissions, you are ready to begin using the MySQL server. In this section, I introduce the predefined MySQL functions, enabling you to easily interface your PHP scripts with a MySQL server. Here is the general order of events that take place during the MySQL server communications process:

1. Establish a connection with the MySQL server. If the connection attempt fails, display an appropriate message and exit process.

2. Select a database on the MySQL server. If you cannot select the database, display an appropriate message and exit process. It's possible to simultaneously have several databases open for querying.

3. Perform necessary queries on selected database(s).

4. Once the querying is complete, close the database server connection.

The example tables (products, customers, orders) in Figure 11-1 are used as the basis for the examples in the remainder of this section. If you would like to follow along with these examples, I suggest going back and creating them now. Alternatively, make a copy of the pages so you do not have to continuously flip back and forth.

With that said, let's begin at the beginning, that is, how to connect to the MySQL database server.

mysql_connect()

The function mysql_connect() is used to establish an initial connection with the MySQL server. Once a successful connection is established, a database residing on that server can be selected. The syntax is:

```
int mysql_connect([string hostname [:port] [:/path/to/socket] [, string username]
[, string password])
```

The hostname is the name of the host as listed in the MySQL server privilege tables. Of course, it is also used to direct the request to the Web server hosting the MySQL server, since it is possible to connect to a remote MySQL server. An optional *port* number can be included along with the host, in addition to an optional path to a socket when a local host is specified. Both the *username* and *password* input parameters should correspond to the username and password, respectively, as specified in the MySQL server privilege tables. Note that all of the input parameters are optional, since the privilege tables can be loosely configured to accept a nonauthenticated connection. If the *hostname* parameter is empty, mysql_connect() attempts to connect to the local host.

An example connection call follows:

```
@mysql_connect("localhost", "web", "4tf9zzzf") or die("Could not connect to MySQL
server!");
```

In this case, localhost is the server host, web is the username, and 4tf9zzzf is the password. The @ preceding the mysql_connect() function will suppress any error message that results from a failed attempt, instead producing the custom one specified in the die() call. Note that no value is returned from the mysql_connect() call. This is fine when there is only one MySQL server connection that will come into play. However, when connections are made to multiple MySQL servers on multiple hosts, a link ID must be generated so that subsequent commands can be directed to the intended MySQL server. For example:

```
<?
$link1 = @mysql_connect("www.somehost.com", "web", "abcde") or die("Could not
connect to MySQL server!");
$link2 = @mysql_connect("www.someotherhost.com", "usr", "secret") or die("Could
not connect to MySQL server!");
?>
```

Now, $link1 and $link2 can be called as needed in subsequent queries. You will soon learn exactly how these link IDs are used in queries to specify the intended server.

> **NOTE** *The function* mysql_pconnect() *offers persistent connection support. In multiuser environments,* mysql_pconnect() *is recommended over* mysql_connect() *as a means for conserving system resources. The* mysql_pconnect() *input and return parameters are exactly the same as in* mysql_connect().

mysql_select_db()

Once a successful connection is established with the MySQL server, a database residing on that server can be selected. This is accomplished with mysql_select_db(). Its syntax is:

```
int mysql_select_db (string database_name [, int link_id])
```

The input parameter `database_name` should be selected and assigned an identification handle (returned by `mysql_select_db()`). Note that the input parameter `link_id` is optional. This is true only when just a single MySQL server connection is open. When multiple connections are open, `link_id` must be specified. An example of how a database is selected using `mysq(_select_db()` follows:

```
<?
@mysql_connect("localhost", "web", "4tf9zzzf")
or die("Could not connect to MySQL server!");
@mysql_select_db("company") or die("Could not select company database!");
?>
```

If there is only one database selection, there is no need to return a database ID. However, as with `mysql_connect()`, when multiple databases are open, the database ID must be returned so there is a way to specify exactly which database you would like to perform a query on; otherwise the most recently *opened* link is used.

mysql_close()

Once you have finished querying the MySQL server, you should close the connection. The function `mysql_close()` will close the connection corresponding to the optional input parameter `link_id`. If the `link_id` input parameter is not specified, `mysql_close()` will close the most recently opened link. The syntax is:

```
int mysql_close ([int link_id])
```

An example of `mysql_close()` follows:

```
<?
@mysql_connect("localhost", "web", "4tf9zzzf")
      or die("Could not connect to MySQL server!");
@mysql_select_db("company") or die("Could not select company database!");
print "You're connected to a MySQL database!";
mysql_close();
?>
```

In the above example, there is no need to specify a link identifier, since only one open server connection exists when `mysql_close()` is called.

> **NOTE** *It is not necessary to close database server connections opened by* `mysql_pconnect()`.

mysql_query()

The function `mysql_query()` provides the functional interface from which a database can be queried. Its syntax is:

```
int mysql_query (string query [, int link_id])
```

The input parameter query corresponds to an SQL query. This query is sent either to the server connection corresponding to the last opened link or to the connection specified by the optional input parameter `link_id`.

People often mistakenly think that the `mysql_query()` function returns the results of the query. This is not the case. Depending on the type of query, `mysql_query()` has different outcomes. In a successful SELECT SQL statement, a result ID is returned that can subsequently be passed to `mysql_result()` so the selected data can be formatted and displayed to the screen. If the query fails, FALSE is returned. The function `mysql_result()` is introduced later in this section. Furthermore, the number of rows that have been selected can be determined by executing `mysql_num_rows()`. This function is also introduced later in this section.

In the case of SQL statements involving INSERT, UPDATE, REPLACE, or DELETE, the function `mysql_affected_rows()` can be called to determine how many rows were affected by the query. (The function `mysql_affected_rows()` is introduced next.)

With that said, I will delay presenting an example until the `mysql_result()` and `mysql_affected_rows()` functions are introduced.

> **TIP** *If you are concerned that you are using up too much memory when making various query calls, call the predefined PHP function* `mysql_free_result()`. *This function, which takes as input the* `result_id` *returned from* `mysql_query()`, *will free up all memory associated with that query call.*

mysql_affected_rows()

It is often useful to return the number of rows affected by an SQL query involving an INSERT, UPDATE, REPLACE, or DELETE. This is accomplished with the function `mysql_affected_rows()`. Its syntax is:

```
int mysql_affected_rows ([int link_id])
```

Notice that the input parameter `link_id` is optional. If it is not included, `mysql_affected_rows()` attempts to use the last opened `link_id`. Consider the following example:

```
<?
// connect to the server and select a database.
@mysql_connect("localhost", "web", "4tf9zzzf")
        or die("Could not connect to MySQL server!");
@mysql_select_db("company") or die("Could not select company database!");
// declare query
$query = "UPDATE products SET prod_name = \"cantaloupe\"
        WHERE prod_id = \"1001pr\"";
// execute query
$result = mysql_query($query);
// determine the number of rows that have been affected.
print "Total row updated: ".mysql_affected_rows();
mysql_close();
?>
```

Executing this code example returns this:

```
Total rows updated: 1
```

This will not work for queries involving a SELECT statement. To determine the number of rows returned from a SELECT, use the function `mysql_num_rows()` instead. This function is introduced next.

> **CAUTION** *There seems to be a quirk when using* `mysql_affected_rows()` *in one particular situation. If you execute a DELETE without a WHERE clause,* `mysql_affected_rows()` *will return 0.*

mysql_num_rows()

The function `mysql_num_rows()` is used to determine the number of rows returned from a SELECT query statement. Its syntax is:

```
int mysql_num_rows (int result)
```

A usage example of `mysql_num_rows()` follows:

```
<?
@mysql_connect("localhost", "web", "4tf9zzzf")
        or die("Could not connect to MySQL server!");
@mysql_select_db("company") or die("Could not select company database!");
// select all product names where the product name begins with a 'p'
$query = "SELECT prod_name FROM products WHERE prod_name LIKE \"p%\"";
// execute the query
$result = mysql_query($query);

print "Total rows selected: ".mysql_num_rows($result);

mysql_close();
?>
```

Since there is only one product name beginning with *p* (pears), only one row is selected. This is the result:

```
Total rows selected: 1
```

mysql_result()

The function `mysql_result()` is used in conjunction with `mysql_query()` (when a SELECT query is involved) to produce a data set. Its syntax is:

```
int mysql_result (int result_id, int row [, mixed field])
```

The input parameter `result_id` refers to a value returned by `mysql_query()`. The parameter `row` refers to a particular row in the dataset specified by the `result_id`. Lastly, the optional input parameter `field` can be used to specify the following:

- Field offset in the table.

- Field name

- Field name specified in dot format. Dot format is simply another way to specify the field name, specified as `fieldname.tablename`.

Consider Listing 11-1, which makes use of the database displayed in Figure 11-1.

271

Listing 11-1: Retrieving and formatting data in a MySQL database

```
<?
@mysql_connect("localhost", "web", "ffttss") or die("Could not connect to MySQL
server!");
@mysql_select_db("company") or die("Could not select company database!");
// Select all rows in the products table
$query = "SELECT * FROM products";
$result = mysql_query($query);
$x = 0;
print "<table>";
print "<tr><th>Product ID</th><th>Product Name</th><th>Product Price</th></tr>";
while ($x < mysql_numrows($result)) :
     $id = mysql_result($result, $x, 'prod_id');
     $name = mysql_result($result, $x, 'prod_name');
     $price = mysql_result($result, $x, 'prod_price');
     print "<tr>";
     print "<td>$id</td><td>$name</td><td>$price</td>";
     print "</tr>";
     $x++;
endwhile;
</table>
mysql_close();
?>
```

Executing this example using our sample data returns the results you see in Listing 11-2:

Listing 11-2: Output generated from execution of Listing 11-1

```
<table>
<tr>
<th>Product ID</th><th>Product Name</th><th>Product Price</th>
</tr>
<tr>
<td>1000pr</td>
<td>apples</td>
<td>1.23</td>
</tr>
<tr>
<td>1001pr</td>
<td>oranges</td>
<td>2.34</td>
</tr>
<tr>
```

```
<td>1002pr</td>
<td>bananas</td>
<td>3.45</td>
</tr>
<tr>
<td>1003pr</td>
<td>pears</td>
<td>4.45</td>
</tr>
</table>
```

While this function works fine when dealing with relatively small result sets, there are other functions that operate much more efficiently, namely, mysql_fetch_row() and mysql_fetch_array(). These functions are described below.

mysql_fetch_row()

It is typically much more convenient to simultaneously assign an entire row to an indexed array (starting at offset 0), rather than make multiple calls to mysql_result() to assign column values. This is accomplished with mysql_fetch_row() Its syntax is:

```
array mysql_fetch_row() (int result)
```

Using the array function list() in conjunction with mysql_fetch_row() can eliminate several lines of code necessary when using mysql_result(). In Listing 11-3, I reconsider the code used in Listing 11-1, this time using list() and mysql_fetch_row().

Listing 11-3: Retrieving data with mysql_fetch_row()
```
<?
@mysql_connect("localhost", "web", "ffttss") or die("Could not connect to MySQL
server!");
@mysql_select_db("company") or die("Could not select company database!");
$query = "SELECT * FROM products";
$result = mysql_query($query);
print "<table>\n";
print "<tr>\n<th>Product ID</th><th>Product Name</th><th>Product
Price</th>\n</tr>\n";
```

```
while (list($id, $name, $price) = mysql_fetch_row($result)) :
    print "<tr>\n";
    print "<td>$id</td>\n<td>$name</td>\n<td>$price</td>\n";
    print "</tr>\n";
endwhile;
print "</table>";
mysql_close();
?>
```

Execution of Listing 11-3 will produce the same results as Listing 11-1. However, Listing 11-3 accomplishes this with fewer lines of code.

mysql_fetch_array()

The function mysql_fetch_array() accomplishes the same result as mysql_fetch_row(), except that by default it assigns a returned row to an *associative* array. However, you can specify the type of array mapping (associative, numerically indexed, or both). The syntax is:

```
array mysql_fetch_array (int result [, result_type])
```

The input parameter result is the result returned by a call to mysql_query(). The optional input parameter result_type can be one of three values:

- MYSQL_ASSOC directs mysql_fetch_array() to return an associative array. This is the default should result_type not be specified.

- MYSQL_NUM directs mysql_fetch_array() to return a numerically indexed array.

- MYSQL_BOTH directs mysql_fetch_array() to allow for the returned row to be accessed either numerically or associatively.

Listing 11-4 is a variation of Listing 11-1 and Listing 11-3, this time using mysql_fetch_array() to return an associative array of row values.

Listing 11-4: Retrieving data with mysql_fetch_array()

```
<?
@mysql_connect("localhost", "web", "ffttss")
        or die("Could not connect to MySQL server!");
@mysql_select_db("company") or die("Could not select products database!");
$query = "SELECT * FROM products";
```

```
$result = mysql_query($query);

print "<table>\n";
print "<tr>\n<th>Product ID</th><th>Product Name</th>
             <th>Product Price</th>\n</tr>\n";
// No result type, therefore It defaults to MYSQL_ASSOC
while ($row = mysql_fetch_array($result)) :
    print "<tr>\n";
    print "<td>".$row["prod_id"]."</td>\n
           <td>".$row["prod_name"]."</td>\n
           <td>".$row["prod_price"]."</td>\n";
    print "</tr>\n";
endwhile;
print "</table>";
mysql_close();
?>
```

Executing Listing 11-4 yields the same results as Listings 11-1 and 11-3.

At this point, you have been introduced to enough of PHP's MySQL function-ality to begin building interesting database applications. The first application that I will consider is a basic search engine. This example will illustrate how HTML forms (introduced in the preceding chapter) are used to supply information that is subsequently used to mine information from a database.

Building a Search Engine

While all of us are certainly familiar with using a Web-based search engine to retrieve data, how is one built? A simple search engine must be able to accept at least one keyword, which is then passed to a SQL query, which in turn polls the database for matches. There are many ways that a search engine could format results (for example, by category or match consistency).

The search engine illustrated in Listing 11-5 is actually geared toward mining for customer information. The search form prompts the user for a keyword and a category (customer name, customer ID, or customer email) from which the search will take place. If the user enters an existing customer name, ID, or email, the engine will query the database for the remaining pieces of information. Then it makes use of the customer ID to poll the orders table for an order history based on that customer. All orders placed by that customer are displayed in descending order. If the input keyword is not in the category chosen by the user, then the search will cease, and the user is provided with an appropriate message, and the form is again displayed.

Listing 11-5: A simple search engine (searchengine.php)

```php
<?
$form =
"<form action=\"searchengine.php\" method=\"post\">
<input type=\"hidden\" name=\"seenform\" value=\"y\">
Keyword:<br>
<input type=\"text\" name=\"keyword\" size=\"20\" maxlength=\"20\" value=\"\"><br>
Search Focus:<br>
<select name=\"category\">
<option value=\"\">Choose a category:
<option value=\"cust_id\">Customer ID
<option value=\"cust_name\">Customer Name
<option value=\"cust_email\">Customer Email
</select><br>
<input type=\"submit\" value=\"search\">
</form>
";
// If the form has not been displayed, show it.
if ($seenform != "y") :
    print $form;
else :
    // connect to MySQL server and select database
    @mysql_connect("localhost", "web", "ffttss")
            or die("Could not connect to MySQL server!");
    @mysql_select_db("company") or die("Could not select company database!");
    // form and execute query statement
    $query = "SELECT cust_id, cust_name, cust_email
            FROM customers WHERE $category = '$keyword'";
    $result = mysql_query($query);
    // If no matches found, display message and redisplay form
    if (mysql_num_rows($result) == 0) :
        print "Sorry, but no matches were found. Please try your search again:";
        print $form;
    // matches found, therefore format and display results
    else :
        // format and display returned row values.
        list($id, $name, $email) = mysql_fetch_row($result);
        print "<h3>Customer Information:</h3>";
        print "<b>Name:</b> $name <br>";
        print "<b>Identification #:</b> $id <br>";
        print "<b>Email:</b> <a href=\"mailto:$email\">$email</a> <br>";

        print "<h3>Order History:</h3>";
```

```
        // form and execute 'orders' query
        $query = "SELECT order_id, prod_id, quantity
                  FROM orders WHERE cust_id = '$id'
                  ORDER BY quantity DESC";
        $result = mysql_query($query);

        print "<table border = 1>";
        print "<tr><th>Order ID</th><th>Product ID</th><th>Quantity</th></tr>";
        // format and display returned row values.
        while (list($order_id,$prod_id,$quantity) = mysql_fetch_row($result)):
            print "<tr>";
            print "<td>$order_id</td><td>$prod_id</td><td>$quantity</td>";
            print "</tr>";
        endwhile;
        print "</table>";
    endif;
endif;
?>
```

Entering the keyword Milano and selecting Customer Name from the pull-down menu, will cause the following information to be displayed on the screen:

Customer Information:

Name: Milano
Identification #: 2000cu
Email: felix@milano.com

Order History:

Order ID	Product ID	Quantity
100003	1000pr	12
100005	1002pr	11

Of course, this is just one of many ways that a search engine could be implemented. Consider adding the possibility to allow multiple keywords, partial keywords, or automated suggestions for keywords not in the table, but with similar matches. I'll leave these features to your creativeness as a programming exercise.

Building a Table Sorter

It is particularly useful for users to be able to sort data as they wish when displaying database data. For example, consider the output shown from the search engine example, in particular the data following the Order History: header. What if the list was particularly long, and you wanted to reorder the data by the product ID? Or by order ID? To illustrate this concept, take a moment to check out one of my favorite sites, http://download.cnet.com. When viewing a particular software category, notice that when you click each header (Title, Date Added, Downloads, and File Size), the list is resorted accordingly. The following code shows just how a feature such as this can be constructed.

In Listing 11-6, I select the data from the orders table. By default, the data is ordered by descending quantity. However, clicking any of the table headers will cause the script to again be called, but this time reordering the table information in accordance with the column in which the user clicked.

Listing 11-6: A table sorter (tablesorter.php)

```
<?
// connect to MySQL server and select database
@mysql_connect("localhost", "web", "ffttss")
        or die("Could not connect to MySQL server!");
@mysql_select_db("company") or die("Could not select company database!");
// If the $key variable is not set, default to 'quantity'
if (! isset($key)) :
    $key = "quantity";
endif;
// create and execute query. Any retrieved data is sorted in descending order
$query = "SELECT order_id, cust_id, prod_id, quantity
        FROM orders ORDER BY $key DESC";
$result = mysql_query($query);
// create table header
print "<table border = 1>";
print "<tr>
<th><a href=\"tablesorter.php?key=order_id\">Order ID</a></th>
<th><a href=\"tablesorter.php?key=cust_id\">Customer ID</a></th>
<th><a href=\"tablesorter.php?key=prod_id\">Product ID</a></th>
<th><a href=\"tablesorter.php?key=quantity\">Quantity</a></th></tr>";
// format and display each row value
while (list($order_id, $cust_id, $prod_id, $quantity) =
mysql_fetch_row($result)) :
    print "<tr>";
    print "<td>$order_id</td><td>$cust_id</td>
            <td>$prod_id</td><td>$quantity</td>";
```

```
      print "</tr>";
endwhile;
// close table
print "</table>";
?>
```

Using the information retrieved from the company database (Figure 11-1), the default table displayed by Listing 11-6 follows.

Order ID	Customer ID	Product ID	Quantity
100003	2000cu	1000pr	12
100005	2000cu	1002pr	11
100004	2002cu	1000pr	9
100002	2003cu	1001pr	5
100001	2001cu	1002pr	3

Notice that there are four links shown as table headers. Since Quantity is designated as the default sorting attribute, the rows are sorted in descending order according to quantity. If you click the Order_ID link, you will see that the page reloads, but this time the rows are sorted in accordance with descending order IDs. Thus, the following table would be shown:

Order ID	Customer ID	Product ID	Quantity
100005	2000cu	1002pr	11
100004	2002cu	1000pr	9
100003	2000cu	1000pr	12
100002	2003cu	1001pr	5
100001	2001cu	1002pr	3

As you can see, this feature can prove immensely useful for formatting database information. Just by changing the SELECT clause, you can perform any number of ordering arrangements, including ascending, descending, and grouping information.

And thus finishes the introduction to MySQL. Keep in mind that there is still quite a bit more to be learned about MySQL. For a complete listing of PHP's supported MySQL commands, check out the manual at http://www.php.net/manual.

ODBC

Using a database-specific set of commands is fine when you are sure that you only need to interface with one specific type of database. However, what happens when you need to connect with MySQL, Microsoft SQL Server, and IBM DB2, all in the same application? The same problem arises when you want to develop database-independent applications that can be layered on top of a potential client's existing database infrastructure. ODBC, an acronym for Open Database Connectivity, is an API (application programming interface) used to abstract the database interface calls, resulting in the ability to implement a single set of commands to interact with several different types of databases. The advantageous implications of this should be obvious, since it eliminates the need for you to rewrite the same code repeatedly just to be able to interact with different database brands.

For ODBC to be used in conjunction with a particular database server, that server must be ODBC compliant. In other words, ODBC drivers must be available for it. Check the database's documentation for further information if you are unsure. Once you locate these drivers, you then need to download and install them. Although ODBC, originally created by Microsoft and now an open standard, is predominantly used to access databases developed for the Windows platform, ODBC drivers are also available for the Linux platform. The following links point to some of the more popular drivers available:

- Windows 95/98/NT database drivers
  (http://www.microsoft.com/data/odbc/)

- Automation Technologies (http://www.odbcsdk.com)

- Easysoft (http://www.easysoft.com/products/oob/main.phtml)

- MySQL's MyODBC drivers (http://www.mysql.com)

- OpenLinkSoftware (http://www.openlinksw.com)

Each ODBC application may vary slightly in usage, platform, and purpose. I would advise reading through the documentation of each to gain a better understanding of the various issues involved with ODBC and these third-party applications. Regardless of their differences, all are known to work well with PHP.

Once you've determined the ODBC application that best fits your purposes, download it and follow the installation and configuration instructions. Then it's time to move on to the next section, "PHP's ODBC Support."

PHP's ODBC Support

PHP's ODBC support, collectively known as the *Unified ODBC Functions*, provide the typical ODBC support in addition to the ability to use these functions to access certain databases that have based their own API on the already existing ODBC API. These database servers are listed in below:

- Adabas D

- IODBC

- IBM DB2

- Solid

- Sybase SQL Anywhere

It is important to note that when using any of these databases, there is actually no ODBC interaction involved. Rather, PHP's Unified ODBC Functions can be used to interface with the database. This is advantageous in the sense that should you choose to use any other ODBC database (or other database listed above), you already have the necessary scripts at your disposal.

> **NOTE** *PHP's ODBC support is built in to the PHP distribution, so there is no need for special configuration options unless otherwise stated.*

There are currently almost 40 predefined Unified ODBC Functions. However, you only need to know a few to begin extracting information from an ODBC-enabled database. I will introduce these necessary functions presently. If you would like a complete listing of all of PHP's predefined ODBC functions, please refer to the PHP manual (http://www.php.net/manual).

odbc_connect()

Before querying an ODBC-enabled database, you must first establish a connection. This is accomplished with odbc_connect(). Its syntax is:

```
int odbc_connect (string data_source, string username, string password [,int
cursor_type])
```

The input parameter `data_source` specifies the ODBC-enabled database to which you are attempting to connect. The parameters `username` and `password` specify, logically enough, the username and password required to connect to the `data_source`. The optional input parameter `cursor_type` is used to resolve quirks among some ODBC drivers. There are four possible values for the optional parameter `cursor_type`:

- SQL_CUR_USE_IF_NEEDED

- SQL_CUR_USE_ODBC

- SQL_CUR_USE_DRIVER

- SQL_CUR_DEFAULT

These cursor types attempt to resolve certain errors that arise from use of ODBC drivers. Chances are you won't need to use them, but keep them in mind in case you experience problems when attempting to execute certain queries that your ODBC distribution may not be able to handle.

Implementing `odbc_connect()` is easy. Here is an example:

```
<?
odbc_connect("myAccessDB", "user", "secret")
    or die("Could not connect to ODBC database");
?>
```

> **TIP** *The function* `odbc_pconnect()` *is used to open a persistent database connection. This can save system resources, because* `odbc_pconnect()` *first checks for an already open connection before opening another. If a connection is already open, that connection is used.*

odbc_close()

After you have finished using the ODBC database, you should close the connection to free up any resources being used by the open connection. This is accomplished with `odbc_close()`. Its syntax is:

```
void odbc_close (int connection_id)
```

The input parameter `connection_id` refers to the open connection identifier. Here is a short example:

```
<?
$connect = @odbc_connect("myAccessDB", "user", "secret")
                or die("Could not connect to ODBC database!");
print "Currently connected to ODBC database!";
odbc_close($connect);
?>
```

odbc_prepare()

Before a query is executed, the query must be "prepared." This is accomplished with odbc_prepare(). Its syntax is:

```
int odbc_prepare (int connection_ID, string query)
```

The input parameter `connection_ID` refers to the connection identification variable returned by odbc_connect(). The parameter query refers to the query that is to be executed by the database server. If the query is invalid and therefore cannot be executed, FALSE is returned; Otherwise, a result identifier is returned that can subsequently be used with odbc_execute() (introduced next).

odbc_execute()

After the query is prepared by odbc_prepare(), it can then be executed with odbc_execute(). Its syntax is:

```
int odbc_execute (int result_ID [, array parameters])
```

The input parameter `result_ID` is a result identifier returned from a successful execution of odbc_prepare(). The optional parameter parameters only needs to be used if you are passing serializable data into the function.

Consider the following example:

```
<?
$connect = @odbc_connect("myAccessDB", "user", "secret")
                 or die("Could not connect to ODBC database");
$query = "UPDATE customers set cust_id = \"Milano, Inc.\"
          WHERE cust_id \"2000cu\"";
$result = odbc_prepare($connect, $query) or die("Couldn't prepare query!");
$result = odbc_execute($result) or die("Couldn't execute query!");
odbc_close($connect);
?>
```

This example illustrates a complete ODBC transaction when the query does not result in the need to display data to the browser (as would likely be the case with a SELECT statement). A complete ODBC transaction using a SELECT query is shown later in this chapter, under "odbc_result_all()".

odbc_exec()

The function odbc_exec() accomplishes the roles of both odbc_prepare() and odbc_execute(). Its syntax is:

```
int odbc_exec (int connection_ID, string query)
```

The input parameter connection_ID refers to the connection identification variable returned by odbc_connect(). The parameter query refers to the query to be executed by the database server. If the query fails, FALSE is returned; otherwise a result identifier is returned, which can be then used in subsequent functions.

```
<?
$connect = @odbc_connect("myAccessDB", "user", "secret")
                 or die("Could not connect to ODBC database!");
$query = "SELECT * FROM customers";
$result = odbc_exec($connect, $query) or die("Couldn't execute query!");
odbc_close($connect);
?>
```

In the above example, odbc_exec() will attempt to execute the query specified by $query. If it is successfully executed, $result is assigned a result identifier. Otherwise, $result is assigned FALSE, and the string enclosed in the die() function is displayed.

odbc_result_all()

This very cool function will format and display all rows returned by a result identifier produced by odbc_exec() or odbc_execute(). Its syntax is:

```
int odbc_result_all (int result_ID [, string table_format])
```

The input parameter result_ID is a result identifier returned by odbc_exec() or odbc_execute(). The optional parameter table_format takes as input HTML table characteristics. Consider this example:

```
<?
$connect = @odbc_connect("myAccessDB", "user", "secret")
               or die("Could not connect to ODBC database!");
$query = "SELECT * FROM customers";
$result = odbc_exec($connect, $query) or die("Couldn't execute query!");
odbc_result_all($result, "BGCOLOR='#c0c0c0' border='1'");
odbc_close($connect);
?>
```

Execution of this example would produce a table characterized by a light gray background and a border size of 1 containing the contents of the customers table. Assuming that this table contained the data shown back in Figure 11-1, the table would be displayed as seen in Figure 11-2.

cust_id	cust_name	cust_email
2000cu	Milano	felix@milano.com
2001cu	Apress	info@apress.com
2002cu	ABC, Inc.	jeff@abc.com
2003cu	XYZ, Inc.	web@xyz.com

Figure 11-2. ODBC data as displayed to the browser

odbc_free_result()

It is generally good programming practice to restore any resources consumed by operations that have been terminated. When working with ODBC queries, this is accomplished with odbc_free_result(). Its syntax is:

```
int odbc_free_result (int result_id)
```

The input result_id refers to the result identifier that will not be used any-more. Keep in mind that all memory resources are automatically restored when the script finishes; therefore it is only necessary to use odbc_free_result() when particularly large queries are involved that could consume significant amounts of memory. The following example illustrates the syntax of odbc_free_result(). Remember that this function isn't really necessary unless you plan on making several queries throughout a single script, since all memory is returned anyway at the conclusion of the script.

```
<?
$connect = @odbc_connect("myAccessDB", "user", "secret")
                  or die("Could not connect to ODBC database!");
$query = "SELECT * FROM customers";
$result = odbc_exec($connect, $query) or die("Couldn't execute query!");
odbc_result_all($result, "BGCOLOR='#c0c0c0' border='1'")
odbc_free_result($result);
odbc_close($connect);
?>
```

After odbc_result_all() has finished using the result identifier, the memory is recuperated using odbc_free_result().

This concludes the summarization of those PHP ODBC functions that are particularly indispensable when creating simple ODBC interfaces through the Web In the next section, "Microsoft Access and PHP," many of these functions are used to illustrate just how easily PHP can be used to interface with one of the more popular database servers, Microsoft Access.

Microsoft Access and PHP

Microsoft's Access Database (http://www.microsoft.com/office/access/) is a pop-ular database solution due in large part to its user-friendly graphical interface. It alone can be used as the database solution, or its graphical interface can be used as a front end to interface with other databases, such as MySQL or Microsoft's SQL Server.

To illustrate the use of PHP's ODBC support, I'll describe how you can con-nect to an MS Access database using PHP. It is surprisingly easy and is a great addition to your PHP programming repertoire, due to the popularity of Microsoft Access. I'll detail this process step by step:

1. Go ahead and create an Access database. I'll assume that you know how to do this already. If you don't, but still want to follow along with this example, just quickly create a database using the Access Wizard. For this example, I created the predefined Contact Management Database using

the wizard. Be sure to insert some information into a table and take note of that table name, as you will need it in a while!

2. Save the database somewhere on your computer.

3. Now it's time to make that Access database available using ODBC. Go to Start -> Settings -> Control Panel. You should see an icon entitled "ODBC Data Sources (32 bit)." This is the ODBC Administrator, used to handle the various drivers and database sources on the system. Open this icon by double-clicking it. The window will open to the default tabbed sub-window entitled "User DSN (User Data Sources)." The User DSN contains the data sources specific to a single user and can be used only on this machine. For sake of this example, we'll use this.

4. Click the Add... button on the right side of this window. A second window will open, prompting you to select a driver for which you want to set up a data source. Choose the Microsoft Access Driver (*.mdb) and click Finish.

5. A new window will open, entitled "ODBC Microsoft Access Setup." You'll see a form text box labeled "Data Source Name." Enter a name relative to the Access database that you created. If you would like, enter a description in the text box directly below that of the Data Source Name.

6. Now click the Select... button displayed on the middle left of the window. An Explorer-style window will open, prompting you to search for the database that you would like to make accessible via ODBC.

7. Browse through the Windows directories to your database. When you find it, double-click it to select it. You will return to the ODBC Microsoft Access Setup window. You'll see the path leading to the selected database directly above the Select... button. Click OK.

8. That's it! Your Access database is now ODBC enabled.

Once you have completed this process, all you need to do is create the PHP script that will communicate via ODBC with the database. The script uses the Unified ODBC Functions introduced earlier to display all information in the Contacts table in the Access Contact Management database that I created using the Access wizard. However, before reviewing the script, take a look at the Contacts table in Figure 11-3, as seen in Access.

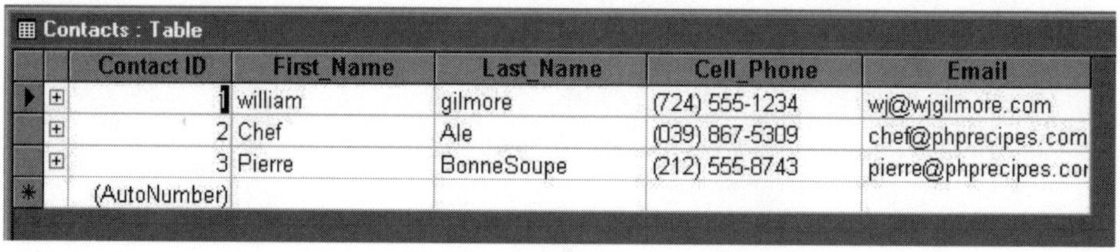

Figure 11-3. Contacts table as seen in MS Access

Now that you have an idea of what information will be extracted, take a look at the script. If you are unfamiliar with any of the functions, please refer to the introductory material at the beginning of this section. The outcome of Listing 11-7 is illustrated in Figure 11-4.

Listing 11-7: Using PHP's ODBC functions to interface with MS Access

```
<?
// Connect to the ODBC datasource 'ContactDB'
$connect = odbc_connect("ContactDB","","")
                or die("Couldn't connect to datasource.");

// form query statement
$query = "SELECT First_Name, Last_Name, Cell_Phone, Email FROM Contacts";

// prepare query statement
$result = odbc_prepare($connect,$query);

// execute query statement and display results
odbc_execute($result);
odbc_result_all($result,"border=1");
// We're done with the query results, so free memory
odbc_free_result($result);

// close connection
odbc_close($connect);
?>
```

First_Name	Last_Name	Cell_Phone	Email
william	gilmore	7245551234	wj@wjgilmore.com
Chef	Ale	0398675309	chef@phprecipes.com
Pierre	BonneSoupe	2125558743	pierre@phprecipes.com

Figure 11-4. Contacts table extracted and displayed to the Web browser

Pretty easy, right? The really great part is that this script is completely reusable with other ODBC-enabled database servers. As an exercise, go ahead and run through the above process, this time using a different database server. Rerun the script, and you will witness the same results as those shown in Figure 11-4.

Project: Create a Bookmark Repository

Probably the easiest way to build content on your site is to provide users with the capability of doing it for you. An HTML form is perhaps the most convenient way for accepting this information. Of course, the user-supplied information must also be processed and stored. In the project covered in the last chapter, you saw that this was easily accomplished with PHP and a text file. But what if you needed a somewhat more robust solution for storing the data? Sure, a text file works when storing relatively small and simple pieces of data, but chances are you will need a database to implement any truly powerful Web application. In this project, I explain how a MySQL database can be used to store information regarding Web sites. These sites are separated into categories to allow for more efficient navigation. Users can use an HTML form to enter information regarding their favorite sites, choosing a fitting category from those predefined by the administrator. Furthermore, users can go to an index page and click one of these predefined categories to view all of the sites under it.

The first thing you need to do is decide what site information should be stored in the MySQL database. To keep the project simple, I'll limit this to the following: site name, URL, category, date added, and description. Therefore, the MySQL table would look like the following:

```
mysql>create table bookmarks (
        category INT,
        site_name char(35),
        url char(50),
        date_added date,
        description char(254) );
```

There are a couple of points to be made regarding the bookmarks table. First of all, you may be curious as to why I chose to store the category information as an integer. After all, you want to use category names that are easily intelligible by the user, right? Don't worry, as you will soon create an array in an initialization file that will be used to create integer-to-category name mappings. This is useful because you may wish to modify or even delete a category in the future. Doing so is considerably easier if you use an array mapping to store the categories. Furthermore, an integer column will take up less information than would repetitive use of category names. Another point regarding the table is the choice to designate only 254 characters to the description. Depending on how extensive you would like the descriptions to be, you may want to change this column type to a medium text or even text. Check out the MySQL documentation for further information regarding possible column types.

The next step in creating this application will be to create an initialization file. Other than holding various global variables, two functions are defined within, add_bookmark() and view_bookmark(). The function add_bookmark() takes as input the user-entered form information and adds it to the database. The function view_bookmark() takes as input a chosen category and extracts all information from the database having that category, in turn displaying it to the browser. This file is shown in Listing 11-8, with accompanying comments.

Listing 11-8: Bookmark repository initialization file (init.inc)

```
<?
// file: init.inc
// purpose: provides global variables for use in bookmark project

// Default page title
$title = "My Bookmark Repository";

// Background color
$bg_color = "white";

// Posting date
$post_date = date("Ymd");

// bookmark categories
$categories = array(
                    "computers",
                    "entertainment",
                    "dining",
                    "lifestyle",
                    "government",
                    "travel");
```

```php
// MySQL Server Information
$host = "localhost";
$user = "root";
$pswd = "";

// database name
$database = "book";

// bookmark table name
$bookmark_table = "bookmarks";

// Table cell color
$cell_color = "#c0c0c0";

// Connect to the MySQL Server
@mysql_pconnect($host, $user, $pswd) or die("Couldn't connect to MySQL server!");

// Select the database
@mysql_select_db($database) or die("Couldn't select $database database!");

// function: add_bookmark()
// purpose: Add new bookmark to bookmark table.

function add_bookmark ($category, $site_name, $url, $description) {
    GLOBAL $bookmark_table, $post_date;

    $query = "INSERT INTO $bookmark_table
                VALUES(\"$category\", \"$site_name\", \"$url\",
                \"$post_date\", \"$description\")";

    $result = @mysql_query($query)
                or die("Couldn't insert bookmark information!");

} // add_bookmark

// function: view_bookmark()
// purpose: View bookmarks following under
// the category $category.

function view_bookmark ($category) {

    GLOBAL $bookmark_table, $cell_color, $categories;
```

```
$query = "SELECT site_name, url, DATE_FORMAT(date_added,'%m-%d-%Y') AS
            date_added, description
            FROM $bookmark_table WHERE category = $category
            ORDER BY date_added DESC";

$result = @mysql_query($query);

print "<div align=\"center\"><table cellpadding=\"2\" cellspacing=\"1\"
border = \"0\" width = \"600\">";

print "<tr><td bgcolor=\"$cell_color\"><b>Category:
$categories[$category]</b></td></tr>";

if (mysql_numrows($result) > 0) :

    while ($row = mysql_fetch_array($result)) :

        print "<tr><td>";
        print "<b>".$row["site_name"]."</b> | Posted:
        ".$row["date_added"]."<br>";
        print "</td></tr>";

        print "<tr><td>";
        print "<a href = \"http://".$row["url"]."\">
            http://".$row["url"]."</a><br>";
        print "</td></tr>";

        print "<tr><td valign=\"top\">";
        print $row["description"]."<br>";
        print "</td></tr>";

        print "<tr><td><hr></td></tr>";

    endwhile;

else :
    print "<tr><td>There are currently no bookmarks falling under
        this category. Why don't you
        <a href=\"add_bookmark.php\">add one</a>?</td></tr>";

endif;

print "</table><a href=\"index.php\">Return to index</a> |";
```

```
        print "<a href=\"add_bookmark.php\">Add a bookmark</a></div>";


} // view_bookmark


?>
```

The next file, add_bookmark.php, provides the interface for adding new bookmark information to the database. Additionally, it calls the function add_bookmark() to process the user information. The file is shown in Listing 11-9.

Listing 11-9: The add_bookmark.php program

```
<html>
<?
INCLUDE("init.inc");
?>
<head>
<title><?=$title;?></title>
</head>

<body bgcolor="#ffffff" text="#000000" link="#808040" vlink="#808040"
alink="#808040">

<?
if (! $seenform) :
?>

<form action="add_bookmark.php" method="post">
<input type="hidden" name="seenform" value="y">

Category:<br>
<select name="category">
<option value="">Choose a category:
<?
while (list($key, $value) = each($categories)) :

        print "<option value=\"$key\">$value";

endwhile;
?>
</select><br>

Site Name:<br>
<input type="text" name="site_name" size="15" maxlength="30" value=""><br>
```

```
URL: (do <i>not</i> include "http://"!)<br>
<input type="text" name="url" size="35" maxlength="50" value=""><br>

Description:<br>
<textarea name="description" rows="4" cols="30"></textarea><br>
<input type="submit" value="submit">
</form>
<?
else :

    add_bookmark($category, $site_name, $url, $description);

    print "<h4>Your bookmark has been added to the repository. <a
href=\"index.php\">Click here</a> to return to the index.</h4>";

endif;
?>
```

When the user first requests this file, the interface shown in Figure 11-5 will be displayed to the browser.

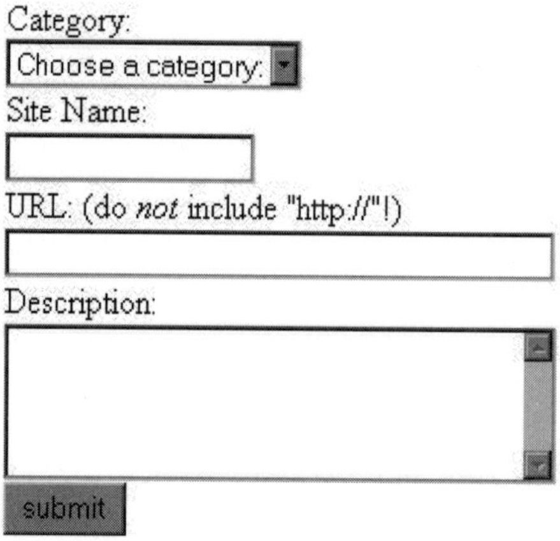

Figure 11-5. Form interface displayed in add_browser.php

Once a bookmark has been added to the database, the user is notified accordingly, and a link is provided for returning to the home page of the repository, entitled "index.php." This file is located in Listing 11-11, displayed below.

The next file, view_bookmark.php, simply calls the function view_bookmark(). The file is shown in Listing 11-10.

Listing 11-10: The view_bookmark.php program

```
<html>
<?
INCLUDE("init.inc");
?>
<head>
<title><?=$title;?></title>
</head>

<body bgcolor="<?=$bg_color;?>" text="#000000" link="#808040" vlink="#808040"
alink="#808040">
<?
view_bookmark($category);
?>
```

Assuming that you had entered a few sites under the dining category, executing view_bookmark.php would result in an interface similar to the one in Figure 11-6.

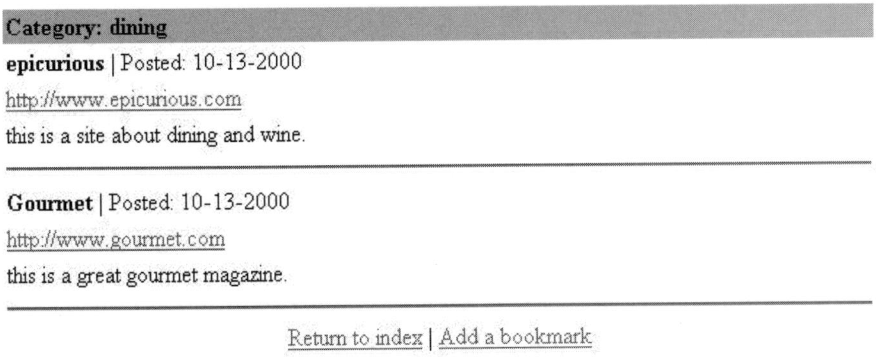

Figure 11-6. Executing view_bookmark.php under the dining category

Finally, you need to provide an interface in which the user can choose the categorical list of bookmarks. I call this file index.php. The file is shown in Listing 11-11.

Listing 11-11: The index.php program

```
<html>
<?
INCLUDE("init.inc");
?>
<head>
<title><?=$title;?></title>
</head>
<body bgcolor="<?=$bg_color;?>" text="#000000" link="#808040" vlink="#808040"
alink="#808040">
<h4>Choose bookmark category to view:</h4>
<?
// cycle through each category and display appropriate link
while (list($key, $value) = each($categories)) :
    print "<a href = \"view_bookmark.php?category=$key\">$value</a><br>";
endwhile;
?>
<p>
<b><a href="add_bookmark.php">Add a new bookmark</a></b>
</body>
</html>
```

Assuming you don't change the default values in the $categories array in init.inc, the HTML in Listing 11-12 would be output to the browser when index.php is executed.

Listing 11-12: Output generated from index.php execution

```
<html>
<head>
<title></title>
</head>
<body bgcolor="white" text="#000000" link="#808040" vlink="#808040"
alink="#808040">
<h4>Choose bookmark category to view:</h4>
<a href = "view_bookmark.php?category=0">computers</a><br>
<a href = "view_bookmark.php?category=1">entertainment</a><br>
<a href = "view_bookmark.php?category=2">dining</a><br>
<a href = "view_bookmark.php?category=3">lifestyle</a><br>
<a href = "view_bookmark.php?category=4">government</a><br>
<a href = "view_bookmark.php?category=5">travel</a><br>
<p>
<b><a href="add_bookmark.php">Add a new bookmark</a></b>
</body>
</html>
```

Clicking any of the links in the preceding HTML source would result in the request of the file view_bookmark.php, which would then call the function `view_bookmark()`, passing the variable $category into it.

What's Next

This chapter covered a great deal of material, some of which may be the most important of the entire book for certain users. Database interfacing is certainly one of the most prominent features of the PHP language, as it can truly lend a hand to extending the functionality of a Web site. In particular, these topics were covered:

- Introduction to SQL

- An overview of PHP's predefined database support

- Case study of the MySQL database server

- PHP's predefined MySQL functions

- A simple search engine example

- A table resorting example

- Introduction to ODBC

- PHP's predefined ODBC functions

- Interfacing Microsoft Access with PHP

- A Web-based bulletin board

For those readers interested in developing large and truly dynamic Web sites with PHP, databasing will be an issue brought up time and time again. I recommend thoroughly reading not only the PHP documentation, but any other data warehousing resources available. As with most other technologies today, even the experts can't seem to learn enough about this rapidly advancing subject.

Next chapter, I delve into one of the more complicated topics of Web development: templates. In particular, I focus on how PHP can be used to create these templates, ultimately saving time and headaches when developing large-scale Web sites.

Templates

You can think of templates as an extension to programming. Not only do they automate an otherwise rigorous process, but they also facilitate the division of design and coding in a team environment. This division of labor becomes increasingly important as a project and team grow in size and complexity due to logistics surrounding the initial design as well as subsequent maintenance of the Web application.

To put this into perspective, consider the developmental logistics of a team divided between Web designers and programmers. The ideal situation would be that the Web design team could embark on building the most eye-appealing, user-friendly site they can, while at the same time the programming team codes the most efficient, powerful Web application possible. Fortunately, templates make this process much easier. Creating a site templating system that facilitates this separation of labor is the subject of this chapter.

What You've Learned So Far

To this point, I've introduced two systems for creating PHP templates:

- HTML embedded in PHP code

- Including files in a page structure

Although the first strategy is the easier to understand and implement, it is also the more restrictive. A major problem lies in the fact that the actual PHP coding is intermingled with the components making up the page design. This presents a problem not only in terms of the need to provide support for the potential simultaneous access and modification to a single page, but also in regards to the increased possibility of introducing errors due to constant scrutiny and editing.

The second strategy can be a substantial improvement over the first in many situations. However, while a patchwork system of header, body, and footer files (see Chapter 9 for further information) works fine for piecing together relatively small sites of specific format, limitations become apparent as the project grows in size and complexity. Attempts to resolve these problems led to the development of another templating strategy, which, although more complex than the other two strategies, is substantially more flexible and superior in many situations. This system calls for the separation of the two main components of a Web application: design and coding. Separating the design and coding of a Web application makes it possible for simultaneous development (Web design and programming) without the need of extensive coordination throughout the lifetime of the initial development cycle. Furthermore, it allows for the later exclusive modification of either component without interfering with the other. In the next section, I'll elaborate on how one of these advanced templating systems is constructed. Keep in mind that this problem is not specific to PHP. In fact, this general strategy certainly precedes PHP's lifetime, and is currently used in several languages, including PHP, Perl, and Java Server Pages. What is described in this chapter is merely an adaptation of this strategy as it would apply to PHP.

Developing an Advanced Template System

As you may have already surmised, the major hurdle to overcome when developing this type of templating system is efficiently dividing the labor between design and functionality. After all, the intended goal of this system is to allow both coders and designers to independently maintain their end of the application *without* interfering with the work of the other group.

Thankfully, this isn't as difficult as it sounds, provided that some planning takes place *before* the development process begins. To illustrate how this is accomplished, Listing 12-1 presents a basic template that you will actually be able to implement with the code provided in this chapter.

Listing 12-1: Sample template file

```
<html>
<head>
<title>::::::{page_title}::::::</title>
</head>
<body bgcolor="{bg_color}">
Welcome to your default home page, {user_name}!<br>
You have 5 MB and 3 email addresses at your disposal<br>
Have fun!
</body>
</html>
```

Notice that there are three strings enclosed in curly brackets ({}), namely page_title, bg_color, and user_name. The brackets are of special meaning to the template parsing engine, signifying that the enclosed string specifies the name of a variable that should be replaced with its respective value. Other than ensuring that these key strings are placed where necessary in the document, the designer is free to structure the page as desired. Of course, the coder and the designer must come to terms with what exactly is to be placed in each page!

So how will the templating system operate? To start, you may be dealing with several templates simultaneously, all having the same general characteristics. This could be well suited for object-oriented programming (OOP). Therefore, all functions used to build and manipulate the templates will actually be methods in a class. The class definition starts as follows:

```
class template {
    VAR $files = array();
    VAR $variables = array();
    VAR $opening_escape = '{';
    VAR $closing_escape = '}';
```

The attribute $files is an array that will store the file identifiers and the corresponding contents of each file. The attribute $variables is a two-dimensional array used to store a file identifier (key) and all of the corresponding variables to be parsed in the template system. Finally, the attributes $opening_escape and $closing_escape refer to the variable delimiters that specify which parts of the template are to be replaced by the system. As you have seen in Listing 12-1, I use curly brackets ({}) as delimiters. However, you can use these final two attributes to change the delimiters to anything you please; just make sure the resulting combination will be unique for this purpose.

Each method in the class serves a well-defined purpose, each corresponding to a step in the templating process. At its most basic level, this process can actually be broken down into these four parts:

- **File registration**: Registration of all files that will be parsed by the templating scripts.

- **Variable registration**: Registration of all variables that will be replaced with corresponding values in the registered files.

- **File parsing:** Replacement of all delimited variables in the registered files.

- **File printing:** Display of the parsed registered files in the browser.

> **NOTE** *OOP as it applies to PHP was discussed in Chapter 6. If you are unfamiliar with OOP, I would suggest quickly reviewing Chapter 6 before continuing.*

File Registration

Registering a file simply means assigning its contents to an array key, the key uniquely referring to the said file. This method opens and reads in the contents of the file passed in as an input parameter. Listing 12-2 illustrates this method.

Listing 12-2: The method for registering a file

```
function register_file($file_id, $file_name) {

    // Open $file_name for reading, or exit and print an error message.
    $fh = fopen($file_name, "r") or die("Couldn't open $file_name!");

    // Read in the entire contents of $file_name.
    $file_contents = fread($fh, filesize($file_name));

    // Assign these contents to a position in the array.
    // This position is denoted by the key $file_id
    $this->files[$file_id] = $file_contents;

    // We're finished with the file, so close it.
    fclose($fh);
} // end register_file
```

The input parameter $file_id is just a pseudonym for the file, which will make all subsequent method calls easier to understand. This parameter will serve as the array key for the $files array. Here is an example of how a file would be registered:

```
// Include the template class
include("template.class");

// Instantiate a new object
$template = new template;

// Register the file "homepage.html", assigning it the pseudonym "home"
$template->register_file("home", "homepage.html");
```

Variable Registration

After you register the files, all of the variables that are to be parsed must also be registered with the system. This method operates along the same premise as reg-ister_file(), retrieving each named variable and inserting it into the $variables array. Listing 12-3 illustrates this method.

Listing 12-3: The method for registering a variable

```
function register_variables($file_id, $variable_name) {

    // attempt to create array from passed in variable names
    $input_variables = explode(",", $variable_name);

    // assign variable name to next position in $file_id array
    while (list(,$value) = each($input_variables)) :

        // assign the value to a new position in the $this->variables array
        $this->variables[$file_id][] = $value;

    endwhile;

} // end register_variables
```

The input parameter $file_id refers to the *previously* assigned alias of a file-name. In the previous example, "home" was the assigned alias of "homepage.html." Therefore, if you are registering variable names that are to be parsed in the homepage.html file, you must refer to it by its alias! The input parameter $variable_name refers to one or several variables that are to be registered under that alias name. An example follows:

```
// Include the template class
include("template.class");

// Instantiate a new object
$template = new template;

// Register the file "homepage.html", assigning it the pseudonym "home"
$template->register_file("home", "homepage.html");

// Register a few variables
$template->register_variables("home", "page_title,bg_color,user_name");
```

File Parsing

After the files and variables have been registered in the templating system, you are free to parse the registered files, replacing all variable references with their respective values. Listing 12-4 illustrates this method.

Listing 12-4: The method for parsing a file

```
function file_parser($file_id) {

    // How many variables are registered for this particular file?
    $varcount = count($this->variables[$file_id]);

    // How many files are registered?
    $keys = array_keys($this->files);

    // If the $file_id exists in the $this->files array and it
    // has some registered variables...
    if ( (in_array($file_id, $keys)) && ($varcount > 0) ) :

        // reset $x
        $x = 0;

        // while there are still variables to parse...
        while ($x < sizeof($this->variables[$file_id])) :

            // retrieve the next variable
            $string = $this->variables[$file_id][$x];

            // Retrieve this variable value! Notice that I'm using a
            // variable variable to retrieve this value. This value
            // will be substituted into the file contents, taking the place
            // of the corresponding variable name.
            GLOBAL $$string;

            // What exactly is to be replaced in the file contents?
            $needle = $this->opening_escape.$string.$this->closing_escape;

            // Perform the string replacement.
            $this->files[$file_id] = str_replace(
                        $needle,    // needle
                        $$string,    // string
                        $this->files[$file_id]); // haystack
            // increment $x
            $x++;
        endwhile;
    endif;
} // end file_parser
```

Basically, the $file_id that is passed in is verified to exist in the $this->files array. If it does, it is also verified that this $file_id has some variables registered that need to be parsed. If it does, the values of each of those variables are retrieved and substituted into the contents of $file_id. An example follows:

```
<?

// Include the template class
include("template.class");

$page_title = "Welcome to your homepage!";
$bg_color = "white";
$user_name = "Chef Jacques";

// Instantiate a new object
$template = new template;

// Register the file "homepage.html", assigning it the pseudonym "home"
$template->register_file("home", "homepage.html");

// Register a few variables
$template->register_variables("home", "page_title,bg_color,user_name");
$template->file_parser("home");

?>
```

Since the variables page_title, bg_color, and user_name have been registered, the corresponding values of each (assigned at the beginning of the script) will be substituted into the homepage.html contents, stored in the objects files array attribute. To this point, everything has been done except actually displaying the resulting template to the browser. This is the next step.

File Printing

After parsing the file, you will probably want to print it out, thereby displaying the parsed template to the user. I create this in a separate method shown in Listing 12-5, but you could also integrate this directly into the file_parser() method, depending on your usage.

Listing 12-5: The method for printing a file

```
function print_file($file_id) {

    // print out the contents pointed to by $file_id
    print $this->files[$file_id];

}
```

Quite simply, when print_file() is called, the contents represented by the key $file_id are output to the browser.

Listing 12-6 displays the finished templating system.

Listing 12-6: Complete example of templating system

```
<?

// Include the template class
include("template.class");

// Assign a few variables
$page_title = "Welcome to your homepage!";
$bg_color = "white";
$user_name = "Chef Jacques";

// Instantiate a new object
$template = new template;

// Register the file "homepage.html", assigning it the pseudonym "home"
$template->register_file("home", "homepage.html");

// Register a few variables
$template->register_variables("home", "page_title,bg_color,user_name");
$template->file_parser("home");
// output the file to the browser
$template->print_file("home");

?>
```

If the template first displayed in Listing 12-1 was saved under the name homepage.html and stored in the same directory as the script shown in Listing 12-6, then the following would be displayed in the browser:

```
<html>
<head>
<title>:::::Welcome to your homepage!:::::</title>
</head>
```

```
<body bgcolor=white>
Welcome to your default home page, Chef Jacques!<br>
You have 5 MB and 3 email addresses at your disposal<br>
Have fun!
</body>
</html>
```

As you can see, all of the previously delimited variable names have been replaced with their respected values. Although simple, this template class ensures 100 percent separation of design and coding. The entire contents of the template class are shown in Listing 12-7.

Listing 12-7: Complete template.class file.

```
<?
class template {

VAR $files = array();
VAR $variables = array();
VAR $opening_escape = '{';
VAR $closing_escape = '}';

// Function: register_file()
// Purpose: Store contents of file specified by $file_id

function register_file($file_id, $file_name) {

    // Open $file_name for reading, or exit and print an error message.
    $fh = fopen($file_name, "r") or die("Couldn't open $file_name!");

    // Read in the entire contents of $file_name.
    $file_contents = fread($fh, filesize($file_name));

    // Assign these contents to a position in the array.
    // This position is denoted by the key $file_id
    $this->files[$file_id] = $file_contents;

    // We're finished with the file, so close it.
    fclose($fh);
} // end register_file;

// Function: register_variables()
// Purpose: Store variables passed in via $variable_name under the corresponding
// array key, specified by $file_id
```

```
function register_variables($file_id, $variable_name) {

    // attempt to create array from passed in variable names
    $input_variables = explode(",", $variable_name);

    // assign variable name to next position in $file_id array
    while (list(,$value) = each($input_variables)) :

        // assign the value to a new position in the $this->variables array
        $this->variables[$file_id][] = $value;

    endwhile;

} // end register_variables

// Function: file_parser()
// Purpose: Parse all registered variables  in file contents
//                     specified by input parameter $file_id

function file_parser($file_id) {

    // How many variables are registered for this particular file?
    $varcount = count($this->variables[$file_id]);

    // How many files are registered?
    $keys = array_keys($this->files);

    // If the $file_id exists in the $this->files array and it
    // has some registered variables…
    if ( (in_array($file_id, $keys)) && ($varcount > 0) ) :

        // reset $x
        $x = 0;

        // while there are still variables to parse…
        while ($x < sizeof($this->variables[$file_id])) :

            // retrieve the next variable
            $string = $this->variables[$file_id][$x];

            // retrieve this variable value! Notice that I'm using a
            // variable variable to retrieve this value. This value
```

```
        // will be substituted into the file contents, taking the place
        // of the corresponding variable
        // name.
        GLOBAL $$string;

        // What exactly is to be replaced in the file contents?
        $needle = $this->opening_escape.$string.$this->closing_escape;

        // Perform the string replacement.
        $this->files[$file_id] = str_replace(
                    $needle,    // needle
                    $$string,   // string
                    $this->files[$file_id]); // haystack
        // increment $x
        $x++;
      endwhile;
    endif;
} // end file_parser


// Function: print_file()
// Purpose: Print out the file contents specified by input parameter $file_Id

function print_file($file_id) {
    // print out the contents pointed to by $file_id
    print $this->files[$file_id];
}

} // END template.class
```

Expanding the Template Class

Of course, this template class is rather limited, although it does the trick nicely for projects that need to be created in a hurry. The nice thing about using an object-oriented implementation strategy is that you can easily add functionality without worrying about potentially "breaking" existing code. For example, suppose you wanted to create a method that retrieved values from a database for later template substitution. Although slightly more complicated than the file_parser() method, which just substitutes globally-accessible variable values, an SQL-based file parser can be written with just a few lines and encapsulated in its own method. In fact, I create one of these parsers in the address book project at the conclusion of this chapter.

Several modifications could be made to this template class, the first likely being the consolidation of register_file() and register_variables(). This would automatically add the variables in each registered file. Of course, you will also want to insert error-checking functionality to ensure that invalid file and variable names are not registered.

You are also likely to begin thinking about how this system could be enhanced. Consider the following enhancement questions. How would you create a method that worked with entire arrays? Included Files? I think that you'll find it easier than it first seems. As a reference, check out the implementation I created for an SQL-parser in the address book project at the end of this chapter. You can easily transform this general methodology into whatever implementation you desire.

This basic templating strategy has been implemented in several languages and is certainly not a new concept. Therefore, you can find a wealth of information on the Web pertaining to template implementations. Two particularly interesting resources are this set of related articles, written with JavaScript in mind:

- `http://developer.netscape.com/viewsource/long_ssjs/long_ssjs.html`

- `http://developer.netscape.com/viewsource/schroder_template/schroder_template.html`

The following article touches upon templates as it applies to Java Server Pages:

- `http://www-4.ibm.com/software/webservers/appserv/doc/guide/asgdwp.html`

There are also quite a few PHP implementations that follow this templating strategy. Several of the more interesting ones include:

- PHPLib Base Library (`http://phplib.netuse.de`)

- Richard Heyes's Template Class (`http://www.heyes-computing.net`)

- Fast Template (`http://www.thewebmasters.net/php/`)

The PHP resource site PHPBuilder (`http://www.phpbuilder.com`) also contains a few interesting tutorials regarding template manipulation. Also check out PHP Classes Repository (`http://phpclasses.UpperDesign.com`). Several similar templating implementations are there.

Drawbacks to This Templating System

While this form of templating fulfills its purpose of completely separating the code from the design, it is not without its disadvantages. I'll highlight these disadvantages here.

Resulting Unfounded Belief in "Silver Bullet" Solution

While templates can aid in clearly defining the boundaries of a project in terms of coding and design, they are not a substitute for communication. In fact, they won't even operate correctly without concise communication between both parties about exactly what information will be templated in the application. As is the case with any successful software project, a thorough survey of the application specifications should always be drawn up before even one line of PHP is coded. This will greatly reduce the possibility for later miscommunication, resulting in unexpected template parsing results.

Performance Degradation

The dependence on file parsing and manipulation will cause the templating system to suffer a loss in performance in terms of speed. Exactly what the degree of this loss is depends on a number of factors, including page size, SQL query size (if any), and machine hardware. In many cases, this loss will be negligible; however there may be instances where it will be noticeable if it becomes necessary to simultaneously manipulate several template files in high-traffic situations.

Designer Is Still PHP-Impaired

One of the main reasons for creating this system at all lies in the fact that it could be problematic if the designer comes into contact with the code when editing the look and feel of the page. In an ideal environment, the designer would also be a programmer or at least know general programming concepts, such as a variable, loop, and conditional. A designer who is not privy to this information stands to gain nothing from using templates except education in a relatively useless syntax (the syntax used to delimit variable keywords). Therefore, regardless of what your final verdict is on using this form of page templating, I strongly recommend taking time to begin educating the designer on the finer points of the PHP language (or better, buy the designer a copy of this book!). This results in a win-win situation for both parties, as the designer will learn an extra skill, and in doing so, become an even more valuable member of the team. The programmer wins, as this person will be an extra brain to pick for new programming ideas, perhaps even a particularly valuable one, since chances are that the designer will look at things from a different perspective than the typical programmer would.

Project: Create an Address Book

Although templating systems are well suited for a variety of Web applications, they are particularly useful in datacentric applications in which formatting is important. One such application is an address book. Think about what a conventional (paper-based) address book looks like: each page looks exactly the same, save for perhaps a letter denoting which set of last names the particular page is reserved for. The same kind of idea could apply to a Web-based address book. In fact, formatting is even more important in this case, since it might be necessary to export the data to another application in a particularly rigorous format. This kind of application works great with the templating system, since the designer is left to create a single page format that will be used for all 26 letters of the alphabet.

To begin, you must decide what kind of data you want to store in the address book and how this data is to be stored. Of course, the most plausible choice for a storage media would be a database, since this also facilitates useful features such as searching and ordering data. I'll use a MySQL database to store the address information. The table looks like this:

```
mysql>CREATE table addressbook (
        last_name char(35) NOT NULL,
        first_name char(20) NOT NULL,
        tel char(20) NOT NULL,
        email char(55) NOT NULL );
```

Of course, you can add street address, city, and state columns. I'll use this abbreviated table for sake of illustration.

Next, I'll play the role of designer and create the templates. For this project, two templates are required. The first template, shown in Listing 12-8, could be considered the "parent" template.

Listing 12-8: Parent address book template, entitled "book.html"

```
<html>
<head>
<title>:::::{page_title}:::::</title>
</head>
<body bgcolor="white">

<table cellpadding=2 cellspacing=2 width=600>
<h1>Address Book: {letter}</h1>
<tr><td>
<a href="index.php?letter=a">A</a> | <a href="index.php?letter=b">B</a> |
<a href="index.php?letter=c">C</a> | <a href="index.php?letter=d">D</a> |
<a href="index.php?letter=e">E</a> | <a href="index.php?letter=f">F</a> |
```

```
<a href="index.php?letter=g">G</a> | <a href="index.php?letter=h">H</a> |
<a href="index.php?letter=i">I</a> | <a href="index.php?letter=j">J</a> |
<a href="index.php?letter=k">K</a> | <a href="index.php?letter=l">L</a> |
<a href="index.php?letter=m">M</a> | <a href="index.php?letter=n">N</a> |
<a href="index.php?letter=o">O</a> | <a href="index.php?letter=p">P</a> |
<a href="index.php?letter=q">Q</a> | <a href="index.php?letter=r">R</a> |
<a href="index.php?letter=s">S</a> | <a href="index.php?letter=t">T</a> |
<a href="index.php?letter=u">U</a> | <a href="index.php?letter=v">V</a> |
<a href="index.php?letter=w">W</a> | <a href="index.php?letter=x">X</a> |
<a href="index.php?letter=y">Y</a> | <a href="index.php?letter=z">Z</a>
</td></tr>

{rows.addresses}
</table>
</body>
</html>
```

As you can see, the bulk of this file is given to the links displaying each letter of the alphabet. Clicking a particular letter, the user will be presented with all persons stored in the address book having a last name beginning with that letter.

There are also three delimited variable names: page_title, letter, and rows.addresses. The purpose of the first two variables should be obvious: the title of the page and the letter of the address book currently used to retrieve address information, respectively. The third variable refers to the child template and is used to specify which table configuration file should be inserted into the parent. I say "table configuration file" because, in a complex page, you might be simultaneously using several templates, each employing HTML tables for formatting data. Therefore, "rows" specifies that a table template will be inserted, and "addresses" tells us that it is the table used to format addresses.

The second template, shown in Listing 12-9, is the "child" template, because it will be embedded in the parent. Why this is necessary will soon become clear.

Listing 12-9: Child address book template, entitled "rows.addresses"
```
<tr><td bgcolor="#c0c0c0">
<b>{last_name},{first_name}</b>
</td></tr>
<tr><td>
<b>{telephone}</b>
</td></tr>
<tr><td>
<b><a href = "mailto:{email}">{email}</a></b>
</td></tr>
```

There are four delimited variable names in Listing 12-9: `last_name`, `first_name`, `telephone`, and `email`. The meanings of each should be obvious. It is important to notice that this file only contains table row (`<tr>…</tr>`) and table cell (`<td>…</td>`) tags. This is because this file will be repeatedly inserted into the template, one time for each address retrieved from the database. Since the `rows.addresses` variable name is enclosed in table tags in Listing 12-8, the HTML formatting will parse correctly. To illustrate how this works, take a look at Figure 12-1, which is essentially a screenshot of the completed address book in address. Then examine Listing 12-10, which contains the source code for that screen shot. You'll see that the rows.addresses file is used repeatedly in the source code.

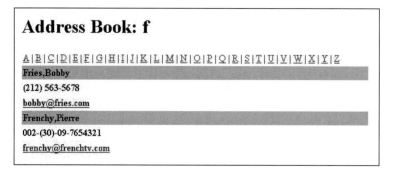

Figure 12-1. Screenshot of the address book in action

Listing 12-10: Source code for Figure 12-1

```
<html>
<head>
<title>:::::Address Book:::::</title>
</head>
<body bgcolor="white">

<table cellpadding=2 cellspacing=2 width=600>
<h1>Address Book: f</h1>
<tr><td><a href="index.php?letter=a">A</a> | <a href="index.php?letter=b">B</a> |
<a href="index.php?letter=c">C</a> |
<a href="index.php?letter=d">D</a> | <a href="index.php?letter=e">E</a> | <a
href="index.php?letter=f">F</a> | <a href="index.php?letter=g">G</a> | <a
href="index.php?letter=h">H</a> | <a href="index.php?letter=i">I</a> | <a
href="index.php?letter=j">J</a> | <a href="index.php?letter=k">K</a> | <a
```

```
href="index.php?letter=l">L</a> | <a href="index.php?letter=m">M</a> | <a
href="index.php?letter=n">N</a> | <a href="index.php?letter=o">O</a> | <a
href="index.php?letter=p">P</a> | <a href="index.php?letter=q">Q</a> | <a
href="index.php?letter=r">R</a> | <a href="index.php?letter=s">S</a> | <a
href="index.php?letter=t">T</a> | <a href="index.php?letter=u">U</a> | <a
href="index.php?letter=v">V</a> | <a href="index.php?letter=w">W</a> | <a
href="index.php?letter=x">X</a> | <a href="index.php?letter=y">Y</a> | <a
href="index.php?letter=z">Z</a></td></tr>

<tr><td bgcolor="#c0c0c0">
<b>Fries,Bobby</b>
</td></tr>
<tr><td>
<b>(212) 563-5678</b>
</td></tr>
<tr><td>
<b><a href = "mailto:bobby@fries.com">bobby@fries.com</a></b>
</td></tr>
<tr><td bgcolor="#c0c0c0">
<b>Frenchy,Pierre</b>
</td></tr>
<tr><td>
<b>002-(30)-09-7654321</b>
</td></tr>
<tr><td>
<b><a href = "mailto:frenchy@frenchtv.com">frenchy@frenchtv.com</a></b>
</td></tr>
</table>
</body>
</html>
```

As you can see, there are apparently two persons having a last name that begins with *F* stored in the address book, Bobby Fries and Pierre Frenchy. Therefore, two table rows have been inserted in the table.

The design process for the address book project is complete. Now, I'll don the hat of a coder. You'll be surprised to know that there are no changes to the template.class file in Listing 12-7, save for one new method, address_sql(). This method is displayed in Listing 12-11.

Listing 12-11: SQL parsing method, address_sql()

```
class template {

    VAR $files = array();
    VAR $variables = array();
    VAR $sql = array();
    VAR $opening_escape = '{';
    VAR $closing_escape = '}';

    VAR $host = "localhost";
    VAR $user = "root";
    VAR $pswd = "";
    VAR $db = "book";
    VAR $address_table = "addressbook";

. . .

    function address_sql($file_id, $variable_name, $letter) {

    // Connect to MySQL server and select database
    mysql_connect($this->host, $this->user, $this->pswd)
            or die("Couldn't connect to MySQL server!");
    mysql_select_db($this->db) or die("Couldn't select MySQL database!");

    // Query database
    $query = "SELECT last_name, first_name, tel, email
                    FROM $this->address_table WHERE last_name LIKE '$letter%'";
    $result = mysql_query($query);

    // Open "rows.addresses" file and read contents into variable.
    $fh = fopen("$variable_name", "r");

    $file_contents = fread($fh, filesize("rows.addresses") );

    // Perform replacements of delimited variable names with table data
    while ($row = mysql_fetch_array($result)) :

        $new_row = $file_contents;

        $new_row = str_replace(
                $this->opening_escape."last_name".$this->closing_escape,
                $row["last_name"],
                $new_row);
```

```
        $new_row = str_replace(
                $this->opening_escape."first_name".$this->closing_escape,
                $row["first_name"],
                $new_row);

        $new_row = str_replace(
                $this->opening_escape."telephone".$this->closing_escape,
                $row["tel"],
                $new_row);

        $new_row = str_replace(
                $this->opening_escape."email".$this->closing_escape,
                $row["email"],
                $new_row);

        // Append new table row onto complete substitution string
        $complete_table .= $new_row;

    endwhile;

    // Assign table substitution string to SQL array key
    $sql_array_key = $variable_name;

    $this->sql[$sql_array_key] = $complete_table;

    // add the key to the variables array for later lookup
    $this->variables[$file_id][] = $variable_name;

    // Close the filehandle
    fclose($fh);

    } // end address_sql
    . . .
} // end template.class
```

The comments in Listing 12-11 should suffice for understanding the mechanics of what is taking place. However, there are still a few important points to make. First, notice that the rows.addresses file is opened only *once*. An alternative way to code this method would be to repeatedly open and close the rows.addresses file, replacing information each time and appending it to the $complete_table variable. However, this would be highly inefficient coding practice. Therefore, take some time to review how the loop is used to continuously append new table information to the $complete_table variable.

A second point to make about Listing 12-11 is that five new class attributes are used: $host, $user, $pswd, $db, and $address_table. Each of these pertains to information that the MySQL server requires, and the meaning of each should be obvious. If it isn't obvious, take a moment to read through Chapter 11, "Databases."

All that's left to do now is code the file that triggers the template parsing. This file is shown in Listing 12-12. By clicking one of the letter links (index.php?letter=someletter) in book.html (Listing 12-8), this file will be called, in turn regenerating the book.html file with appropriate information.

Listing 12-12: Template parser index.php

```
<?
include("template.class");

$page_title = "Address Book";

// The default page will retrieve persons having last name beginning with 'a'
if (! isset($letter) ) :
    $letter = "a";
endif;

$tpl = new template;
$tpl->register_file("book", "book.html");
$tpl->register_variables("book", "page_title,letter");
$tpl->address_sql("book", "rows.addresses","$letter");
$tpl->file_parser("book");
$tpl->print_file("book");
?>
```

There you have it: a practical example of how templates can be used to efficiently divide labor between coder and designer. Take some time to think about how you can use templates to further streamline your development process. I'll bet that you find a number of different implementations for templates.

What's Next?

This chapter introduced a particularly useful concept of both PHP and Web programming in general: advanced template usage. It began with a synopsis of the two templating systems covered thus far, simple variable substitution via PHP embedding, and the use of INCLUDE files to separate page components. I then introduced the third and most advanced template strategy, which completely separates the code from the design of the page. The remainder of the chapter was spent examining a class built to implement this type of template, concluding with a practical implementation of the template system, using a Web-based address book as an example. This example also built on the simple template class, implementing an SQL parser.

In particular, the following topics were discussed in this chapter:

- Why templates?

- Simple template #1: embedding PHP in HTML

- Simple template #2: using INCLUDE files to separate components

- Advanced templating through the complete division of design and code

- The template class

- File registration

- Variable registration

- File parsing

- File printing

- Disadvantages to using templates

- Address book project that expands on the default class, implementing an SQL parser

Next chapter, I continue the discussion of dynamic Web application development, introducing how cookies and session tracking can add a new degree of user interactivity to your Web site!

Cookies and Session Tracking

The ability to track users and customize user information based on personal preferences has become both one of the hottest and most debated features to be offered on the Web. While the advantages of being able to offer users services based on exactly what they desire are obvious, many questions have been raised regarding privacy in terms of the ramifications of being able to "follow" a user as that user navigates from page to page, and even from site to site.

Barring privacy concerns, the process of tracking user information through cookies or other technologies can be immensely beneficial to both the user and the site offering these services. It is to the user's benefit that these services provide the opportunity to customize content, weeding out any information that may be uninteresting or useless. This capability is also highly beneficial to the site administrators, as tracking user preferences and habits opens up a whole new realm of possibilities for user interaction, including targeted marketing and a vastly superior analysis of the popularity of their onsite content. On the commerce-dominated Web, these capabilities are by now practically the de facto standard.

This idea of tracking a user while navigating through your site can be defined as session tracking. Given the vast amount of knowledge that could be gained from introducing session tracking into your site architecture, it could be said that the advantages of session tracking and providing customized content far outweigh the disadvantages. With that said, this could hardly be considered a complete PHP textbook without devoting a chapter to PHP's session-tracking capabilities. In this chapter, I introduce several concepts closely intertwined with session tracking, namely, session cookies and their uses, unique session identification numbers, before concluding the chapter with a synopsis of PHP's predefined session-tracking configuration and predefined functions.

What Is a Cookie?

A *cookie* is nothing more than a small parcel of information that is sent by a Web server and stored on a client browser. This can be advantageous to the developer because useful data regarding the user session can be stored and then later retrieved, resulting in the creation of a state of persistence between the client and server. Cookies are commonly used by many Internet sites as a means to enhance both user experience and site efficiency, providing a way to track user navigation, actions, and preferences. The ability to store this information is a key feature for sites offering such services as online shopping, site personalization, and targeted advertising.

Due to the usercentric purpose of cookie usage, the key piece of information stored is likely to be a unique user identification number (UIN). This ID is subsequently stored in a database and is used as the key for retrieving any information stored in the database that is mapped to this UIN. Of course, it is not mandatory that the cookie is used to store a UIN; you could store anything you like in the cookie, provided that its total size does not surpass four kilobytes (4096 bytes).

Cookie Components

Interestingly, other pieces of information are also stored in the cookie, enabling the developer to tailor its usage in terms of domain, time frame, path, and security. Here are descriptions of the various cookie components:

- **name**—The cookie name is a mandatory parameter because the name is the parameter from which the cookie is referenced. The cookie name can be essentially thought of in terms of a variable name.

- **value**—A cookie value is simply a piece of data mapped to the cookie name. This could be a user identification number, background color, date, anything.

- **expiration date**—This date defines the lifetime of the cookie. Once this timestamp equals the current date and time, the cookie will expire and be rendered unusable. According to cookie specifications, inclusion of the expiration date is optional. However, PHP's cookie-setting functionality requires that this expiration date is set. According to the cookie specifications, if an expiration date is not included, the cookie will expire at the end of the user session (that is, when the user exits the site).

- **domain**—This is the domain that both created and can read the cookie. If a domain has multiple servers and would like all servers to be able to access the same cookie, then the domain could be set in the form of .phprecipes.com. In this case all potential third-level domains falling under the PHPrecipes site, such as wap.phprecipes.com or news.phprecipes.com, would have access to the cookie. For security reasons, a cookie cannot be set for any domain other than the one mapped to the server attempting to set the cookie. This parameter is optional. If it is not included, it will default to the domain name from which the cookie is emanating.

- **path**—The path setting specifies the URL path from which the cookie is valid. Any attempt to retrieve a cookie from outside of this path will fail. Setting path is optional. If it is not set, then the path will be set to the path of the document from which the cookie is created.

- **security**—This determines whether or not the cookie can be retrieved in a nonsecure setting. Because the cookie will be primarily used in a nonsecure setting, this optional parameter will default to FALSE.

Although all cookies must abide by the same set of syntax rules when they are set, the cookie storage format is browser dependent. For example, Netscape Communicator stores a cookie in a format similar to the following:

```
.phprecipes.com   FALSE   /   FALSE   971728956   bgcolor   blue
```

In Internet Explorer, the same cookie would be stored as:

```
bgcolor
blue
localhost/php4/php.exe/book/13/
0
2154887040
29374385
522625408
29374377
*
```

To correctly view a cookie stored by Internet Explorer, just open it up using a text editor. Keep in mind that certain text editors do not properly process the newline character found at the end of each line, causing them to appear as squares in the cookie document.

> **NOTE** *Internet Explorer stores its cookie information in a folder aptly entitled "Cookies," while Netscape Communicator stores it in a single file entitled "cookies." Just perform a search on your drive to find these files.*

Cookies and PHP

OK, enough background information. By now, I'm sure you're eager to learn how you can begin using PHP to store and retrieve your own cookies. You'll be happy to know that it is surprisingly easy, done with a simple call to the predefined function setcookie().

The function setcookie() stores a cookie on a user's machine. Its syntax is:

```
int setcookie (string name [, string val [, int date [, string path [, string
domain [, int secure]]]]])
```

If you took a moment to read the introduction to cookies, you are already familiar with the parameters in the setcookie() syntax. If you've skipped ahead and are not familiar with the mechanics of persistent cookies, I suggest that you return to the beginning of this section and read through the introduction, as all of the setcookie() parameters are introduced there.

Before proceeding, I ask that you read the following sentence not once, not twice, but three times. A cookie must be set *before* any other page-relevant information is sent to the browser. Write this 500 times on a blackboard, get a tattoo stating this rule, teach your parrot to say it: I don't care, just get it straight. In other words, you cannot just set a cookie where you wish in a Web page. It must be sent before any browser-relevant information is sent; otherwise *it will not work.*

Another important restriction to keep in mind is that you cannot set a cookie and then expect to use that cookie in the same page. Either the user must refresh the page (don't count on it), or you will have to wait until the next page request before that cookie variable can be used.

This example illustrates how setcookie() is used to set a cookie containing a user identification number:

```
$userid = "4139b31b7bab052";
$cookie_set = setcookie ("uid", $value, time()+3600, "/", ".phprecipes.com", 0);
```

After analyzing this code, you'll notice these results of setting the cookie:

- After reloading or navigating to any subsequent page, the variable $userid becomes available, producing the user id 4139b31b7bab052.

- This cookie will expire (thus be rendered unusable) exactly one hour (3600 seconds) after it has been sent.

- The cookie is available for retrieval in all directories on the server.

- This cookie is only accessible via the phprecipes.com domain.

- This cookie is accessible via a nonsecured protocol.

The next example, shown in Listing 13-1, illustrates how a cookie can be used to store page-formatting preferences, in this case the background color. Notice how the cookie will only be set *if* the form action has been executed.

Listing 13-1: Storing a user's favorite background color

```
<?
// If the variable $bgcolor exists…
if (isset($bgcolor)) :
    setcookie("bgcolor", $bgcolor, time()+3600);
?>

<html>
<body bgcolor="<?=$bgcolor;?>">

<?
// else, $bgcolor is not set, therefore show the form
else :
?>
<body bgcolor="white">
<form action="<? print $PHP_SELF; ?>" method="post">
    What's your favorite background color?
    <select name="bgcolor">
        <option value="red">red
        <option value="blue">blue
        <option value="green">green
        <option value="black">black
    </select>
        <input type="submit" value="Set background color">
</form>

<?
endif;
?>
</body>
</html>
```

On loading of this page to the browser, the script will verify whether the cookie entitled "bgcolor" has been set. If it has, then the background color of the page will be set to the value specified by the variable $bgcolor. Otherwise, an

HTML form will appear, prompting the user to specify a favorite background color. Once the color is specified, subsequent reloading of the page or traversal to any page using the cookie value $bgcolor will be recognized.

Interestingly, you can also use array notation to specify cookie names. You could specify cookie names as uid[1], uid[2], uid[3], and so on, and then later access these values just as you would a normal array. Check out Listing 13-2 for an example of how this works.

Listing 13-2: Assigning cookie names according to array index value

```
<?
setcookie("phprecipes[uid]", "4139b31b7bab052", time()+3600);
setcookie("phprecipes[color]", "black", time()+3600);
setcookie("phprecipes[preference]", "english", time()+3600);

if (isset ($phprecipes)) {
   while (list ($name, $value) = each ($phprecipes)) {
      echo "$name = $value<br>\n";
   }
}
?>
```

Executing this script results in the following output, in addition to three cookies being set on the user's computer:

```
uid = 4139b31b7bab052
color = black
preference = english
```

> **NOTE** *Although the use of array-based cookies may seem like a great idea for storing all kinds of information, keep in mind that certain browsers (such as Netscape Communicator) limit the number of cookies to 20 per domain.*

Perhaps the most common use of cookies is for storage of a user identification number that will be later used for retrieving user-specific information. This process is illustrated in the next listing, where a UIN is stored in a MySQL database. The stored information is subsequently retrieved and used to set various pieces of information regarding the formatting of the page.

To set the stage for the next listing, assume that a table entitled user_info resides on a database named user. The user_info table contains three pieces of information: a user ID, first name, and email address. This table was created using the following syntax:

```
mysql>create table user_info (
->user_id char(18),
->fname char(15),
->email char(35));
```

Listing 13-3 actually picks up about halfway through what would be a complete "registration" script, starting where the user information (user ID, first name, and email address) has already been inserted into the database. To eliminate the need for the user to later log in, the user ID (set to 15 in Listing 13-3 for the sake of illustration) is stored on the user's computer by way of a cookie.

Listing 13-3: Retrieving user information from a database

```
<?
if (! isset($userid)) :
    $id = "15";
    setcookie ("userid", $id, time()+3600);
    print "A cookie containing your userID has been set on your machine. Please
refresh the page to retrieve your user information";
else:
    @mysql_connect("localhost", "web", "4tf9zzzf")
            or die("Could not connect to MySQL server!");
    @mysql_select_db("user") or die("Could not select user database!");
    // declare query
    $query = "SELECT * FROM user_info WHERE user_id = '$userid'";
    // execute query
    $result = mysql_query($query);

    $row = mysql_fetch_array($result);
    print "Hi ".$row["fname"].",<br>";
    print "Your email address is ".$row["email"];

    mysql_close();
endif;
?>
```

Listing 13-3 highlights just how useful cookies can be for identifying users. The above scenario could be applied to any number of situations, ranging from eliminating the need to log in to effectively tracking user preferences.

The listing in the next section, "Unique Identification Numbers," illustrates the complete process of user registration and subsequent storage of the unique user ID.

> **NOTE** *The MySQL functions used in Listing 13-3 are introduced in Chapter 11, "Databases."*

Unique Identification Numbers

By now you are probably curious just how easy it is to create a unique UIN. Put your college calculus books away; there is no need for funky 17th-century algorithms. PHP provides an easy way to create a unique UIN through its predefined function uniqid().

The function uniqid() generates a 13-character unique identification number based on the current time. Its syntax is:

```
int uniqid (string prefix [, boolean lcg])
```

The input parameter prefix can be used to begin the UIN with a particular string value. Since prefix is a required parameter, you must designate at least an empty value. If set to TRUE, the optional input parameter lcg will cause uniqid() to produce a 23-character UIN. To quickly create a unique ID, just call uniqid() using an empty value as the sole input parameter:

```
$uniq_id = uniqid("");
// Some 13 character value such as ' 39b3209ce8ef2' will be generated.
```

Another way to create a unique ID is to prepend the derived value with a string, specified in the input parameter prefix, as shown here:

```
$uniq_id = uniqid("php", TRUE);
// Some 16 character value such as 'php39b3209ce8ef2' will be generated.
```

Given the fact that uniqid() creates its UIN based on the current time of the system, there is a remote possibility that it could be guessed. Therefore, you may want to ensure that its value is truly random by first randomly choosing a prefix using another of PHP's predefined functions, rand(). The following example demonstrates this usage:

```
srand ((double) microtime() * 1000000);
$uniq_id = uniqid(rand());
```

The function srand() acts to initiate the random number generator. If you want to ensure that rand() consistently produces a random number, you must execute srand() first. Placing rand() as an input parameter to uniqid() will result in rand() first being executed, returning a prefix value to uniqid(), which will then execute, producing a UIN that would be rather difficult to guess.

Armed with the knowledge of how to create unique user IDs, you can now create a practical user registration scheme. On first request of the script in Listing 13-4, the user is greeted with a short form requesting a name and email address. This information will be then inserted along with a generated unique ID into the table user_info, first described along with Listing 13-3. A cookie containing this unique ID is then stored on the user's computer. Any subsequent visit to the page will prompt the script to query the database based on the unique user ID stored in the cookie, displaying the user information to the screen.

Listing 13-4: A complete user registration process

```
<?
// build form
$form = "
<form action=\"Listing13-4.php\" method=\"post\">
<input type=\"hidden\" name=\"seenform\" value=\"y\">
Your first name?:<br>
<input type=\"text\" name=\"fname\" size=\"20\" maxlength=\"20\" value=\"\"><br>
Your email?:<br>
<input type=\"text\" name=\"email\" size=\"20\" maxlength=\"35\" value=\"\"><br>
<input type=\"submit\" value=\"Register!\">
</form>
";
// If the form has not been displayed and the user does not have a cookie.
if ((! isset ($seenform)) && (! isset ($userid))) :

     print $form;

// If the form has been displayed but the user information
// has not yet been processed
elseif (isset ($seenform) && (! isset ($userid))) :

     srand ((double) microtime() * 1000000);
     $uniq_id = uniqid(rand());
     // connect to the MySQL server and select the users database
     @mysql_pconnect("localhost", "web", "4tf9zzzf")
             or die("Could not connect to MySQL server!");
     @mysql_select_db("user") or die("Could not select user database!");
```

```
        // declare and execute query
        $query = "INSERT INTO user_info VALUES('$uniq_id', '$fname', '$email')";
        $result = mysql_query($query) or die("Could not insert user information!");

        // set cookie "userid" to expire in one month.
        setcookie ("userid", $uniq_id, time()+2592000);

        print "Congratulations $fname! You are now registered! Your user information
        will be displayed on each subsequent visit to this page.";
// else if the cookie exists, use the userID to extract
// information from the users database
elseif (isset($userid)) :
        // connect to the MySQL server and select the users database
        @mysql_pconnect("localhost", "web", "4tf9zzzf")
                or die("Could not connect to MySQL server!");
        @mysql_select_db("user") or die("Could not select user database!");

        // declare and execute query
        $query = "SELECT * FROM user_info WHERE user_id = '$userid'";
        $result = mysql_query($query) or die("Could not extract user information!");

        $row = mysql_fetch_array($result);
        print "Hi ".$row["fname"].",<br>";
        print "Your email address is ".$row["email"];

endif;

?>
```

The judicious use of several *if* conditionals makes it possible to use one script to take care of each step of the registration and subsequent user recognition process. There are three scenarios involved in this script:

- The user has not seen the form and does not have a valid cookie. This is the step where the user is presented with the form.

- The user has filled in the form and does not yet have a valid cookie. This is the step where the user information is entered into the database, and the cookie is set, due to expire in one month.

- The user returns to the script. If the cookie is still valid (has not expired), the cookie is read in and the relevant information is extracted from the database.

The general process shown in Listing 13-4 could of course be applied to any database. This illustrates, on a very basic level, how many of the larger sites are able to apply user-specified preferences to their site, resulting in a "tailor-made" look for each user.

This ends the introduction to PHP and cookies. If you are interested in learning more about the cookie mechanism, check out the online resources that I've cited in the sidebar "Relevant Links."

Relevant Links

For more information regarding cookies and their usage, take a moment to read through a few of the resources that I've gleaned from the Web:

- http://www.cookiecentral.com

- http://home.netscape.com/newsref/std/cookie_spec.html

- http://builder.com/Programming/Cookies/ss01.html

- http://www.w3.org/Protocols/rfc2109/rfc2109

As you have learned, cookies can be very useful for "remembering" user-specific information that can be retrieved in subsequent visits to your site. However, cookies can not be solely relied on since users can set their browsers to refuse to accept cookies. Thankfully, PHP offers an alternative methodology for storing persistent information; This method is called *session tracking* and is the subject of the next section.

Session Handling

A *session* is best defined as the period of time beginning when a user enters your site and ending when the user exits. Throughout this session, you may wish to assign various variables that will accompany the user while navigating around your site, without having to manually code a bunch of hidden forms or appended URL variables. This otherwise tedious process becomes fairly easy with *session handling*.

Consider the following scenario. Using session handling, a user entering your site would be assigned a unique session id (SID). This SID is then sent to the user's browser in a cookie entitled PHPSESSID. If cookie support is disabled or not supported, this SID can be automatically appended to all local URLs throughout the user session. At the same time, a file with the same name as the SID is stored on the server. As the user navigates throughout the site, you may wish to record certain variables as session variables. These variables are stored in that user's file. Any subsequent call to any of those variables deemed to be of the "session" type will cause the server to grab that user's session file and search it for the session variable in question. And voilà! The session variable is displayed. In a nutshell, this is the essence of session handling. Of course, you can also direct this user information to be stored in databases or other files, whatever you wish.

Sounds interesting? You bet it does. Armed with this information, you will surely have a better understanding of the various configuration issues at hand, which I will now discuss. There are three particularly important configuration flags. The first, entitled –enable-trans-id, must be included in the configuration process if you wish to take advantage of its features (described below). The other two, entitled track_vars and register_globals, can be enabled and disabled as necessary in the php.ini file. The ramifications of activating these three flags are discussed next.

–enable-trans-sid

When PHP is compiled with this flag, all relative URLs will automatically be rewritten with the session ID attached. This appendage of the session ID is written in the form session-name=session-id, where session-name is defined in the php.ini file (explained later in this section). If you decide not to do so, you can use the constant SID.

track_vars

Enabling track_vars allows $HTTP_*_VARS[] arrays, where * is one of the EGPCS (Environment, Get, Post, Cookie, Server) values. This must be enabled in order for the SID to propagate from one page to another. As of PHP 4.03, this setting is always enabled.

register_globals

Enabling this option will result in all EGCPS variables being globally accessible. You want this disabled if you don't want your global array filling with perhaps unnecessary data. If this is disabled and track_vars is enabled, all GPC variables can be accessed through the *$HTTP_*_VARS[]* arrays. As an example, if register_globals is disabled, you would have to refer to the predefined variable $PHP_SELF as $HTTP_SERVER_VARS["PHP_SELF"].

There are also a number of preferential configuration issues that you should take care of. These directives are described in Table 13-1, shown in their default form as seen in the php.ini file. They are introduced in the order that they actually appear in the file.

Table 13-1. Session-handling directives in the php.ini file

DIRECTIVE		DESCRIPTION
`session.save_handler`	`= files`	Specifies how the session information will be stored on the server. There are three ways to do so: in a file (`files`), shared memory (`mm`), or through user-defined functions (`User`). The user-defined functions allow you to easily store the information in any format you wish, for example, in a database.
`session.save_path`	`= /tmp`	Designates the directory in which the PHP session files will be stored. On the Linux platform, the default setting (`'/tmp'`) is probably just fine. On the Windows platform, you will need to change this to some Windows path; otherwise errors will occur.
`session.use_cookies`	`= 1`	When enabled, cookies are used to store the session ID on the user's computer.
`session.name`	`= PHPSESSID`	If `session.use_cookies` is enabled, then `session.name` will be used as the cookie name. The characters comprising the name can only be alphanumeric.
`session.auto_start`	`= 0`	When enabled, `session.auto_start` will automatically initiate a session when a client makes an initial request.
`session.cookie_lifetime`	`= 0`	If `session.use_cookies` is enabled, then `session.cookie_lifetime` will determine the lifetime of the sent cookies. If it is set to 0, then any sent cookies will expire on the termination of the user session.
`session.cookie_path`	`= /`	If `session.use_cookies` is enabled, then `session.cookie_path` determines the parent path directory for which sent cookies are valid.
`session.cookie_domain`	`=`	If `session.use_cookies` is enabled, then `session.cookie_domain` determines the domain for which sent cookies are valid.
`session.serialize_handler`	`= php`	This specifies the name of the handler that will be used to serialize data. There are currently two possible values for this: `php` and `WDDX`.

Table 13-1. (Continued)

DIRECTIVE		DESCRIPTION
session.gc_probability	= 1	This specifies the percentual probability that PHP's garbage collection routine will be activated.
session.gc_maxlifetime	= 1440	Specifies the time (in seconds) before session data is considered invalid and will be destroyed. This timer begins counting down after the last access to the session.
session.referer_check	=	When set to a string, each request to a session-enabled page will begin with a verification that the specified string is in the global variable $HTTP_REFERER. If it is not found, any accompanying session ID will be ignored.
session.entropy_file	=	Points to an external file that supplies additional random information used during the creation of the session ID. There are typically two devices on UNIX systems made for this purpose, /dev/random and /dev/urandom. The /dev/random device collects random data from inside the kernel, while the /dev/urandom device relies on the MD5 hashing algorithm to produce a random string. In short, /dev/random is faster, but /dev/urandom produces a more "random" string.
session.entropy_length	= 0	Assuming session.entropy_file is set, session.entropy_length specifies the number of bytes to be read from the file specified by session.entropy_length.
session.cache_limiter	= nocache	Determines the cache control method for session pages. There are three possible values for this setting: nocache, public, and private.
session.cache_expire	= 180	Determines the TTL (time to live) in minutes for cached session pages.

Now that you have presumably made any necessary configuration adjustments to your server, I will turn attention toward the mechanics of how you can implement session handling on your site. It is actually a rather simple process, made possible through the use of several predefined functions. The first concept that you need to know is that a session is initiated with the function session_start(). Of course, you could eliminate the need to use this function if you had enabled session.auto_start in the php.ini file as discussed earlier in this section. However, for the remainder of this section, I will assume that you have not done this so to ensure consistency in my examples. The syntax of session_start() is simple, as it requires no input parameters and returns only a boolean informing the developer as to its success.

session_start()

The function session_start() is twofold in purpose. Once called, it checks to see if the user has already started a session, and if the user has not, it starts one. Its syntax is:

```
boolean session_start()
```

If it starts a session, it performs three functions, assigning the user a SID, sending a cookie (if session.use_cookies is enabled in the php.ini file), and creating the session file on the server. Its second purpose is that it informs the PHP engine that other session variables may be used in the script from which it (session_start()) is executed.

A session is started simply by calling session_start() like this:

```
session_start();
```

Just as a session can be created, it can be destroyed. This is accomplished via the function session_destroy().

session_destroy()

The function session_destroy() will destroy all persistent data corresponding to the current user session. Its syntax is:

```
boolean session_destroy()
```

Keep in mind that this will *not* destroy any cookies on the user's browser. However, if you are not interested in using the cookie beyond the end of the session, just set session.cookie_lifetime to 0 (its default value) in the php.ini file. An example of the function's usage is:

```
<?
session_start();
// do some session stuff
session_destroy();
?>
```

Now that you know how to create and destroy sessions, you are ready to begin working with the various session variables. Perhaps the most important one is the SID. This is easily obtainable through using the session_id() function.

session_id()

The function session_id() returns the user's SID originally created by session_start(). This is its syntax:

```
string session_id([string sid])
```

If you supply a session ID as the optional input parameter sid, the user's session ID will be changed. Keep in mind, however, that this will *not* resend the cookie. Executing this example:

```
<?
session_start ();
print "Your session identification number is ".session_id();
session_destroy();
?>
```

results in output similar to the following being displayed to the browser:

```
Your session identification number is 967d992a949114ee9832f1c11cafc640
```

So how can you begin creating your own session variables? The function ses-
sion_register() takes care of this job handily.

session_register()

The function session_register() registers one or more variable names with the
user's current session. Its syntax is:

```
boolean session_register (mixed varname1 [, mixed varname2 …])
```

Keep in mind that you are *not* registering variables, but rather the names of
the variables. Session_register() will also call session_start() internally,
implicitly beginning a new session if one does not already exist.

Before exemplifying the usage of session_register(), I would like to introduce another session-oriented function that can verify whether or not a particular variable has been registered. The function is entitled
session_is_registered().

session_is_registered()

It is often useful to determine whether or not a variable has already been registered. This task can be accomplished with session_is_registered(). Its syntax is:

```
boolean session_is_registered (string varname)
```

To illustrate the usage of session_register() and session_is_registered(),
I'll refer to what seems to be everyone's favorite basic session example: a hit
counter. This is illustrated in Listing 13-5.

Listing 13-5: A user-specific hit counter
```
<?
session_start();
if (! session_is_registered('hits')) :
    session_register('hits');
endif;
$hits++;
print "You've seen this page $hits times";
?>
```

Just as you can create session variables, you can destroy them. This is accomplished with session_unregister().

session_unregister()

A session variable can be destroyed with a call to session_unregister(). Its syntax is:

```
boolean session_unregister (string varname)
```

The input parameter varname is the name of the session variable that you would like to destroy.

```
<?
session_start();
session_register('username');
// ...use the variable $username as needed, then destroy it.
session_unregister('username');
session_destroy();
?>
```

As is the case with session_register(), remember that you do not specify the input parameter varname as an actual variable (that is, with a preceding dollar sign [$]). Instead, you just use the *name* of the variable.

session_encode()

The function session_encode() offers a particularly convenient method for formatting session variables for storage, for example in a database. Its syntax is:

```
boolean session_encode()
```

Executing this function will result in all session data being formatted into a single string. This string can then be inserted into a database for storage purposes.

Consider Listing 13-6 for an example of how session_encode() is used. Assume that a "registered" user has a cookie containing that user's unique ID stored on a computer. When the user requests the page containing Listing 13-6, the user ID is retrieved from the cookie. This value is then assigned to be the session ID. Certain session variables are created and assigned values, and then all of this information is encoded using session_encode() and inserted into a MySQL database.

Listing 13-6: Using session_encode() to store data in a MySQL database

```
<?
// Initiate session and create a few session variables
session_register('bgcolor');
session_register('fontcolor');

// assume that the variable $usr_id (containing a unique user ID)
// is stored in a cookie on the user's machine.

// use session_id() to set the session ID to be the user's
// unique user ID stored in the cookie and In the database
$id = session_id($usr_id);

// these variables could be set by the user via an HTML form
$bgcolor = "white";
$fontcolor = "blue";

// encode all session data into a single string
$usr_data = session_encode();

// connect to the MySQL server and select users database
@mysql_pconnect("localhost", "web", "4tf9zzzf") or die("Could not connect to MySQL
server!");
@mysql_select_db("users") or die("Could not select user database!");

// update the user's page preferences
$query = "UPDATE user_info set page_data='$usr_data' WHERE user_id= '$id'";
$result = mysql_query($query) or die("Could not update user information!");
?>
```

As you can see, the capability to quickly convert all of the session variables into a single string eliminates the need to keep track of several column names when storing and retrieving data and eliminates several lines of code that would otherwise be needed to store and retrieve this data.

session_decode()

Any session data previously encoded with session_encode() can be decoded with session_decode(). Its syntax is:

```
string session_decode(string session_data)
```

The input parameter session_data is the encoded string of session variables, presumably returned from a file or database retrieval. The string is decoded, and all session variables in the string are regenerated back to their original variable format.

Listing 13-7 illustrates how previously encoded session variables are regenerated by using session_decode(). Assume that a MySQL table entitled "user_info" is built from just two columns: user_id and page_data. The user's UID, stored in a cookie on the user's computer, is used to retrieve encoded session data stored in the page_data column. The page_data column stores an encoded string of variables, one of which is the user's preferential background color, stored in the variable $bgcolor.

Listing 13-7: Decoding session data stored in a MySQL database

```
<?
// assume that the variable $usr_id (containing a unique user ID)
// is stored in a cookie on the user's machine.

$id = session_id($usr_id);

// connect to the MySQL server and select user's database
@mysql_pconnect("localhost", "web", "4tf9zzzf") or die("Could not connect to MySQL
server!");
@mysql_select_db("users") or die("Could not select company database!");

// select data from the MySQL table
$query = "SELECT page_data FROM user_info WHERE user_id= '$id'";
$result = mysql_query($query);
$user_data = mysql_result($result, 0, "page_data");

// decode the data
session_decode($user_data);

// output one of the regenerated session variables
print "BGCOLOR: $bgcolor";

?>
```

As you can see from the previous two listings, session_encode() and session_decode() are enormously useful and efficient for storing and retrieving session data.

Specifying User Callbacks as Storage Modules

While storing session information in files works pretty well, you may be interested in storing data using other mediums, probably a database. Or perhaps you are interested in reusing the same scripts on different sites, but with different databases. Another common dilemma is the need to share session data across various servers, something that is rather difficult when using PHP's default routines of storing session data in a file. You'll be happy to know that realizing all of these extensions to PHP's session handling is really an easy task, given PHP's capability to allow users to specify their own storage routines via a predefined function called `session_set_save_handler()`.

The function `session_set_save_handler()` defines the user-level session storage and retrieval functions. Its syntax is:

```
void session_set_save_handler (string open, string close, string read, string
write, string destroy, string gc)
```

The six input parameters correspond to the six functions that are transparently called by PHP's session-handling functions. The function `session_set_save_handler()` allows you to redefine these functions without affecting the scripts that call PHP's predefined session functions. Although you can change the names of the functions to be whatever you wish, each must take as input a specified set of parameters. Before proceeding to an example, take a look at Table 13-2 to understand the roles of these six functions and their input parameters.

> **NOTE** *In order to make use of* `session_set_save_handler()`, *you must set* `session.save_handler` *to* `user` *in the php.ini file.*

Table 13-2: Six input parameters for the function session_set_savehandler()

PARAMETER	DESCRIPTION
sess_close()	Called when a script implementing the session functions finishes. This is *not* the same as sess_destroy(), which is used to actually destroy the session variables. There aren't any input parameters for sess_close().
sess_destroy($session_id)	Deletes all session data. The input parameter $session_id specifies which session is to be destroyed.
sess_gc($maxlifetime)	Deletes any sessions that have expired. The expiration time is denoted by the input parameter $maxlifetime, specified in seconds. This parameter is read from the php.ini file and corresponds to session.gc_lifetime.
sess_open($sess_path, $sess_name)	Called when a new session is initialized, either by session_start() or session_register(). The two input parameters $sess_path and $sess_name are read from the php.ini file and correspond to the session.save_path and session.name parameters, respectively.
sess_read($key)	Used to retrieve the value corresponding to a session variable, denoted by the input parameter $key.
sess_write($key, $value)	Used to write the session data. Any data saved by sess_write() can later be retrieved by sess_read(). The input parameter $key corresponds to a session variable name, and $value corresponds to the value assigned to $key.

Now that you know more about the functions that you need to define, I'll provide an example of a MySQL-based implementation of the session-handling functions. This example is given in Listing 13-8.

Listing 13-8: MySQL implementation of the session-handling functions

```php
<?
// MySQL implementation of session-handling functions

// mysql server host, username, and password values
$host = "localhost";
$user = "web";
$pswd = "4tf9zzzf";

// database and table names
$db = "users";
$session_table = "user_session_data";
$SESS_TBLNAME = "user_session_data";

// retrieve sess.gc_lifetime value from php.ini file
$sess_life = get_cfg_var("sess.gc_lifetime");

// Function: mysql_sess_open()
// mysql_sess_open() connects to the MySQL server
// and selects the database.

function mysql_sess_open($save_path, $session_name) {
    GLOBAL $host, $user, $pswd, $db;

    @mysql_pconnect($host, $user, $pswd)
            or die("Can't connect to MySQL server!");
    @mysql_select_db($SESS_$db) or die("Can't select session database!");
}

// Function: mysql_sess_close()
// mysql_sess_close() is not needed in the MySQL implementation.
// *However*, it still must be defined.

function mysql_sess_close() {
    return true;
}

// Function: mysql_sess_read()
// mysql_sess_read() reads the information from the MySQL database.

function mysql_sess_read($key) {
    GLOBAL $session_table;
```

```php
    $query = "SELECT value FROM $session_table WHERE sess_key = '$key' AND
                    sess_expiration >". time();
    $result = mysql_query($query);

    // If session value Is found, return it
    if (list($value) = mysql_fetch_row($result)) :
        return $value;
    endif;

    return false;
}


// Function: mysql_sess_write()
// mysql_sess_write() writes the information to the MySQL database.

function mysql_sess_write($key, $val) {
    GLOBAL $sess_life, $session_table;

    // set expiration time
    $expiration = time() + $sess_life;

    $query = "INSERT INTO $session_table VALUES('$key', '$expiration',
            '$value')";
    $result = mysql_query($query);

    // if the insert query failed because of the primary key already exists,
    // perform an update instead.

    if (! $result) :
    $query = "UPDATE $session_table SET sess_expiration = '$expiration',
                        sess_value='$value' WHERE sess_key = '$key'";
            $result = mysql_query($result);
    endif;
}

// Function: mysql_sess_destroy()
// mysql_sess_destroy() deletes all table rows having the session key = $sess_id

function mysql_sess_destroy($sess_id) {
    GLOBAL $session_table;

    $query = "DELETE FROM $session_table WHERE sess_key = '$sess_id'";
    $result = mysql_result($query);
```

```
        return $result;
}


// Function: mysql_sess_gc()
// mysql_sess_gc() deletes all table rows
// having an expiration < current time - session.gc_lifetime

function mysql_sess_gc($max_lifetime) {
    GLOBAL $session_table;

    $query = "DELETE FROM $session_table WHERE sess_expiration < " . time();
    $result = mysql_query($query);

    return mysql_affected_rows();
}


session_set_save_handler("mysql_sess_open", "mysql_sess_close", "mysql_sess_read",
"mysql_sess_write", "mysql_sess_destroy", "mysql_sess_gc");
?>
```

Once you have defined these six functions, you are then free to execute each
through its abstract name (sess_close(), sess_destroy(), sess_gc(),
sess_open(), sess_read(), or sess_write()). The convenience in this lies in the
fact that you could then build as many implementations as necessary and then
redefine session_set_save_handler() whenever necessary.

Project: Create a Visitor Log

It's often useful to record information about your site's visitors. As you already
know, this is a common practice among Web advertising agencies, portals, and
any of a number of other sites interested in learning more about their visitors.
While these systems can get enormously complicated, there are still a number of
benefits that can be obtained from the creation of a relatively simple logging system. I'll show you how to build just such a simple system using PHP, MySQL, and
cookies.

> **CAUTION**   *This project incorporates the Chapter 8 browser detection proj-
> ect. If you skipped over either Chapter 8 or the project, I would strongly rec-
> ommend at least reviewing the project code before proceeding.*

As I've already said, our system will be relatively simple, monitoring only visits to the site index page. When the visitor arrives, the PHP script checks to see whether or not a valid cookie resides on the visitor's computer. If one does, this signifies that the user has previously visited in a specified time frame (preset by the site administrator in an initialization file), and the script will not count this visit. If there is no cookie (or there is a previously set cookie that has expired), then either the user has never visited or the preset time frame between visits has been surpassed, and the information is recorded to the MySQL table. Furthermore, a new cookie is sent to the visitor's computer.

How can this script be constructed using PHP? First, you need to create the MySQL table that holds the information:

```
mysql>create table visitors (
        ->browser char(85) NOT NULL,
        ->ip char(30) NOT NULL,
        ->host char(85) NOT NULL,
        ->timeOfVisit datetime NOT NULL
        ->);
```

What is the purpose of each column? The column browser contains information directly relating to the user's browser. This information is supplied by the PHP variable $HTTP_USER_AGENT. The column ip contains the user's IP address. The column host contains ISP information from where the IP address emanates. Finally, the column timeOfVisit specifies the date and time that the visitor arrived at the site.

> **NOTE** *A powerful visitor-logging application is available for free download from the PHP resource site phpinfo.net (http://www.phpinfo.net). You can also check out a live implementation onsite. However, you'll need to dust off that French textbook before going there!*

Next, create the application initialization file, init.inc, as shown in Listing 13-9. It holds both the global variables and core functions. Notice that the functionality of the Chapter 8 project script sniffer.php is used in the viewStats() function. This script will be included along with the init.inc file when necessary. Take a moment to review this script and its comments.

Listing 13-9: Creating the application initialization file (init.inc)

```php
<?
// file: init.inc
// purpose: initialization file for Visitor Logging project

// Database connection variables
$host = "localhost";
$user = "web";
$pswd = "4tf9zzzf";

// database name
$database = "myTracker";

// polls table name
$visitors_table = "visitors";

// Connect to the MySQL Server
@mysql_pconnect($host, $user, $pswd) or die("Couldn't connect to MySQL server!");

// Select the database
@mysql_select_db($database) or die("Couldn't select $database database!");

// Number of recent visitors to display in table
$maxNumVisitors = "5";

// Cookie Name. You can set this to whatever you wish.
// However, the current setting will work just fine.
$cookieName = "visitorLog";

// Value stored in the cookie.
$cookieValue="1";

/*
Timeframe between acknowledgement of subsequent visit by same user
If $timeLimit is set to 0, every user visit to that page will be recorded
regardless of the frequency. All other integer settings will be regarded as number
of SECONDS that must pass between visits in order to be recorded.
*/
$timeLimit = 3600;
```

```
// How would you like the table displayed?
$header_color = "#cbda74";
$table_color = "#000080";
$row_color = "#c0c0c0";
$font_color = "#000000";
$font_face = "Arial, Times New Roman, Verdana";
$font_size = "-1";


// function: recordUser
// purpose: Record user Information in the MySQL table $visitors_table
function recordUser() {

    GLOBAL $visitors_table, $HTTP_USER_AGENT, $REMOTE_ADDR, $REMOTE_HOST;

/*
If the visitor is operating on the internal site server, set the $REMOTE_HOST to
'localhost'. Alternatively, you may want to eliminate the recording of all
internal visitors, since it's likely to be yourself or another development team
member.
/*
    if ($REMOTE_HOST == "") :
        $REMOTE_HOST = "localhost";
    endif;

    // format a valid MySQL datetime format
    $timestamp = date("Y-m-d H:i:s");

    // Insert the user data into the MySQL table
    $query = "INSERT INTO $visitors_table VALUES
            ('$HTTP_USER_AGENT', '$REMOTE_ADDR',
             '$REMOTE_HOST', '$timestamp')";

    $result = @mysql_query($query);

} // recordUser

// function: viewStats
// purpose: Extract and format information  in the MySQL table $visitors_table
function viewStats() {

    // Include some global variables
    GLOBAL $visitors_table, $maxNumVisitors, $table_color, $header_color;
```

```
        GLOBAL $row_color, $font_color, $font_face, $font_size;

        // Select the most recent $maxNumVisitors from the MySQL table.
        $query = "SELECT browser, ip, host, timeOfVisit FROM $visitors_table
                     ORDER BY timeOfVisit desc LIMIT 0, $maxNumVisitors";

        $result = @mysql_query($query);

        // format and print the retrieved data
        print "<table cellpadding=\"2\" cellspacing=\"1\" width = \"800\" border =
        \"0\" bgcolor=\"$table_color\">";
        print "<tr bgcolor= \"$header_color\">
              <th>Browser</th><th>IP</th><th>Host</th><th>TimeofVisit</th>
              </tr>";

        while($row = mysql_fetch_array($result)) :

            // These functions are in 'sniffer.inc'
            list ($browse_type, $browse_version) = browser_info ($row["browser"]);
            $op_sys = opsys_info ($row["browser"]);

            print "<tr bgcolor=\"$row_color\">";
            print "<td><font color=\"$font_color\" face=\"$font_face\"
            size=\"$font_size\">";
            print "$browse_type $browse_version - $op_sys</font></td>";
            print "<td><font color=\"$font_color\" face=\"$font_face\"
            size=\"$font_size\">".$row["ip"]."</font></td>";
            print "<td><font color=\"$font_color\" face=\"$font_face\"
            size=\"$font_size\">".$row["host"]."</font></td>";
            print "<td><font color=\"$font_color\" face=\"$font_face\"
            size=\"$font_size\">";
            print $row["TimeofVisit"]."</font></td>";
            print "</tr>";

        endwhile;
        print "</table>";
} // viewStats
?>
```

Next, insert the script you see in Listing 13-10; it will be used to check for a valid cookie and call the recordUser() function when necessary. I'll include this code along with a very simple index file entitled "index.php."

Listing 13-10: Checking for a valid cookie (index.php)

```
<?
include("init.inc");
// If no valid cookie is found
if (! isset($$cookieName)) :
    // Set a new cookie
    setcookie($cookieName, $cookieValue, time()+$timeLimit);
    // Record the visitor information
    recordUser();
endif;
?>

<html>
<head>
<title>Welcome to My Site!</title>
</head>
<body bgcolor="#c0c0c0" text="#000000" link="#808040" vlink="#808040"
alink="#808040">
Welcome to my site. <a href = "visitors.php">Check out who else has recently
visited</a>.
</body>
</html>
```

How is the information that is stored in the MySQL database viewed in the browser? This is accomplished simply by placing the function viewStats()in a separate file(visitors.php), as shown here:

```
<html>
<?
// Include browser detection functionality
include("sniffer.inc");
// Include the initialization file
include("init.inc");
?>
<head>
<title>Most recent <?=$maxNumVisitors;?> visitors</title>
</head>
<body bgcolor="#ffffff" text="#000000" link="#808040" vlink="#808040"
alink="#808040">
<?
viewStats();
?>
</body>
</html>
```

Alternatively, you could place the entire HTML code in the `viewStats()` function and then just include sniffer.inc, init.inc, and a call to `viewStats()` in a separate file. It depends on how much you would like to consolidate the formatting of the page. Using the current table format settings in init.inc, a sample output produced by `viewStats()` is shown in Figure 13-1.

Browser	IP	Host	TimeofVisit
Netscape 4.75 - Linux	134.43.112.41	host12.cob.ohio-state.edu	2000-10-16 12:16:00
Opera 4.02 - Windows	212.23.456.123	nat-7.cat.com	2000-10-16 11:55:00
IE 5.0 - Windows	62.4.156.931	paris11-nas4-46-208.dial.proxad.net	2000-10-16 11:24:00
IE 5.0 - Windows	213.43.48.52	ppp-127.dialup.osu.edu	2000-10-16 11:21:00
IE 5.0 - Windows	245.12.234.512	ca.ol23.att.net	2000-10-16 11:20:00

Figure 13-1. Sample output produced by `viewStats()`

There are many modifications that you could make to this script to expand its practicality. One commonly used way to track visitors is to assign an identification number to each page that you would like to log and then track users as they navigate from page to page. This could be accomplished using the above project by simply expanding your MySQL table to include a column that stores a page identification number. Then modify the `recordUser()` function to have an input parameter from which this ID number could be passed in for recording. You could then vary each cookie to hold that page ID and check for that specific cookie as the visitor requests each logged page.

What's Next?

This chapter introduced one of the most exciting features of the PHP language: session handling. In particular, the following topics were covered:

- Cookie basics

- Cookies and PHP

- Unique identification numbers

- User registration scenarios

- Introduction to sessions

- The php.ini session parameters

- PHP's predefined session functions

- The `session_set_save_handler()` function

- A visitor-logging application

Sessions offer an enormous administrative advantage to developers interested in creating truly user-oriented Web sites. I strongly urge you to experiment with PHP's session-handling functionality, as I think you will find it particularly useful.

This chapter concludes Part II of this book. Part III, "Advanced PHP," begins with a survey of PHP and XML integration. Stay tuned, as things are about to get really interesting.

Advanced PHP

PART THREE

PHP and XML

It can hardly be argued that the Web has not vastly changed the landscape on which we share information. The sheer vastness of this electronic network has made the establishment of certain standards not only a convenience, but a requirement if organizations are ever going to exploit the Web to its fullest capability. XML (eXtensible Markup Language) is one such standard, providing a means for the seamless interchange of data between organizations and their applications. The implications of this are many, resulting in the facilitation of media-independent publishing, electronic commerce, customized data retrieval, and many other data-oriented services.

In the first part of this chapter, I provide a general introduction to XML, highlighting the general syntactical elements that comprise the language. The second half of this chapter is dedicated to PHP's XML-parsing capabilities, elaborating on its predefined XML functionality and the language's general XML-parsing process. This material is geared toward providing you with a better understanding of both why XML is so useful and how you can begin coming to terms with how PHP can be used to develop useful and interesting XML-based applications.

Before delving directly into the issue of XML, many newcomers to this subject may find it useful to learn more about the history behind the concepts that ultimately contributed to the development of the XML standard.

A Brief Introduction to Markup

As its name so implies, HTML (HyperText Markup Language) is what is known as a *markup language*. The term *markup* is defined as the general description for the document annotation that, instead of being displayed to whatever media the document is destined for, is used for describing *how* parts of that document should be formatted. For example, you may want a particular word to be **boldfaced** and another *italicized*. You may wish to use a particular font for one paragraph and a larger font size for a header. As I type this paragraph, my word processor is using its own form of *markup* in order to properly present the formatting as I specify it to be. Therefore, the word processor is using its own particular *formatting markup language* implementation. In short, the markup language used by my word processor is a means for specifying the visual format of the text in my document.

There are many types of markup languages in the world today. For example, communication applications use a form of markup to specify the meaning of each group of 1's and 0's sent over the Internet. Humans use a sort of markup language when underlining or crossing out words in a textbook. Regardless of its format, a markup language accomplishes two important tasks:

- **It defines what is considered to be valid markup syntax.** In the case of the HTML specification, *<b>text</b>* would be a valid markup statement, but *<xR5t>text</x4rt>* would be invalid, due to mismatching opening and closing tags.

- **It defines what is meant by a particular valid markup syntax.** Surely you know that *<b>text</b>* is an HTML command to format in boldface the word *text*. That is an example of the markup defining what is to result when a particular markup *document component* is declared.

HTML is a particularly popular markup language, as is obvious when watching the explosive growth of the Web over the past few years. But how was this language derived? Who thought to use tags such as <b> and </b> to specify meaning in a document? The answer to this lies in HTML's forefather, SGML (Standard Generalized Markup Language).

The Standard Generalized Markup Language (SGML)

SGML is an internationally recognized standard for exchanging electronic information between varied hardware and software implementations. Judging from its name, you would think that SGML is some sort of language. This is perhaps a bit misleading, since SGML is actually defined as a formalized set of rules from which languages can be created. Two particularly popular languages derived from SGML are HTML and XML. As you already know, HTML is a platform- and hardware-independent language used to format and display text. The same is true of XML.

SGML was born out of the necessity to share data between different applications and operating systems. As far back as the 1960s, this was already fast becoming a problem for computer users. Realizing the constraints of the many nonstandard markup languages, three IBM researchers, Charles Goldfarb, Ed Mosher, and Ray Lorie, began unearthing three general concepts that would make it possible to begin sharing documents across operating systems and applications:

- **The document-processing programs must all be able to communicate using a common formatting language.** This makes sense, since we know from our own experiences that communication among individuals speaking different languages is difficult. However, if we are all provided with the same set of syntax and semantics, communication becomes much easier.

- **The formatting language should be specific to its purpose.** The ability to custom-build a language based on a particular set of predefined rules frees the developer from having to depend on a third-party implementation of what is assumed that the end user requires.

- **The document format must closely follow a set of specific rules.** These rules relate to such things as the number and label of the language constructs used in the document. A standard document format ensures that all users know exactly what the structural outline of that document contains. This last pillar of document sharing is particularly important because it does *not* specify how the document is displayed. Rather, it specifies how the document is structurally formatted. The set of rules used to create this document format is better known as a *document type definition*, or DTD.

These three rules form the basis for SGML's predecessor, Generalized Markup Language, or GML. Research and development of GML continued over the next decade or so, until SGML was born out of an agreement made by an international group of developers.

As the need for a common ground for information exchange became increasingly prevalent in the 1980s, SGML soon became the industry standard (1986 was the year that SGML became an ISO standard) for making it happen. In fact, the standard is still going strong today, with agencies in charge of maintaining enormous amounts of information relying on SGML as a dependable and convenient means for data storage. To put it in perspective, the U.S. Patent and Trademark Office (http://www.uspto.gov), U.S. Internal Revenue Service (http://www.irs.gov), and Library of Congress (http://lcweb.loc.gov) are all prominent users of SGML in their mission-critical applications. Just imagine the amount of documentation that each of these agencies handles each year!

> **TIP** *Arguably the best resource on the Internet for learning more about SGML, XML, and various other markup languages is the Robin Cover/OASIS XML Cover Pages at http://www.oasis-open.org/cover/.*

The idea of passing hypertext documents via a Web browser, as was envisioned by Tim Berners-Lee, did not require many of the features offered by the robust SGML implementation. This resulted in the creation of a well-known markup language called HTML.

The Advent of HTML

Interestingly, the concept of the World Wide Web fit only too perfectly in the idea of using a generalized markup language to facilitate information exchange in an environment harboring a multitude of different hardware, operating system, and software implementations. And in fact, Berners-Lee must have had this matter in mind, as he modeled the first version of HTML after the SGML standard. HTML shares several of SGML's characteristics, including a simple generalized tag set and the angled bracket convention. These simple documents could be effectively read on any computer system, offering a means for viewing text documents. And the rest is history.

However, HTML suffers from the major drawback that it does not offer developers the capability of creating their own document types. This resulted in the onset of the "browser wars," where browser developers begin building their own enhancements to the HTML language. These HTML add-ons severely detracted from the idea of working with a unique HTML standard, not to mention wreaking havoc for developers wishing to create cross-browser Web sites. Furthermore, years of a lax definition standard resulted in developers greatly stretching the boundaries of the original intent of the language. I would not be surprised if the vast majority of Web pages on the Internet today failed to comply with the current HTML specification.

The W3C's (`http://www.w3.org`) reaction to this rapidly worsening situation began with a concerted attempt to steer HTML development back toward the right path: that is, a return to the underlying foundations of SGML. The result of their concentrated efforts? XML.

Irrefutable Evidence of Evolution: XML

XML is essentially the culmination of the efforts of the W3C to offer an Internet-based standard that is in conformance with the three major principles of SGML, first introduced in the previous section, "The Standard Generalized Markup Language (SGML)." Like SGML, XML is not in itself a language; it too is composed of a standard set of guidelines from which other languages can be derived. More specifically, XML is the product of the conglomeration of three separate specifications:

- **XML (Extensible Markup Language)**: This specification defines the core XML syntax.

- **XSL (Extensible Style Language)**: XSL is a specification geared toward separating page style from page content through the practice of applying separate style sheets to documents to satisfy specific formatting requirements.

- **XLL (Extensible Linking Language)**: XLL specifies how links between re-sources are represented.

XML not only makes it possible for developers to create their own custom languages for Internet application production; it also allows for the validation of these documents for conformance to the XML specification. Furthermore, XML truly promotes the idea of implementation-independent data, since the XSL can be used to specify exactly how the document will be displayed. For example, assume that you have reformatted your Web site to be stored as XML source. You could use a "wireless" style sheet to format the XML source for use on a PDA, such as a Palm Pilot, and another ""personal computer" style sheet to format it for display on a regular computer monitor. Remember, it's the same XML source, just formatted differently to suit the user's device.

> **NOTE**   *The Wireless Markup Language (WML) is an example of a popular language derived from XML.*

An Introduction to XML Syntax

Those of you already familiar with SGML or HTML will find the structure of an XML document to be nothing new. Consider Listing 14-1, which illustrates a simple XML document.

Listing 14-1: A simple XML document

```
<?xml version="1.0"?>
<!DOCTYPE cookbook SYSTEM "cookbook.dtd">
<cookbook>
<recipe category="italian">
<title>Spaghetti alla Carbonara</title>
<description>This traditional Italian dish is sure to please even the most
discriminating critic.</description>
<ingredients>
<ingredient>2 large eggs</ingredient>
<ingredient>4 strips of bacon</ingredient>
<ingredient>1 clove garlic</ingredient>
<ingredient>12 ounces spaghetti</ingredient>
<ingredient>3 tablespoons olive oil</ingredient>
</ingredients>
<process>
<step>Combine oil and bacon in large skillet over medium heat. Cook until bacon is
brown and crisp.</step>
<step>Whisk eggs in bowl. Set aside.</step>
```

```
<step>Cook pasta in large pot of boiling water to taste, stirring occasionally.
Add salt as necessary.</step>
<step>Drain pasta and return to pot, adding whisked eggs. Stir over medium-low
heat for 2-3 minutes.</step>
<step>Mix in bacon. Season with salt and pepper to taste.</step>
</process>
</recipe>
</cookbook>
```

There you have it! Your first XML document. Now turn your attention toward the following components of just such a document, elaborating on parts of Listing 14-1 to illustrate their usage:

- XML prolog

- Tag elements

- Attributes

- Entity references

- Processing instructions

- Comments

XML Prolog

All XML documents must begin with a document prolog. This line basically says that XML will be used to build the document and which version of XML will be used to do so. Since the current XML version is 1.0, all of your XML documents should begin with:

```
<?xml version="1.0">
```

The next line of Listing 14-1 points to an external DTD. Don't worry too much about this right now. I introduce DTDs in detail in the upcoming section "The Document Type Definition (DTD)."

```
<!DOCTYPE cookbook SYSTEM "cookbook.dtd">
```

The rest of Listing 14-1 contains elements very similar to those of an HTML document. The first element, cookbook, is what is known as the root element, since its tag set encloses all of the other tags in the document. Of course, you can name your root element whatever you like. The important thing to keep in mind is that its tag set encloses all other elements.

There are other instructions that could be placed in the prolog. For example, you could extend the first above-described declaration by specifying that the document is complete by itself:

```
<?xml version="1.0" standalone="yes">
```

Setting standalone to "yes" tells the parser that no other files should be imported into this document, such as a DTD.

Although this extension and others are certainly useful, I'll keep document syntax to a minimum in order to better illustrate the central topic of this chapter: how PHP and XML work together.

Elements

The rest of the document consists largely of varied elements and corresponding data. Elements are easily identified, as they are enclosed within angle brackets like those in HTML markup. An element may be empty, consisting of only one tag set, or it may contain information, in which case it must have an opening and closing tag. If it is not empty, then the tag names describe the nature of the informational data (also known as CDATA) enclosed in the tags. As you can see from Listing 14-1, these tags are very similar to those in an HTML document. However, there are a few important distinctions to keep in mind:

- All XML elements must consist of both an opening and closing tag.

- Those elements that are not empty consist of both opening and closing tags. Those tags that would not logically have a closing tag can use an alternative form of syntax <element />. At first, you may wonder what tag would not have a complement. Keep in mind that certain HTML formatting tags like <br>, <hr>, and <img> don't have closing tags. Tags of the same format can be created in XML documents.

- **XML elements must be properly nested**. Listing 14-1 illustrates an XML document that is properly nested; that is, no element tags appear where they shouldn't. For example, you couldn't do the following:

```
<title>Spaghetti alla Carbonara

<ingredients></title>
```

Other than not making sense, it just doesn't make for good form. Subsequent parsing of this XML document would fail.

- **XML elements are case-sensitive** Those of you used to cranking out HTML at 3 a.m. won't like this rule too much. In XML, the tag <tag> is different from <Tag> is different from <TAG>. Get used to it, or this will soon drive you crazy.

Attributes

Just as HTML tags can be assigned attributes, so can XML tags. In short, *attributes* provide further information about the content that could later be used for formatting or processing the XML. These attributes are assigned in name-value pairs, and unlike in HTML, XML attributes *must* be properly enclosed in either single or double quotation marks, or subsequent parsing will fail. Listing 14-1 contains one such element attribute:

```
<recipe category="italian">
```

This attribute basically says that the category of this particular recipe is italian. This could facilitate subsequent grouping and organizational operations.

Entity References

Entities are a way to facilitate document maintenance by referencing some content through the use of some keyword. This keyword could point to something as simple as an abbreviation expansion or as complicated as an entirely new piece of XML content. The convenience in entities lies in the fact that they can be used repeatedly throughout an XML document. When this document is later parsed, all references to that entity will be replaced with the content referred to in the entity declaration. The entity declaration is placed in the DTD referred to by the XML document.

You can refer to an entity in your XML document by calling its name, preceded by an ampersand (&), and followed by a semicolon (;). For example, assume that you had declared an entity that pointed to copyright information. Throughout the XML document, you could then refer to this entity by using the following syntax:

```
&Copyright;
```

Using this in an applicable manner, a line of the XML document might read:

```
<footer>
…various other footer information…
&Copyright;
</footer>
```

Like variables or templates, entities are useful when a certain piece of information may change in the future or continued explicit referencing of that information is too tedious a process to repeat. I'll delve further into the details of referencing and declaring entities in the upcoming section "The Document Type Definition (DTD)."

Processing Instructions

Processing instructions, commonly referred to as *PIs,* are external commands that are used by the application that is working with the XML document. The general syntax for a PI is:

```
<?PITarget instructions?>
```

PITarget specifies which application should make use of the ensuing instructions. For example, if you wanted PHP to execute a few commands in an XML document, you could make use of a PI:

```
<?php print "Today's date is: ".date("m-d-Y");?>
```

Processing instructions are useful because they make it possible for several applications to work with the same document in unison.

Comments

Comments are always a useful feature of any language. XML comment syntax is exactly the same as that of HTML comment syntax:

```
<!– Descriptive comments go here –>
```

Okay, so you've seen your first XML document. However, there is another very important aspect of creating valid XML documents: the document type definition, or DTD.

The Document Type Definition (DTD)

A *DTD* is a set of syntax rules that form the basis for validation of an XML document. It explicitly details an XML's document structure, elements, and element attributes, in addition to various other pieces of information relevant to any XML document derived from that DTD.

Keep in mind that it is not a requirement that an XML document has an accompanying DTD. If a DTD does exist, then the XML system can use this DTD as a reference for how to interpret the XML document. If a DTD is not present, it is assumed that the XML system will be able to apply its own rules to the document. However, chances are that you want to include a DTD with your XML document to verify its structure and interpretation.

A DTD may be placed directly in the XML document itself, referenced via a URL or via some combination of both methods. If you wanted to place the DTD directly in the XML document, you would do this by defining the DTD directly after the prolog as follows:

```
<!DOCTYPE root_element_name [
…various declarations…
] >
```

The reference to root_element_name will correspond to the name of the root element surrounding your XML document. The section specified by "various declarations" is where the element, attribute, and various other declarations are defined.

Chances are you will want to place your DTD in a separate file to facilitate modularity. Therefore, let's begin by showing how a DTD can be referenced from within an XML document. This is accomplished with a simple command:

```
<!DOCTYPE root_element_name SYSTEM "some_dtd.dtd">
```

As was the case with the internal DTD declaration, root_element_name refers to the name of the root element surrounding your XML document. The keyword SYSTEM refers to the fact that some_dtd.dtd is located on the local server. You could also point to some_dtd.dtd by referring to its absolute URL. Finally, the URL referenced in quotations points to the external DTD. This DTD could reside either locally or on some other server.

So how would you create a DTD for Listing 14-1? First of all, you want to call the DTD from within the XML document. As discussed in the previous section, the DTD is referenced with the following command:

```
<!DOCTYPE cookbook SYSTEM "cookbook.dtd">
```

Looking back to Listing 14-1, you see that cookbook is the `root_element_name`. The name of the DTD being referenced is cookbook.dtd. The DTD itself is shown in Listing 14-2. A line-by-line description of the listing ensues.

Listing 14-2: DTD for Listing 14-1, entitled "cookbook.dtd"

```
<?xml version="1.0"?>
<!DOCTYPE cookbook [
<!ELEMENT cookbook (recipe+)>
<!ELEMENT recipe (title, description, ingredients, process)>
<!ELEMENT title (#PCDATA)>
<!ELEMENT description (#PCDATA)>
<!ELEMENT ingredients (ingredient+)>
<!ELEMENT ingredient (#PCDATA)>
<!ELEMENT process (step+)>
<!ELEMENT step (#PCDATA)>
   <!ATTLIST recipe category CDATA  #REQUIRED>
] >
```

So what does this rather strange-looking document mean? Although seemingly cryptic at first, it is actually rather simple. Let's go over Listing 14-2 line by line:

```
<?xml version="1.0"?>
```

The first line is essentially the XML prolog. You have already been introduced to this.

```
<!DOCTYPE cookbook [
```

The second line states that a DTD is beginning, and the DTD title is cookbook.

```
<!ELEMENT cookbook (recipe+)>
```

The third line refers to an actual tag element in the XML document, in this case the root element, which is cookbook. Immediately following is the word recipe enclosed in parentheses. This means that enclosed in the cookbook tags will be a *child* tag element named recipe. The plus sign following recipe means that there will be at least one set of the recipe tags in the *parent* cookbook tags.

```
<!ELEMENT recipe (title, description, ingredients, process)>
```

The fourth line defines the recipe tag. It states that in the recipe tag, four distinct child tags will be found: title, description, ingredients, and process. Since no occurrence indicators (more about occurrence indicators in the following section, "DTD Components") follow any of the tag declarations, it is assumed that one set of each will appear in the recipe tag.

```
<!ELEMENT title (#PCDATA)>
```

Here we happen on the first tag definition that does not contain any nested tags. Instead it is said to hold #PCDATA. The keyword #PCDATA stands for character data, that is, any data that is not considered to be markup oriented.

```
<!ELEMENT description (#PCDATA)>
```

The element definition of description, like title, states that the description tags will not hold anything else except character data.

```
<!ELEMENT ingredients (ingredient+)>
```

The definition of the ingredients element states that it will contain one or more tags named ingredient. Check out Listing 14-1, and you will realize how logical this is.

```
<!ELEMENT ingredient (#PCDATA)>
```

Since the tag element ingredient refers to a single ingredient in the list, it only makes sense that this element will contain character data.

```
<!ELEMENT process (step+)>
```

The element process is expected to contain one or more instances of the element step.

```
<!ELEMENT step (#PCDATA)>
```

The element step, like ingredient, is a component of a larger list. Therefore, it is expected to contain character data.

```
<!ATTLIST recipe category CDATA  #REQUIRED>
```

Notice that the recipe element in Listing 14-1 contains an attribute. This attribute, category, refers to a general category in which the recipe would fall, in this case Italian. Note that both the element name and the attribute name are specified in this ATTLIST definition. Furthermore, because of the fact that for referential purposes it would be useful to categorize every single recipe, we specify that this attribute is #REQUIRED.

```
] >
```

This final line simply closes the DTD definition. You must always properly enclose the definition, or an error will occur.

Let's finish this section with a synopsis of the major components of a typical DTD:

- Element type declarations

- Attribute declarations

- ID, IDREF, and IDREFS

- Entity declarations

You were introduced to several of these components in the preceding review of Listing 14-2. Now I'll cover each component in further detail.

Element Declarations

All elements used in an XML document must be properly defined if a DTD accompanies the document. You've already seen two commonly used element definition variations: defining an element to contain other elements, and defining an element to contain character data. To recap, the following definition of the tag element description specifies that it will contain only character data:

```
<!ELEMENT description (#PCDATA)>
```

The following definition of the element process specifies that it will contain exactly one occurrence of the element named step:

```
<!ELEMENT process (step)>
```

Of course, it might not make too much sense to just have one step in a process, and chances are you would have more. Therefore you can use the occurrence indicator to specify that there will be *at least* one occurrence of the element step:

```
<!ELEMENT process (step+)>
```

You can specify the frequency of occurrence of elements in several different ways. A listing of available element operators is shown in Table 14-1.

Table 14-1. Element Operators

INDICATOR	MEANING
?	Zero or one occurrences
*	Zero or more occurrences
+	One or more occurrences
[none]	Exactly one time
		Either element
,	The first element must follow the second element.

If you intended on including several different tags in a specific tag element, you delimit each with a comment in the element definition:

```
<!ELEMENT recipe (title, description, ingredients, process)>
```

Since there are no occurrence indicators, each of these tags must appear *only once.*

You can also use Boolean logic to further specify the definition of an element. For example, assume that you were dealing with recipes that always specified pasta accompanied with one or more types of either cheese or meat. You could define the ingredient element as follows:

```
<!ELEMENT ingredient (pasta+, (cheese | meat)+)>
```

Since you always want the pasta tag to appear, you place the plus (+) occurrence indicator after it. Then, either the cheese *or* meat element is expected; therefore you separate them with a vertical bar and proceed the parentheses block with a plus (+), since one or the other is always expected.

There are many other element definition variations. This is only the beginning. However, what has been covered thus far should suffice for you to effectively follow the examples presented throughout the rest of this chapter.

Attribute Declarations

Element attributes describe what kind of value an element may have. Like HTML tag elements, XML elements may have zero, one, or several attributes. The general syntax for an attribute declaration is:

```
<!ATTLIST element_name
attribute_name1 datatype1 flag1
...
>
```

Where `element_name` is the name of the tag element. The attributes for this tag element then ensue. There are three main components of each attribute, the name, specified by `attribute_name1`; its datatype, specified by `datatype1`; and a flag specifying how that attribute value is handled, specified by `flag1`. The ellipsis (...) signifies that more than one attribute declaration can be placed here.

You've already seen a simple example of an attribute declaration in Listing 14-2:

```
<!ATTLIST recipe category CDATA  #REQUIRED>
```

However, as you can see from the general syntax definition, you can also simultaneously declare multiple attributes. For example, suppose that you wanted to assign the recipe element not only a category attribute, but a difficulty (in preparation) attribute as well. This would be a multiple-attribute declaration. You could declare both of these attributes in the same list:

```
<!ATTLIST recipe category CDATA  #REQUIRED
                 difficulty CDATA  #REQUIRED>
```

You are not required to format the declaration as I've done; However, it improves readability over just letting the declarations run together on a single line. Also, since both attributes are required, you cannot just use the recipe tag with only one or the other; both must be used. For example, this would be wrong:

```
<recipe difficulty="hard">
```

Why? Because the category attribute is not present. However, this would be correct:

```
<recipe category="Italian" difficulty="hard">
```

There are actually three different flags that can be used to indicate how an attribute value is handled. These flags and their descriptions are shown in Table 14-2.

Table 14-2. Attribute Flags

FLAG	DESCRIPTION
#FIXED	Specifies that the attribute can only be assigned one specific value for every element instance in the document.
#IMPLIED	Specifies that a default attribute value can be used if the attribute is not included with the element.
#REQUIRED	Specifies that the attribute is not optional and must always be present with each element instance.

Attribute Types

An element attribute can be declared as one of a number of types. Each type is described in further detail in this chapter.

CDATA Attributes

Many times, you will be interested in just ensuring that the attributes contain general character data. These are known as CDATA attributes. The following example was already shown at the beginning of this section:

```
<!ATTLIST recipe category CDATA #REQUIRED>
```

ID, IDREF, and IDREFS Attributes

Throughout several chapters of this book I introduced the idea of using identification numbers to uniquely identify data, such as user or product information stored in a database table. The use of unique IDs is also particularly useful in the world of XML, since cross-referencing information across documents is common not only in general information management but also on the World Wide Web (via hyperlinks).

Element IDs are assigned the ID attribute. For example, assume that you want to assign each recipe a unique identification number. The DTD syntax might look like the following:

```
...
<!ELEMENT recipe (title, description, ingredients, process)>
<!ATTLIST recipe recipe-id ID #REQUIRED>
<!ELEMENT recipe-ref EMPTY>
<!ATTLIST recipe-ref go IDREF #REQUIRED>
...
```

You could then declare the recipe element in a document as follows:

```
<recipe recipe-id="ital003">
<title>Spaghetti alla Carbonara</title>
...
```

The identifier `ital003` uniquely identifies this recipe. Keep in mind that since `recipe-id` is of type ID, the same identifier cannot be used in any other recipe `recipe-id` value, or the document will be invalid. Now suppose that later on you want to reference this recipe somewhere else, for example, in a user's list of favorite recipes. This is where the element cross-reference and the IDREF attribute come into play. IDREF can be assigned an ID value for referring to the element specified by ID, kind of like a hyperlink refers to a page specified by a particular URL. Consider the following XML snippet:

```
<favoriteRecipes>
<recipe-ref go="ital003">
</favoriteRecipes>
```

Once the XML document is parsed, the `recipe-ref` element would be replaced with a more user-friendly reference pointing to the recipe having that ID, such as the recipe title. Also, it would probably be formatted as a hyperlink to facilitate navigation to that recipe.

Enumerated Attributes

You can also specify a restricted list of potential values for an attribute. This would actually work quite well to improve the above declaration, since you could assume that you would have a specific list of recipe categories and could limit the levels of difficulty to a select few adjectives. Let's refine the previous declaration to read:

```
<!ATTLIST recipe category (Italian | French | Japanese | Chinese)  #REQUIRED
                          difficulty (easy | medium |  hard) #REQUIRED>
```

Notice that when using restricted value sets, you are no longer required to include CDATA. This is because all of the values are already of CDATA format.

Default Enumerated Attributes

It is sometimes useful to declare a default value. Chances are you have probably done this in the past when building forms that have drop-down lists. For example, if the majority of your recipe submissions are from Italians, chances are the majority of the recipes will be of the Italian category. You could set Italian as the default category like this:

```
<!ATTLIST recipe category (Italian | French | Japanese | Chinese) "Italian">
```

In the above declaration, if no other category value has been set, then the category will automatically default to Italian.

Entities and Entity Attributes

Not all of the data in an XML document is necessarily text based. Binary data such as graphics may appear as well. This data can be referred to by using entity attributes. You could specify that a (presumably) graphic named recipePicture will appear within the description element as follows:

```
<!ATTLIST description recipePicture ENTITY #IMPLIED>
```

Similarly, you could simultaneously declare several entities by using the entities attribute in place of the entity attribute. Each ENTITY value is separated by white space.

NMTOKEN and NMTOKENS Attributes

An NMTOKEN, or name token, is a string composed of a restricted range of characters. Therefore, declaring an attribute to be of type NMTOKEN would suggest that the attribute value be in accordance with the restriction posed by NMTOKEN. Typically, an NMTOKEN attribute value consists of only one word:

```
<!ATTLIST recipe category NMTOKEN  #REQUIRED>
```

Similarly, you could simultaneously declare several entities by using the NMTOKENS attribute in place of the NMTOKEN attribute. Each NMTOKEN value is separated by white space

Entity Declarations

An entity declaration works similarly to the `define` command in many programming languages, PHP included. I briefly introduced entity references in the preceding section, "An Introduction to XML Syntax." To recap, an entity reference acts as a substitute for another piece of content. When the XML document is parsed, all occurrences of this entity are replaced with the content that it represents. There are two types of entities: internal and external.

Internal Entities

Internal entities are used much like string variables are, correlating a name with a piece of text. For example, if you wanted to associate a name that pointed to your company's copyright statement you would declare the entity as follows:

```
<!ENTITY Copyright "Copyright 2000 YourCompanyName. All Rights Reserved.">
```

When the document is parsed, all occurrences of &Copyright are replaced with "Copyright 2000 YourCompanyName. All Rights Reserved." Any XML in the replacement content would be parsed as if it had originally appeared in the document!

An internal reference works fine when you plan on using an entity for a specific or limited number of XML documents. However, if your company is processing quite a few XML documents, then perhaps using an external entity is your best bet.

External Entities

External entities also can be used to reference content in another file. This entity type can reference text, but it can also reference binary data, such as a graphic. Referring back to the previous copyright example, you may want to store this information in another file to facilitate its later modification. You could declare an external entity pointing to it as follows:

```
<!ENTITY Copyright SYSTEM http://yoursite.com/administration/copyright.xml">
```

When the XML document is later parsed, any references to &Copyright; will be substituted with the content in the copyright.xml document. This information will be parsed just as if it originally appeared in the document.

It is also useful to use external entities to point to graphics. For example, if you wanted to place a logo in certain XML documents, you could declare an external entity pointing to it, as shown here:

```
<!ENTITY food_picture SYSTEM http://yoursite.com/food/logo.gif>
```

Just as is the case with the copyright example, any reference to &food_picture will be replaced with the graphic to which the external entity points. However, since this data is binary and not text, it will not be parsed.

XML References

Although the preceding XML introduction is sufficient for understanding the basic framework of XML documents, there is still quite a bit more to be learned. The following links point to some of the more comprehensive XML resources available on the Internet:

- `http://www.w3.org/XML/`

- `http://www.xml.com/pub/ArticlesbyTopic`

- `http://www.ibm.com/developer/xml/`

- `http://www.oasis-open.org/cover/`

The remainder of this chapter is devoted to how PHP can be used to parse XML documents. Although it seems complicated (parsing any type of document can be a daunting task), I think you'll be rather surprised at how easy it is once you've learned the basic strategy used by PHP for doing so.

PHP and XML

PHP's XML functionality is implemented using James Clark's Expat (XML Parser Toolkit) package, at http://www.jclark.com/xml/. Expat comes packaged with Apache 1.3.7 and later, so you won't need to specifically download it if you are using a recent version of Apache. To use PHP's XML functionality, you'll need to configure PHP using –with-xml.

> **NOTE** *Expat 2.0 is currently being developed by Clark Cooper. More information is at http://expat.sourceforge.net/.*

Although at first the idea of parsing XML data using PHP (or any language) seems intimidating, much of the work is already done for you by PHP's predefined functionality. All that you are left to do is define new functions tailored to your own DTD definitions and then apply these functions to PHP's easy-to-follow XML parsing process.

Before I begin introducing PHP's XML function set, take a moment to reconsider the very basic pieces that comprise an XML document. This will help you understand the mechanics behind why certain functions are an indispensable part of any XML parser. On the most general level, there are nine components of an XML document:

- Opening tags

- Attributes

- Character data

- Closing tags

- Processing instructions

- Notation declarations

- External entity references

- Unparsed entities

- Other components (comments, XML declaration, etc.)

Given these nine components, in order to effectively parse an XML document, functions need to be defined that handle each of these components. Once they are defined, you use PHP's various predefined callback functions that act to integrate your custom handler functions into the overall XML parsing process. You can think of PHP's general XML parsing process as a series of five steps:

1. Create your customer handler functions. Of course, if you intend on working with XML documents in a consistent fashion, you will only need to create these functions once and subsequently concentrate on maintaining them.

2. Create the XML parser that will be used to parse the document. This is accomplished by calling `xml_parser_create()`.

3. Use the predefined callback functions to register your handler functions with the XML parser.

4. Open the XML file, read the data contained in it, and pass this data to the XML parser. Note that to parse the data, you only need to call `xml_parse()`! This function is responsible for implicitly calling all of the previously defined handler functions.

5. Free up the XML parser, essentially clearing the data from it. This is accomplished by calling `xml_parser_free()`.

The purpose of each of these steps will become apparent as you read the next section, "PHP's Handler Functions."

PHP's Handler Functions

There are eight predefined set functions that act to register the functions that will be used to handle the various components of an XML document:

Keep in mind that you *must* define the functions that will be tied into the handler functions; otherwise an error will occur. Each predefined register function and the specifications for the corresponding handler functions are presented in this section.

xml_set_character_data_handler()

This function registers the handler function that works with character data. Its syntax is:

```
int xml_set_character_data_handler(int parser, string characterHandler)
```

The input parameter parser refers to the XML parser handler. The input parameter characterHandler refers to the name of the function created to handle the character data. The function specified by characterHandler is defined here:

```
function characterHandler(int parser, string data) {
...
}
```

The input parameter parser refers to the XML parser handler, and data to the character data that has been parsed.

xml_set_default_handler()

This function specifies the handler function that is used for all components of the XML document that do not need to be registered. Examples of these components include the XML declaration and comments. Its syntax is:

```
int xml_set_default_handler(int parser, string defaultHandler)
```

The input parameter parser refers to the XML parser handler. The input parameter defaultHandler refers to the name of the function created to handle the XML element. The function specified by defaultHandler is defined here:

```
function defaultHandler(int parser, string data) {
    ...
}
```

The input parameter parser refers to the XML parser handler, and data to the character data that will be handled by default.

xml_set_element_handler()

This function registers the handler functions that work with the parse starting and ending element tags. Its syntax is:

```
int xml_set_element_handler(int parser, string startTagHandler, string endTagHandler)
```

The input parameter parser refers to the XML parser handler. The input parameters startTagHandler and endTagHandler refer to the names of the functions created to handle the starting and ending tag elements, respectively. The function specified by startTagHandler is defined as:

```
function startTagHandler(int parser, string tagName, string attributes[]) {
    ...
}
```

The input parameter parser refers to the XML parser handler, tagName to the name of the opening tag element being parsed, and attributes to the array of attributes that may accompany the tag element.

The function specified by endTagHandler is defined as:

```
function endTagHandler(int parser, string tagName) {
    ...
}
```

The input parameter parser refers to the XML parser handler, tagName to the name of the closing tag element being parsed.

xml_set_external_entity_ref_handler()

This function registers the handler function that works with external entity references. Its syntax is:

```
int xml_set_external_entity_ref_handler(int parser, string externalHandler)
```

The input parameter `parser` refers to the XML parser handler. The input parameter `externalHandler` refers to the name of the function created to handle the external entity. The function specified by `externalHandler` is defined here:

```
function externalHandler(int parser, string entityReference, string base, string systemID, string publicID) {
…
}
```

The input parameter `parser` refers to the XML parser handler, `entityReference` to the name of the entity reference, `systemID` to the system identifier of the entity reference, and `publicID` to the public identifier of the entity reference. The parameter base is currently not used by the function, but needs to be declared anyway.

xml_set_notation_declaration_handler()

This function registers the handler function that works with notation declarations. Its syntax is:

```
int xml_set_notation_declaration_handler(int parser, string notationHandler)
```

The input parameter `parser` refers to the XML parser handler. The input parameter `notationHandler` refers to the name of the function created to handle the notation declaration. The function specified by `notationHandler` is defined here:

```
function notationHandler(int parser, string notationDeclaration, string base, string systemID, string publicID) {
…
}
```

The input parameter `parser` refers to the XML parser handler, `notationDeclaration` to the name of the notation declaration, `systemID` to the system identifier of the notation declaration, and `publicID` to the public identifier of the notation declaration. The parameter base is currently not used by the function, but needs to be declared anyway.

xml_set_object()

This function makes it possible to use the XML parser from within an object. Its syntax is:

```
void xml_set_object(int parser, object &object)
```

The input parameter parser refers to the XML parser handler, and the object reference refers to the object containing the methods used to handle the XML components. The specific purpose of this function is to identify the parser with that specific object. Typically you'll use this function in an object's constructor method, following it with the various handler function definitions:

```
class xmlDB {
VAR $xmlparser;

    function xmlDB() {
        $this->xmlparser = xml_parser_create();
        // associate the parser with the object
        xml_set_object($this->xmlparser,&$this);
        // define the callback functions
        xml_set_element_handler($this->xmlparser,"startTag","endTag");
        xml_set_character_data_handler($this->xmlparser,"characterData");
    }

. . . The handler functions startTag, endTag, characterData and others are created
here

} // end class xmlDB
```

As an exercise, try commenting out the call to xml_set_object(). You'll see that subsequent execution results in error messages regarding the inability to call the handler methods belonging to the object.

xml_set_processing_instruction_handler()

This function registers the handler function that works with processing instructions. Its syntax is:

```
xml_set_processing_instruction_handler(int parser, string processingIntHandler)
```

The input parameter parser refers to the XML parser handler. The input parameter processingHandler refers to the name of the function created to handle the processing instruction. The function specified by processingIntHandler is defined here:

```
function processingIntHandler(int parser, string processingApp, string
instruction) {

    …

}
```

The input parameter parser refers to the XML parser handler, processingApp to the name of the application that should process the instruction, and instruction to the instruction that is passed to the application.

xml_set_unparsed_entity_decl_handler()

This function registers the handler function that works with external entity references. Its syntax is:

```
int xml_set_unparsed_entity_decl_handler(int parser, string unparsedEntityHandler)
```

The input parameter parser refers to the XML parser handler. The input parameter unparsedEntityHandler refers to the name of the function created to handle the unparsed entity. The function specified by unparsedEntityHandler is defined here:

```
function unparsedEntityHandler(int parser, string entDec, string base, string
sysID, string pubID, string NName) {

    …

}
```

The input parameter parser refers to the XML parser handler, entDec to the name of the entity being defined, sysID to the system identifier of the notation declaration, and pubID to the public identifier of the notation declaration. The parameter base is currently not used by the function, but needs to be declared anyway. Finally, NName refers to the name of the notation declaration.

This concludes the introduction of the register and handler functions. However, these are not the only functions you need to effectively parse XML documents. The remainder of PHP's predefined XML functionality is presented next.

PHP's Parsing Functions

While it is not necessary to implement each one of PHP's handler functions (an XML document does not have to use every type of element), there are three functions that should be in every parsing script. These functions are described below.

xml_parser_create()

Before parsing an XML document, you must first create a parser. The syntax for doing so is:

```
int xml_parser_create([string encoding])
```

The optional input parameter encoding can be used to specify the source encoding. Currently, there are three supported source encodings:

- UTF-8

- US-ASCII

- ISO-8859-1 (Default)

Much like fopen() returns a handle to an opened file, xml_parser_create() returns a parser handle. This handle will then be passed into the various other functions throughout the parsing process. If you are simultaneously parsing several documents, you can also define multiple parsers.

xml_parse()

This function does the actual parsing of the document. Its syntax is:

```
int xml_parse(int parser, string data [int isFinal])
```

The parameter parser specifies which XML parser to use. This is the variable returned by xml_parser_create(). The optional input parameter isFinal, when set and true, tells the parser to stop. Typically this would be when the end of the file being parsed is reached.

xml_parser_free()

This function frees the resources devoted to the parser. Its syntax is:

```
int xml_parser_free(int parser)
```

The input parameter parser refers to the XML parser handler.

Useful Functions

PHP also offers a number of other functions that can further facilitate XML parsing. These functions are presented here.

utf8_decode()

This function will convert data to ISO-8859-1 encoding. It is assumed that the data being converted is of the UTF-8 encoding format. Its syntax is:

```
string utf8_decode(string data)
```

The input parameter data refers to the UTF-8-encoded data that is to be converted.

utf8_encode()

This function will convert data from the ISO-8859-1 encoding format to the UTF-8 encoding format. Its syntax is:

```
string utf8_encode(string data)
```

The input parameter data refers to the ISO-8859-1-encoded data that is to be converted.

xml_get_error_code()

The function xml_get_error_code() retrieves the error value specific to an XML parsing error. This can then be passed to xml_error_string() (introduced next) for interpretation. Its syntax is:

```
int xml_error_code(int parser)
```

The input parameter parser refers to the XML parser handler. An example of usage is shown below, in the introduction to the function xml_get_current_line_number().

xml_error_string()

When a parsing error occurs, it is assigned an error code. The function
xml_error_string() can be passed this code, returning the text description of the
code. Its syntax is:

```
string xml_error_string(int code)
```

The input parameter code refers to the error code assigned to the respective
error. This error code can be retrieved from the function xml_get_error_code().
An example of usage is shown below, in the introduction to the function
xml_get_current_line_number().

xml_get_current_line_number()

This function retrieves the line currently being parsed by the XML parser. Its syntax is:

```
int get_current_line_number(int parser)
```

The input parameter parser refers to the XML parser handler. An example
follows:

```
while ($line = fread($fh, 4096)) :
    if (! xml_parse($xml_parser, $line, feof($fh))) :
        $err_string = xml_error_string(xml_get_error_code($xml_parser));
        $line_number = xml_get_current_line_number($xml_parser);
        print "Error! [Line $line_number]: $err_string";
    endif;
endwhile;
```

If a parsing error occurred in line six of the file pointed to by $fh, you would
see an error message similar to the following in the parsed output:

```
Error! [Line 6]: mismatched tag
```

xml_get_current_column_number()

The function xml_get_current_column_number() can be used in conjunction with
xml_get_current_line_number() to pinpoint the exact location of an error in an
XML document. Its syntax is:

```
int get_current_column_number(int parser)
```

The input parameter parser refers to the XML parser handler. Reconsider the previous example:

```
while ($line = fread($fh, 4096)) :
    if (! xml_parse($xml_parser, $line, feof($fh))) :
        $err_string = xml_error_string(xml_get_error_code($xml_parser));
        $line_number = xml_get_current_line_number($xml_parser);
        $column_number = xml_get_current_column_number($xml_parser);
        print "Error! [Line $line_number, Column $column_number]: $err_string";
    endif;
endwhile;
```

If a parsing error occurred in line six of the file pointed to by $fh, you would see an error message similar to the following in the parsed output:

```
Error! [Line 6 Column 2]: mismatched tag
```

XML Parser Options

PHP currently offers two parser options:

- XML_OPTION_CASE_FOLDING, which is nothing more than converting tag element names to uppercase.

- XML_OPTION_TARGET_ENCODING, which specifies the document encoding output by the XML parser. Currently, UTF-8, ISO-8859-1, and US-ASCII encoding support is available.

These options can be both retrieved and modified using the functions xml_parser_get_option() and xml_parser_set_option(), respectively.

xml_parser_get_option()

The function xml_parser_get_option() retrieves the XML parser's options. Its syntax is:

```
int xml_parser_get_option(int parser, int option)
```

The input parameter parser refers to the XML parser handler. The parameter option specifies the option that will be retrieved, its value specified by the parameter value. An example follows:

```
$setting = xml_parser_get_option($xml_parser, XML_OPTION_CASE_FOLDING);
print "Case Folding: $setting";
```

Assuming that the XML_OPTION_CASE_FOLDING option has not been already explicitly modified, its default option of enabled will be retrieved. Therefore, executing this code would result in the outcome:

```
CASE FOLDING: 1
```

xml_parser_set_option()

The function xml_parser_set_option() configures the XML parser's options. Its syntax is:

```
int xml_parser_set_option(int parser, int option, mixed value)
```

The input parameter parser refers to the XML parser handler. The parameter option specifies the option that will be set, its value specified by the parameter value. An example follows:

```
xml_parser_set_option($xml_parser, XML_OPTION_TARGET_ENCODING, "UTF-8");
```

Execution of this command changes the target encoding option from the default of ISO-8859-1 to UTF-8.

XML-to-HTML Conversion

Suppose that you had an XML document containing a list of bookmarks, entitled bookmarks.xml. It looks similar to the following:

```
<?xml version="1.0"?>
<website>
<title>Epicurious</title>
<url>http://www.epicurious.com</url>
<description>
Epicurious is a great online cooking resource, providing tutorials, recipes,
forums and more.
</description>
</website>
```

Now assume that you wanted to parse bookmarks.xml, displaying its contents in a format readable from within a PC browser. Listing 14-3 will parse this file and reformat as necessary.

Listing 14-3: XML-to-HTML conversion parser

```
<?

class XMLHTML {
    VAR $xmlparser;
    VAR $tagcolor = "#800000";
    VAR $datacolor = "#0000ff";

    function XMLHTML() {
        $this->xmlparser = xml_parser_create();
        xml_set_object($this->xmlparser, &$this);
        xml_set_element_handler($this->xmlparser, "startTag", "endTag");
        xml_set_character_data_handler($this->xmlparser, "characterData");
    }

    // This function is responsible for handling all starting element tags.
    function startTag($parser, $tagname, $attributes) {
        GLOBAL $tagcolor;
        print "<font size=\"-2\" color=\"$this->tagcolor\" face=\"arial,
        verdana\">&lt;$tagname&gt;</font> <br>";
    }

    // This function is responsible for handling all character data.
    function characterData($parser, $characterData) {
        GLOBAL $datacolor;
        print "<font size=\"-2\" color=\"$this->datacolor\" face=\"arial,
        verdana\">   $characterData</font> <br>";
    }

    // This function is responsible for handling all ending element tags.
    function endTag($parser, $tagname) {
        GLOBAL $tagcolor;
        print "<font size=\"-2\" color=\"$this->tagcolor\" face=\"arial,
        verdana\">&lt;/$tagname&gt;</font> <br>";
    }

    function parse($fp) {
        // xml_parse($this->xmlparser,$data);
        // Parse the XML file
        while ( $line = fread($fp, 4096) ) :
```

```
                // If something goes wrong, stop and print an error message.
                    if ( ! xml_parse($this->xmlparser, $line, feof($fp))) :
                    die(sprintf("XML error: %s at line %d",
                    xml_error_string(xml_get_error_code($this->xmlparser)),
                    xml_get_current_line_number($this->xmlparser)));
                endif;
            endwhile;
        }

} // end class

// Open the XML file for parsing
$xml_file = "bookmarks.xml";
$fp = fopen($xml_file, "r");

// create new object
$xml_parser = new XMLHTML;

// parse $xml_file
$xml_parser->parse($fp);

?>
```

Once bookmarks.xml is parsed, you would see it displayed in the browser as shown below.

```
<WEBSITE>
<TITLE>
   Epicurious
</TITLE>
<URL>
   http://www.epicurious.com
</URL>
<DESCRIPTION>
   Epicurious is a great online cooking resource, providing tutorials, recipes,
forums and more.
</DESCRIPTION>
</WEBSITE>
```

Of course, this doesn't accomplish too much; it merely makes the XML viewable within the browser. With just a few modifications to Listing 14-3, you could begin parsing links to ensure that they are displayed as working hyperlinks, convert the data found within the <TITLE>...</TITLE> tags to boldface, etc. As you can see, I also declared two font colors as object attributes to show that you can easily format the data being output to the browser.

A Final Note About PHP and XML

Throughout this chapter I introduced XML and the various functions that PHP uses to parse XML documents. However, as it applies to PHP, I've only actually covered one of the three specifications that define XML and did not delve into issues regarding XSL or XLL. Of course, to truly take advantage of separating content from presentation, all three of these components need to be fully exploited, or at the very least, XML and XSL.

Unfortunately, at the time of this writing, PHP does not provide a complete solution for those wishing to work with XML using PHP as the sole handling language. Of course, as PHP's capabilities continue to expand, I'm fairly confident that these issues will be resolved.

> **NOTE** *One particularly promising development in this area is an XSLT (XSL transformation) processor named Sablotron, developed by Ginger Alliance Ltd. (http://www.gingerall.com). On October 12, 2000, it was announced that PHP 4.03 is now available with the Sablotron module extension on both the Linux and Windows platforms. Be sure to check this out for further developments.*

What's Next?

This chapter covered quite a bit of ground regarding XML and PHP's XML parsing functionality. I began with a brief synopsis of the history of markup languages and subsequently introduced you to XML, its advantages, and a primer of its syntactical constructs. The remainder of the chapter was devoted to introducing the many predefined XML functions offered by PHP, finally concluding with several examples of how PHP can be used to parse and output XML data. In particular, the following topics were covered:

- A brief introduction to markup languages

- SGML

- An introduction to XML

- XML syntax

- The document type definition (DTD)

- PHP and XML

Chapter 15 switches gears, covering two prominent technologies, namely, JavaScript and the Component Object Model (COM), and how PHP can interact with them.

JavaScript and COM

As I've already stated several times throughout this book, one of the greatest aspects of the PHP language is the ease with which it can be integrated with other technologies. To this point, you've seen this in the discussions regarding databasing, ODBC, and XML, for example. In this chapter I introduce two more such possibilities for integration, namely, the ease with which PHP can work alongside JavaScript and COM-based applications.

Brief introductions to each of these technologies are provided in this chapter, in addition to practical examples of how PHP can interact with them. By the conclusion of this chapter, you will have gained useful knowledge about two particularly powerful technologies and how they can be further used through PHP.

JavaScript

JavaScript is a particularly powerful scripting language used to develop both client- and server-oriented Internet applications. One of the most interesting aspects of the language is the fact that it is capable of manipulating not only data but also events. An event is defined as any action that takes place in the realm of the browser, such as a mouse click or loading of a page.

For anyone who has experience working with programming languages such as PHP, C, Pascal, or C++, JavaScript will not be too much of a chore to learn. If you are a novice to these languages, do not be dismayed; JavaScript, like PHP, is a language that can be quickly learned. Like with PHP, its developers were content with creating a language geared toward one thing: getting the job done.

For those of you interested in retaining the event-driven capabilities of JavaScript while implementing the multitude of advantages offered by PHP, have no fear; PHP is as easily integrable with JavaScript as it is with HTML. In fact, it complements PHP unusually well, as it is capable of performing functions that PHP is not well suited for, and vice versa.

However, before attempting to integrate PHP and JavaScript, keep in mind that some users may have JavaScript turned off in their browsers or (gasp!) use a browser that does not even support JavaScript. PHP offers a simple solution for making this judgment.

JavaScript Detection

Correctly determining a browser's capabilities is essential to providing users a hassle-free visit to your site. After all, what could cause a user to leave a site faster than when annoying "JavaScript error" messages begin jumping out at them, or if the site functionality does not work properly due to the fact that the user's browser does not even support the technologies you are using? Fortunately, PHP offers an easy way to discern many of the capabilities supported by the user's browser, by way of a predefined function named get_browser().

get_browser()

The function get_browser() retrieves browser capabilities, returning them in object format. The syntax is:

```
object get_browser([string user_agent])
```

The optional input parameter user_agent can be used to retrieve characteristics about a particular browser. Generally you will probably want to call get_browser() without any input parameter, since by default it uses the PHP global variable $HTTP_USER_AGENT as input.

A predefined list of browser capabilities is stored in the browscap file, its path directory specified by the browscap parameter in the php.ini file. The default setting of this parameter is shown here:

```
;browscap = extra/browscap.ini
```

The browser.ini file is developed by cyScape, Inc. The most recent version can be downloaded from http://www.cyscape.com/browscap/. Download and unzip the file, storing it in some logical location on the server. Take note of this location, as you will need to update the browscap setting in the php.ini file to reflect this location.

Once you have downloaded browscap.ini and configured your php.ini file, you are ready to begin incorporating browser-detection capabilities into your code. However, before doing so I would suggest opening the browser.ini file and scanning through it to get a better idea of how it is structured. After doing this, take a moment to experiment with Listings 15-1 and 15-2. Listing 15-1 is a very simple example that shows how all of a browser's characteristics can be output to the browser. Listing 15-2 focuses on the detection of just one of the browser's characteristics, JavaScript.

Listing 15-1: Showing all browser attributes

```
<?
// retrieve browser information
$browser = get_browser();

// typeset $browser to an array
$browser = (array) $browser;

while (list ($key, $value) = each ($browser)) :

    // clarify which of the browser elements are empty
    if ($value == "") :
        $value = 0;
    endif;

    print "$key : $value <br>";

endwhile;
?>
```

Executing Listing 15-1 in the Microsoft 5.0 browser yields the following output:

```
browser_name_pattern : Mozilla/4\.0 (compatible; MSIE 5\..*)
parent : IE 5.0
browser : IE
version : 5.0
majorver : #5
minorver : #0
frames : 1
tables : 1
cookies : 1
backgroundsounds : 1
vbscript : 1
javascript : 1
javaapplets : 1
activexcontrols : 1
win16 : 0
beta : 0
ak : 0
sk : 0
aol : 0
crawler : 0
cdf : 1
```

Listing 15-2 is a very short yet effective script that uses the browscap.ini file to verify whether or not JavaScript is enabled for a particular browser.

Listing 15-2: Ensuring JavaScript availability

```
<?
$browser = get_browser();

// typeset $browser to an array
$browser = (array) $browser;

if ($browser["javascript"] == 1) :
    print "Javascript enabled!";
else :
    print "No javascript allowed!";
endif;
?>
```

Basically, Listing 15-2 checks to verify whether the JavaScript key is listed for the given browser. If it is and is set to 1, then a message stating that JavaScript is enabled is displayed to the browser. Otherwise, an error message is displayed. Of course, in a practical situation you would likely get rid of the messages and perform other functions better suiting the user's browser capabilities.

The following two examples show just how easily PHP can be integrated with JavaScript. Listing 15-3 illustrates how the screen resolution and color depth can be determined using JavaScript and then subsequently displayed using PHP. The listing in the next section, "Building a Dynamic Pop-Up Window," illustrates how a PHP template can be used in a JavaScript-initiated pop-up window to display information based on the link the user clicks.

Listing 15-3: Detecting Color and Screen Resolution

```
<html>
<head>
<title>Browser Information</title>
</head>
<body>
<script language="Javascript1.2">
<!-//
document.write('<form method=POST action ="<? echo $PHP_SELF; ?>">');
document.write('<input type=hidden name=version value=' + navigator.appVersion +
'>');
document.write('<input type=hidden name=type value=' + navigator.appName + '>');
document.write('<input type=hidden name=screenWidth value=' + screen.width + '>');
```

```
document.write('<input type=hidden name=screenHeight value=' + screen.height +
'>');
document.write('<input type=hidden name=browserHeight value=' + window.innerWidth
+ '>');
document.write('<input type=hidden name=browserWidth value=' + window.innerHeight
+ '>');
//—>
</script>
<input type="submit" value="Get browser information"><p>
</form>

<?
    echo "<b>Browser:</b> $type Version: $version<br>";
    echo "<b>Screen Resolution:</b> $screenWidth x $screenHeight pixels.<br>";
    if ($browserWidth != 0) :
        echo "<b>Browser resolution:</b> $browserWidth x $browserHeight
        pixels.";
    else :
        echo "No JavaScript browser resolution support for this browser!";
    endif;
?>
</body>
</html>
```

Building a Dynamic Pop-Up Window

One of the interesting capabilities of JavaScript is the ease with which it can be used to manipulate browser windows. A useful application of this feature is small pop-up windows to display various parcels of information that perhaps are brief enough that they do not warrant the time taken to request and render another full page. Of course, you may be interested in creating a single template that will be used for each parcel of information. And thus the need for PHP. Listing 15-3 illustrates how a PHP file, window.php, is called from JavaScript. This file provides a very simple template, also incorporating a PHP INCLUDE call to the file ID as passed to window.php by the JavaScript in Listing 15-4.

For those of you not familiar with JavaScript, I have included descriptive comments in the code. The important point to keep in mind is that the variable winID will be passed to the PHP script, window.php This variable is assigned in the actual *link*, in the body of the HTML. Clicking it will trigger the function newWindow( ), specified in the JavaScript. To illustrate how this is done, consider this link:

```
<a href="#" onClick="newWindow(1);">Contact Us</a><br>
```

As you can see, I simply place a '#' in the href, since the link will be generated by the JavaScript onClick event handler. This event handler causes the function newWindow() to be called when the user clicks the link. Finally, notice that the input parameter for the function is 1. This is the identification number that the PHP script will use to display the corresponding contact information. You can use any number you please, as long as it correctly corresponds to the file that will be displayed in the PHP script.

Take a moment to review Listing 15-4. As a guide, I have also built three simple files that correspond to each of the links in Listing 15-4.

Listing 15-4: Building dynamic pop-up windows

```html
<html>
<head>
<title>Listing 15-4</title>
<SCRIPT language="Javascript">
<!-
    // declare a new JavaScript variable
    var popWindow;
    // declare a new function, newWindow
    function newWindow(winID) {
        // declare variable winURL, setting it to the name of the PHP file
        // and accompanying data.
        var  winURL = "window.php?winID=" + winID;
        // If the popup window does not exist, or it is currently closed,
        // open it.
        if (! popWindow || popWindow.closed) {
            // open new window having width of 200 pixels, height of 300
            // pixels, positioned
            // 150 pixels left of the linking window, and 100 pixels from the
            // top of the linking window.
            popWindow = window.open(winURL, 'popWindow',
            'dependent,width=200,height=300,left=150,top=100');
            }
            // If the popup window is already open, make it active and update
            // its location to winURL.
        else {
            popWindow.focus();
            popWindow.location = winURL;
        }
    }
//->
</SCRIPT>
```

```
</head>
<body bgcolor="#ffffff" text="#000000" link="#808040" vlink="#808040"
alink="#808040">
<a href="#" onClick="newWindow(1);">Contact Us</a><br>
<a href="#" onClick="newWindow(2);">Driving Directions</a><br>
<a href="#" onClick="newWindow(3);">Weather Report</a><br>
</body>
</html>
```

Again, once the user has clicked one of the links in Listing 15-4, a pop-up window is created and window.php is displayed in this window. The variable winID is passed to window.php and is in turn used to identify the file that should be included in the PHP script. Listing 15-5 contains window.php:

Listing 15-5: window.php

```
<html>
<head>
<title>Popup Window Fun</title>
</head>

<body bgcolor="#ffffff" text="#000000" link="black" vlink="gray" alink="#808040"
marginheight="0" marginwidth="0" topmargin="0" leftmargin="0">

    <table width="100%" border="0" cellpadding="0" cellspacing="0">
        <tr>
            <td>
            <?
            // Include file specified by input parameter
            INCLUDE("$winID.inc");
            ?>
            </td>
        </tr>
        <tr>
            <td>
            <a href="#" onClick="parent.self.close();">close window</a>
            </td>
        </tr>
    </table>

</body>
</html>
```

The final piece to this puzzle is the creation of the files that correspond to the links in Listing 15-4. Since there are three unique IDs (1, 2, and 3), I need to create three separate files. These files are shown here. The first file, which holds the contact information, should be saved as 1.inc.

```
<table>
    <tr>
        <td>
        <h4>Contact Us</h4>
        <ul>
        <li>email: <a href="mailto:wj@wjgilmore.com">wj@wjgilmore.com</a>
        <li>phone: (555) 867 5309
        <li>mobile: (555) 555 5555
        </ul>
        </td>
    </tr>
</table>
```

The next file, which holds the driving directions, should be saved as 2.inc.

```
<table>
    <tr>
        <td>
        <h4>Driving Directions</h4>
        <ol>
        <li>Turn left on 1st avenue.
        <li>Enter the old Grant building.
        <li>Take elevator to 4th floor.
        <li>We're in room 444.
        </ol>
        </td>
    </tr>
</table>
```

And the final file, which holds the weather report, should be saved as 3.inc. To further illustrate the easy integration of PHP and JavaScript, notice how I make use of a call to PHP's date function:

```
<table>
    <tr>
        <td>
        <h4>Weather Report <?=date("m-d-Y");?></h4>
        <b>Today:</b> Brrr... Brisk, with blowing and drifting snow.<br><br>
        <b>Tonight:</b> Winter Weather Advisory. 7-10 inches snow expected.
        </td>
    </tr>
</table>
```

An example of what a pop-up window would look like if the user clicked the weather report is shown in Figure 15-1.

Figure 15-1. Displaying weather information in a pop-up window

And thus ends this ever-so-brief introduction to PHP and JavaScript integration. Also both examples are relatively simple, and both are useful and can be easily built on to suit more complex needs. Perhaps most important when combining PHP with JavaScript, or any other server-side-oriented technology, is that you must provide adequate means for detecting the capabilities of the user's browser so as not to cause any ugly errors. In summary, it is always a good idea to experiment with other technologies in an attempt to incorporate them into your PHP code; just take heed so as not to scare the user away from your site due to unusable features or nonviewable content.

The next section discusses COM, another technology that can be easily interfaced using PHP.

The Component Object Model

COM, an acronym for *Component Object Model*, is essentially a specification that makes it possible for language- and platform-specific applications to communicate with each other. This capability greatly promotes the idea of building reusable, maintainable, and adaptable programming components, three ideas widely revered in the field of computer science. Although COM support is generally regarded as a Microsoft-centric specification, COM communication capability has actually been built into a number of languages (PHP, Java, C++, and Delphi, for example) and is used on a wide variety of platforms (Windows, Linux, and Macintosh, for example).

So what can COM and PHP do for you? Well, for one thing PHP's COM functionality makes it possible to directly communicate with many Microsoft applications. One interesting application is the formatting and display of Web database information to a Microsoft Word document. In fact, I'll show you just how easily this is accomplished in a later section.

> **NOTE**   *These few pages devoted to COM barely, and I mean barely, scratch the surface of the technology. To make matters worse, it is also largely underdocumented as it relates to the PHP language. Therefore, if you are interested in learning more about the mechanics of COM, I would suggest checking out "Further Reading" at the end of this section.*

PHP has several predefined COM functions. Keep in mind that these functions are *only* available for the Windows version of PHP! Before moving on to some concrete examples of how they are used, please take a moment to review each as they are introduced below.

PHP's COM Functionality

PHP's predefined COM functionality is used to instantiate COM objects and subsequently make use of the objects' properties and methods. Remember that this support is only offered in the Windows version of PHP.

The accompanying examples will be based on working with Microsoft Word 2000. The objects, methods, and events referenced can be found at the Microsoft MSDN Web site (http://msdn.microsoft.com/library/officedev/off2000 /wotocobjectmodelapplication.htm).

Instantiating a COM Object

To instantiate a COM object, just call new, just like you do to instantiate an object when programming the object-oriented way. The syntax is:

```
object new COM("object.class" [, string remote_address])
```

The parameter object.class refers to some COM module present on the server machine. The optional input parameter remote_address is used if you would like to create a COM object on some remote machine. For example, suppose that you want to instantiate an object that points to the MS Word application. This will actually start the Microsoft Word application just as if you had done so manually (of course, you must have MS Word installed on the machine in order for it to open). The syntax for doing so is shown here:

```
$word=new COM("word.application") or die("Couldn't start Word!");
```

Once you have instantiated a new COM object, you can begin working with the various methods and properties comprising that object. In regard to the above example, you may want to make the Word interface the active window. The following line enables the object's visibility attribute, resulting in the display of the application's interface:

```
$word->visible = 1;
```

Don't worry if you don't completely understand this command. Implementation of COM object methods is the subject of the next section.

Implementing a COM Object's Methods

You implement a COM object's methods in typical OOP format, using the object as a referring variable. The syntax for doing so is:

```
object->method_name([method_value, …]);
```

The object refers to a COM object that has been instantiated using the new instantiation process described previously. The parameter method_name refers to a method that is part of the class represented by object. The optional parameter space specified by method_value can be used to input parameters to those methods that allow or require input. Its syntax is just like that of a normal function, with each input parameter separated by a comma.

If you wanted to open a new MS Word document after instantiating a new COM object pointing to the application, as seen in the previous example, you could simply reference the method that accomplishes this. This is the add() method in the Documents subclass of $word:

```
$word->Documents->Add();
```

Notice how this follows a very logical, OOP-style syntax. Executing this will result in a new document being displayed to the MS Word application window.

com_get()

The function com_get() is used to retrieve COM object properties. Its syntax is:

```
mixed com_get(resource object, string property)
```

The input parameter object points to an instantiated COM object, and property refers to an attribute in the class represented by the instantiated object.

```
<?
// Instantiate a new object pointing to the MS Word application
$word=new COM("word.application") or die("Couldn't start Word!");

// The CapsLock property is either 0 for No, or 1 for Yes.
$flag = com_get($word->Application,CapsLock);

// Turn $flag value (0 or 1) into human-readable format
if ($flag == 1) :
    $flag = "YES";
else :
    $flag = "NO";
endif;
// display appropriate message
print "CAPS Lock activated: $flag";
$word->Quit();
?>
```

Alternatively, you could retrieve the `CapsLock` attribute value by calling it just as you would call an object's attribute via OOP syntax. To use this alternative format in the above example, simply replace this line in the above example:

```
$flag = com_get($word->Application,CapsLock);
```

with this line:

```
$flag = $word->Application->CapsLock;
```

Making use of these object attributes, you can retrieve any variety of information about the characteristics of an application. Furthermore, you can also set values for many characteristics. This is accomplished with the function `com_set()`.

com_set()

The function `com_set()` is used to set an object attribute to a specified value.

```
void com_set(resource object, string property, mixed value)
```

The input parameter `object` points to an instantiated COM object, and property erty refers to an attribute in the class represented by the instantiated object. The parameter `value` is the value to which you would like to set `property`.

In Listing 15-6, the Microsoft Word application is started and made the active window. A new document is then created, and one line of text is added to it. Next, I set the default document format (the attribute is called `DefaultSaveFormat`) to Text. This will become apparent once the Save As prompt is displayed, as you will see that the Save As Type setting is set to Text Only. Once you save the document, the Microsoft Word application is closed.

Listing 15-6: Setting the default document type
```
<?
// Instantiate a new object pointing to the MS Word application
$word=new COM("word.application") or die("Couldn't start Word!");

// Make MS Word the active window.
$word->visible =1;

// Create a new document
$word->Documents->Add();

// Insert some text into the document
```

```
$word->Selection->Typetext("php's com functionality is cool\n");

// Set the default document format to Text
$ok = com_set($word->Application, DefaultSaveFormat, "Text");

// Prompt the user to name and save the document.
// Notice that the default document format is Text!
$word->Documents[1]->Save;

// Quit MS Word
$word->Quit();
?>
```

Alternatively, you could set the DefaultSaveFormat attribute by directly calling it almost like you would a variable. To achieve the same results as Listing 15-6 using this alternative format, simply replace the line:

```
$ok = com_set($word->Application, DefaultSaveFormat, "Text");
```

with the line:

```
$word->Application->DefaultSaveFormat = "Text";
```

At this point, you have been introduced to all of the functionality necessary to manipulate Windows applications via PHP's COM functionality. Now I'll move on to a rather interesting example that illustrates just how useful and cool the COM features can be.

Writing Information to a Microsoft Word Document

This example demonstrates just how useful PHP's COM functionality can be. Suppose some of your users wanted to format some database information in a Microsoft Word document for a presentation. Just a few lines of PHP code can automate this entire process. To illustrate this, I'll use the table addressbook first used in the address book project at the end of Chapter 12. The process executed by the script flows as follows:

1. Connect to the MySQL server and select the necessary database.

2. Select all of the data in the table, ordering it by last name.

3. Open the Microsoft Word application and create a new document.

4. Format and output each row of table data to this document.

5. Prompt the user for a name under which the document will be saved.

6. Close Microsoft Word

The code is shown in Listing 15-7.

Listing 15-7: Interacting with Microsoft Word through PHP's COM functionality

```
<?
// Connect to the MySQL server
$host = "localhost";
$user = "root";
$pswd = "";
$db = "book";
$address_table = "addressbook";

mysql_connect($host, $user, $pswd) or die("Couldn't connect to MySQL server!");
mysql_select_db($db) or die("Couldn't select database!");

// Query the company database for all 'addresses' rows
$query = "SELECT * FROM $address_table ORDER BY last_name";
$result = mysql_query($query);

// Instantiate a new COM object. In this case, one pointing to the MS Word
application
$word=new COM("word.application") or die("Couldn't start Word!");

// Make MS Word the active Window
$word->visible =1;

// Declare a new, empty document.
$word->Documents->Add();

// Cycle through each address table row.
while($row = mysql_fetch_array($result)) :
    $last_name = $row["last_name"];
    $first_name = $row["first_name"];
    $tel = $row["tel"];
    $email = $row["email"];

    // Output table data to the open Word document.
```

```
        $word->Selection->Typetext("$last_name, $first_name\n");
        $word->Selection->Typetext("tel. $tel\n");
        $word->Selection->Typetext("email. $email:\n");

endwhile;

// Prompt the user for a document name
$word->Documents[1]->Save;

// Quit the MS Word Application
$word->Quit();
?>
```

Although this example is very simple, it illustrates in a very practical sense how you could write PHP applications that synchronize database information with a user's favorite Windows application. A more complicated application could be written that would allow users to sync Web-viewable information with Microsoft Outlook. All you would need to do is obtain a reference of Outlook's objects, properties, and methods, and you can begin experimentation. (An introduction to the object model of all applications comprising Office is at http://www.microsoft.com/officedev/articles/Opg/toc/PGTOC.htm).

Further Reading

The following links point to several of the more useful COM-related resources that I have found on the Internet:

- http://msdn.microsoft.com/library/techart/msdn_comppr.htm

- http://www.microsoft.com/Com/news/drgui.asp

- http://www.microsoft.com/com/default.asp

- http://www.comdeveloper.com/

What's Next

This chapter further introduced just how easy it is to integrate PHP with third-party technologies, namely, JavaScript and the Component Object Model (COM). In particular, I introduced the following topics:

- What is JavaScript?

- Detecting JavaScript-capable browsers

- Detecting browser properties

- Using pop-up windows in conjunction with PHP

- What is the Component Object Model (COM)?

- PHP's predefined COM functionality

- Using PHP's COM functionality to send database data to Microsoft Word

Integrating these technologies with PHP can expand the functionality of your applications in many ways. Working with JavaScript opens up the possibility of performing certain functions on the client side, such as window and browser manipulation and forms error checking. COM provides you with the possibility to create applications that communicate directly with such popular applications as the Microsoft Office suite, further enhancing the value and user-friendliness of your PHP applications.

In our final chapter (Did it really go by that quickly?), I cover a topic that should be constantly on the minds of every programmer and administrator: security. Important security-related issues such as script protection, encryption, and ecommerce data solutions are introduced.

Security

"Non sum qualis eram." ("I am not as I used to be.")
—Horace

When I happened across this quotation from Horace some time ago, I thought it so fittingly described the true essence of network security that I tucked it into the depths of my harddrive in hopes of being able to later use it. Of course, many of you are scratching your heads wondering what Horace, the ancient Roman poet, could possibly have to say that could be related to network security. In fact, network security is one of those subjects that spews forth a never-ending amount of information and is always changing to the tune of emerging technology. Thus, it is never what it used to be. You can never rely solely on what you already know about the subject, as it became most likely outdated the moment it hit the mainstream information market or is soon doomed to become so. The only way to feel the sense of being *relatively* secure in building reliable server-based applications is either to constantly stay abreast of the latest developments regarding the subject or to hire a reliable third party capable of effectively handling the problem for you.

Security considerations as applicable to PHP take many faces, some of which tie into the security of the server itself. After all, the degree of vulnerability built into the server is paramount in many ways to determining that of the data handled by the PHP scripts I strongly suggest that you read as much as you can about your Web server and be on the watch for upgrades and recommended fixes. Provided that many readers will likely be using the Apache server, I recommend checking out the Apache site (`http://www.apache.org`) and the great Apache resource Apache Week (`http://www.apacheweek.com`). Beyond your server, PHP can be also held accountable for providing some degree of security through its configuration options and cautious coding.

This final chapter, devoted to introducing many of these issues to you, is divided into five sections:

- Configuration Issues

- Coding Issues

- Data Encryption

- Ecommerce Solutions

- User Authentication

Although none of these sections will provide you with *all* of the answers regarding how to build an impregnable PHP application system, they will provide you with the basis from which you can begin your own investigation into this important topic.

Configuration Issues

There are several configuration options you should consider immediately after installing PHP to begin safeguarding your system. Of course, your configuration choices should depend on your particular situation. For example, if solely you or your development team are going to be programming PHP, then your security configuration may be vastly different from an ISP that has decided to allow all clients to develop PHP scripts for use on the server. Regardless of your situation, it is a good idea to evaluate all of the configuration options and implement only those that you deem necessary. These options are in the php.ini file.

safe_mode boolean

Enabling safe_mode places restrictions on several potentially dangerous PHP options. It can be enabled by setting safe_mode to the Boolean value of on, or disabled by setting it to off Its restriction scheme is based on the comparison of the UID (user ID) of the executing script and the UID of the file that that script is attempting to access. If the UIDs are the same, the function can execute; otherwise, the function fails.

It isn't possible to use safe_mode when PHP is compiled as an Apache module. This is because, when run as an Apache module, all PHP scripts run under the same user as Apache, making it impossible to differentiate between script owners. Please see the section "Safe_mode and the PHP Apache Module," later in this chapter, for more information.

Specifically, when safe_mode is enabled, several restrictions come into effect:

- Use of all input/output functions (fopen(), file(), and include(), for example) is restricted to usage only with files that have the same owner as the script that is calling these functions. For example, assuming that safe_mode is enabled, fopen() called from a script owned by Mary calling will fail if it attempts to open a file owned by John. However, if Mary owns the script calling fopen() and the file called by fopen(), the function will be successful.

- Attempts by a user to create a new file will be restricted to creating the file in a directory in which the user is the owner.

- Attempts to execute external scripts via functions like popen(), system(), or exec() are only possible when the external script resides in the directory specified by safe_mode_exec_dir. This directive is discussed later in this section.

- HTTP authentication is further strengthened because the UID of the owner of the authentication script is prepended to the authentication realm. User authentication is discussed in further detail in the later section "User Authentication."

- The username used to connect to a MySQL server must be the same as the username of the owner of the file calling mysql_connect().

Table 16-1 provides a complete list of functions that are affected when safe_mode is enabled.

Table 16-1. Functions restricted by safe_mode

chgrp	include	require
chmod	link	rmdir
chown	passthru	symlink
exec	popen	system
fopen	readfile	unlink
file	rename	

TIP *The PHP documentation for safe_mode has unfortunately not been updated since PHP2.0, although its functionality remains largely unchanged. This documentation is at http://www.php.net/manual/phpfi2.html.*

safe_mode_exec_dir string

This directive specifies the residing directory in which any system programs reside that can be executed by functions such as system(), exec(), or passthru(). Safe_mode must be enabled for this to work.

disable_functions string

You can set this directive equal to a comma-delimited list of function names that you want to disable. Note that this directive is not in any way related to `safe_mode` For example, if you wanted to just disable `fopen()`, `popen()`, and `file()`, just set `disable_functions` as follows:

```
disable_functions = fopen,popen,file
```

doc_root string

This directive can be set to a path that specifies the root directory from which PHP files will be served. If `doc_root` is set to nothing (empty), it will be ignored, and the PHP scripts are executed exactly as the URL specifies. If `safe_mode` is enabled and `doc_root` is not empty, no PHP scripts lying outside of this directory will be executed.

max_execution_time integer

This directive specifies how many seconds a script can execute before being terminated. This can be useful to prevent users' scripts from eating up CPU time. By default, this is set to 30 seconds. If you set it to zero, no time limit will be set.

memory_limit integer

This directive specifies, in bytes, how much memory a script can use. By default, this is set to 8 megabytes (8,388,608 bytes).

sql.safe_mode integer

When enabled, `sql.safe_mode` ignores all information passed to `mysql_connect()` and `mysql_pconnect()`, allowing connection only under the user the Web server is running as.

user_dir string

This directive specifies the name of the directory in a user's home directory where PHP scripts must be placed in order to be executed. For example, if user_dir is set to scripts and user Alessia wants to execute somescript.php, then that user must create a directory named scripts in her home directory and place somescript.php

in it. This script can then be accessed via the URL
http://www.yoursite.com/~alessia/somescript.php. Notice that the URL does not
include the directory scripts. This directive is typically used in conjunction with
Apache's UserDir configuration directive.

safe_mode and the PHP Module

Keep in mind that safe_mode is not useful when using PHP as a server module.
This is because the PHP module runs as a part of the Apache server, and therefore
all PHP scripts are executed under the same UID as the Apache server itself. Since
safe_mode operates under the premise of comparing UIDs to restrict use of certain functions, it can only really be useful when the CGI version of PHP is used in
conjunction with SuExec (http://www.apache.org/docs/suexec.html). This is because the CGI version of PHP runs as a separate process, and therefore the UID
can be changed dynamically through the suExec functionality. If you are particularly interested in making use of PHP's safe_mode features, running PHP as a CGI
along with suExec is probably your best bet, although it will be at a cost of speed
and overall performance.

Another important configuration strategy is the prevention of certain files
from being viewed in the browser. Certainly you wouldn't want those secret passwords or other configuration information to be viewed by an outside user, would
you? That is the topic of this next section.

Hiding Data Files and Configuration Files

This is an extremely important security-oriented procedure to keep in mind, regardless of the programming language. I will use the Apache server configuration
to illustrate just how easily your security can be compromised if sufficient steps
aren't taken to "hide" files not meant to be viewed by the user.

In Apache's httpd.conf file is a configuration directive named DocumentRoot.
This is set to the path from which you would like the server to consider to be the
public HTML directory. Any file in this path is considered fair game in terms of
being served to a user's browser, even if the file does not have a recognized extension. It is not possible for a user to view a file that resides outside of this path.
Therefore, it is a very good idea to *always* place your configuration files outside of
the DocumentRoot path!

As an exercise, create a file and inside this file type "my secret stuff." Save this
file into your public HTML directory under the name of secrets with some really
strange extension like .zkgjg. Obviously, the server isn't going to recognize this extension, but it's going to attempt to serve up the data anyway. Now, go to your
browser and request that file, using the URL pointing to that file. Scary, isn't it?
Fortunately, there are two simple ways to correct this problem.

Maintain the Document Outside of the Document Root

The first solution is to simply place any files that you do not want the user to view outside of document root. Then use include() to include those files into any PHP files. For example, assume that you set your document root to:

```
DocumentRoot C:/Program Files/Apache Group/Apache/htdocs    # Windows
DocumentRoot /www/apache/home                               # non-Windows
```

Suppose you have a file containing access information (hostname, username, password) for your MySQL database. You certainly wouldn't want anyone to view that file, so it would be a good idea to place it outside of the document root. Therefore, in Windows, you could save that file to:

```
C:/Program Files/mysecretdata/
```

or

```
/usr/local/mysecretdata/
```

for UNIX.

When you need to use this access information, just include these files using the full pathname where needed. For example:

```
INCLUDE("C:/Program Files/mysecretdata/mysqlaccess.inc");
```

for Windows, or

```
INCLUDE("/usr/local/mysecretdata/mysqlaccess.inc");
```

for UNIX.

Of course, if you have safe_mode disabled (see the previous section, "Configuration Issues"), this may not prevent other users with the capability to execute PHP scripts on the machine from attempting to include that file into their own scripts. Therefore, in a multiuser environment it would be a good idea to couple this safeguard with the enabling of safe_mode.

Configure httpd.conf File
to Deny Certain File Extension Access

A second way to prevent users from viewing certain files is to deny access to certain extensions by configuring the httpd.conf file FILES directive. Assume that you don't want anyone to access files having the extension .inc. Simply place the following in your httpd.conf file:

```
<Files *.inc>
    Order allow,deny
    Deny from all
</Files>
```

After making this addition, restart the Apache server, and you will find that access is denied to any user making a request to view a file having the extension .inc via the browser. However, you can still include these files in your scripts. Incidentally, if you search through the httpd.conf file, you will see that this is the same premise used to protect access to .htaccess files. These files are used to password-protect certain directories and are discussed at the conclusion of this chapter.

Coding Issues

Even if you have a solid server configuration, you still must be constantly wary of introducing security holes into your PHP code. It's not that PHP is not a secure language. It is possible to introduce potentially dangerous holes in practically any programming language. However, given PHP's propensity to be used in a large-scale distributed environment (that is, the Web), the opportunity for users to attempt to "break" your code increases substantially. It's up to you to make sure that this does not happen.

Accepting User Input

While the ability to accept user input is an important part of practically any useful application, you must constantly be wary of the introduction of malicious data, both accidental and intentional. The danger involved in regard to a Web application is even more pronounced, since it is possible for a user to execute system commands through the use of functions such as system() or exec().

One of the easiest ways to combat malicious user input is by using the predefined function escapeshellcmd().

escapeshellcmd()

The function escapeshellcmd() will escape any questionable characters entered by the user that could result in the execution of a potentially damaging system command. Its syntax is:

```
string escapeshellcmd(str command)
```

To illustrate just how ugly things could get if you were not to control user input, suppose that you offered users the ability to execute system commands such as 'ls -l'. However, what if the user entered something like `rm -rf * ` you were to then either echo this input or insert it into exec() or system(), it could potentially recursively delete files and directories from your server! You can eliminate these problems by first cleaning up the command with escapeshellcmd(). Reconsidering the input `rm -rf * `, if you were to first pass it through escapeshellcmd(), the string would be converted to \`rm -rf \*\`.

> **NOTE** *Backticks are an execution operator, telling PHP to attempt to execute the contents found between backticks. The output can be echoed directly to the screen, or it can be assigned to a return variable.*

Another problem that arises from user input is the introduction of HTML content. This can be particularly problematic when the information is displayed back to the browser, as is the case with a message board. The introduction of HTML tags into a message board could alter the display of the page, causing it to be displayed incorrectly or not at all. This problem can be eliminated by passing the user input through strip_tags().

strip_tags()

The function strip_tags() will remove all HTML tags from a string. Its syntax is:

```
string strip_tags(str string [, str allowed_tags])
```

The input parameter string is the string that will be examined for tags, while the optional input parameter allowed_tags specifies any tags that you would like to be allowed in the string. For example, italic tags (<i></i>) might be allowable, but table tags such as <td></td> could potentially wreak havoc on a page. An example of usage of the function follows:

```
$input = "I <i>really</i> love PHP!";
$input = strip_tags($input);
// $input now equals "I really love PHP!"
```

This sums up the brief synopsis of the two more widely used functions for sanitizing user input. Next I introduce data encryption, highlighting several of PHP's predefined functions capable of encrypting data.

Data Encryption

Encryption can be defined as the translation of data into a format that is, in theory, unreadable by anyone except the intended party. The intended party can then decode, or decrypt, the encrypted data through the use of a secret key or password. PHP offers support for several encryption algorithms. Several of the more prominent ones are described here.

General Encryption Functions

It is important to realize that encryption over the Web is largely useless unless the scripts running the encryption schemes are operating via a secured server. Why? Since PHP is a server-side scripting language, information must first be sent to the server in plain text format *before* it can be encrypted. There are many ways that an unwanted third party can watch this information as it is transmitted from the user to the server if the user is not operating via a secured connection. For more information about setting up a secure Apache server, check out http://www.apache-ssl.org. For those readers implementing a different Web server, refer to your documentation. Chances are that there exists at least one, if not several different, security solutions for your particular server.

md5()

Md5 is a third-party hash algorithm used for creating digital signatures (among other things), which can be used to uniquely identify the sending party. PHP provides support to it:

```
string md5(string string)
```

It is considered to be a "one-way" hashing algorithm, which means there is no way to dehash data that has been hashed using md5().

The Md5 algorithm can also be used as a password verification system. Since it is in theory extremely difficult to retrieve the original string that has been hashed using the Md5 algorithm, you could hash a given password using Md5 and then compare that encrypted password against those that a user enters in order to gain access to restricted information.

For example, assume that our secret password toystore has an Md5 hash of 745e2abd7c52ee1dd7c14ae0d71b9d76. You store this hashed value on the server and compare it to the Md5 hash equivalent of the password the user attempts to enter. Even if an intruder were to get hold of the encrypted password, it wouldn't make much difference, since that intruder couldn't (in theory) decrypt it. An example of hashing a string follows:

```
$val = "secret";
$hash_val = md5 ($val);
// $hash_val = "c1ab6fb9182f16eed935ba19aa830788";
```

Now I'll introduce another way to secure a data string, that is, through another one of PHP's predefined functions: crypt().

crypt()

Crypt() offers a convenient way to one-way encrypt a piece of data. By one-way encrypt, I mean that the data can only be encrypted; there is no known algorithm to decrypt the data once it is encrypted using crypt(). Its syntax is:

```
string crypt(string string [, salt])
```

The input parameter string is the string that will be encrypted by the crypt() algorithm. The optional input parameter, salt, determines the type of encryption that will be used to encrypt string. Specifically, the encryption type is determined by the length of the salt. The various encryption types and their determinant salt lengths are shown in Table 16-2.

Table 16-2. Encryption Types and Corresponding Salt Lengths

ENCRYPTION TYPE	LENGTH
CRYPT_STD_DES	2
CRYPT_EXT_DES	9
CRYPT_MD5	12 (starting with first character of unencrypted password)
CRYPT_BLOWFISH	12 (starting with first two characters of unencrypted password)

Not all encryption formats are available on each system, but you can easily determine which of the formats listed in Table 16-2 are available by printing the encryption type to the browser. A 1 will be displayed if it is available, 0 otherwise.

Listing 16-1 illustrates the use of crypt() to create and compare encrypted passwords.

Listing 16-1: Using `crypt()` **(STD_DES) to store and compare passwords**

```
$user_pass = "123456";
// extract the first two characters of $user_pass for use as salt.
$salt = substr ($user_pass, 0, 2);
// encrypt and store password somewhere
$crypt1 = crypt($user_pass, $salt);
// $crypt1 = "12tir.zIbWQ3c";

// . . . user enters password
$entered_pass = "123456";

// get the first two characters of the stored password
$salt1 = substr ($crypt, 0, 2);
// encrypt $entered_pass using $salt1 as the salt.
$crypt2 = crypt ($entered_pass, $salt1);
// $crypt2 = "12tir.zIbWQ3c";
// Therefore, $crypt1 = $crypt2
```

As you can see in Listing 16-1, $crypt1 equals $crypt2, but *only* because I correctly used the first two characters of $crypt1 as the salt for the encryption of $entered_pass. I suggest that you experiment with this example, inserting different salt values so that you can see firsthand that $crypt1 and $crypt2 will only end up equivalent using this procedure.

> **TIP** *When choosing between* `crypt()` *and* `md5()` *to carry out your site encryption procedures, go with* `md5()`. *It's more secure.*

mhash()

The function `mhash()` offers support for a number of hashing algorithms, allowing developers to implement checksums, message digests, and various other digital signatures into their PHP application. Hashes are also used for storing passwords. Integrating the `mhash()` module into your PHP distribution is rather simple:

1. Go to http://mhash.sourceforge.net and download the source.

2. Extract the contents of the compressed distribution and follow the instructions as specified in the INSTALL document.

3. Compile PHP with the –with-mhash option.

Easy enough. There is, however, one quirk that tends to cause trouble when compiling mhash into a PHP/Apache system. Apparently, many find that they have to configure mhash as follows: "./configure -disable-pthreads". (You'll understand what I'm talking about when you read the mhash INSTALL document.) Keep this in mind when compiling your distribution.

On completion of the installation process, you have the functionality offered by mhash at your disposal. Mhash currently supports the hashing algorithms listed in Table 16-3.

Table 16-3. Hashing Algorithms Currently Supported by mhash()

SHA1	RIPEMD160	MD5
GOST	TIGER	SNEFRU
HAVAL		CRC32
RIPEMD128		
CRC32B		

mcrypt()

Mcrypt is a popular data-encryption package available for use with PHP, providing support for two-way encryption (that is, encryption and decryption). The mcrypt module offers support for the four types of encryption modes discussed here:

> **TIP** *For more information about encryption modes, I recommend the textbook* Applied Cryptography Second Addition, *by Bruce Schneier (John Wiley & Sons, 1996). This is a fantastic resource for learning more about cryptographic protocols, techniques, and algorithms.*

CBC: Cipher Block Chaining

CBC mode is typically the encryption mode that is the most frequently used of the four. Unlike ECB (described below), using CBC results in different encryption patterns of identical plain text blocks, making it more difficult for an attacker to discern patterns. If you don't know which of the four modes you should be using, use this one. However, I would suggest learning more about each mode before making a final decision.

CFB: Cipher Feedback

CFB combines certain characteristics of the stream cipher, resulting in the elimination of the need to amass blocks of data before enciphering takes place. Typically, you won't need to use this mode.

ECB: Electronic Code Book

ECB mode encrypts each plain text block independently with the block cipher, making it susceptible to attack when used to encrypt relatively small block sizes of language text. This is because ECB will encrypt two plain text blocks with identical encipherments, providing an attacker with a means to base a decipherment strategy. Therefore, unless you have a valid reason for using ECB, you'll probably want to use CBC mode instead.

OFB: Output Feedback

OFB mode has many of the same characteristics as the CFB mode. Like CFB, you typically won't need to use this mode.

> **NOTE** *To use the functionality offered by* mcrypt, *you must first download the mcrypt package from ftp://argeas.cs-net.gr/pub/unix/mcrypt/.*

A Final Note About Data Encryption

The methods in this section are only those that are in some way incorporated into the PHP extension set. However, you are not limited to these encryption/hashing solutions. Keep in mind that you can use functions like popen() or exec() to work with any of your favorite third-party encryption technologies, PGP (http://www.pgpi.org) or GPG (http://www.gnupg.org), for example.

You might find the following links particularly useful for learning more about cryptography and information privacy:

- http://jya.com/crypto-free.htm

- http://www.io.com/~ritter/LEARNING.HTM

- http://www.rsasecurity.com/rsalabs/faq/

- http://www.cs.auckland.ac.nz/~pgut001/links.html

- http://www.thawte.com/support/crypto/contents.html

To close out this section, I would like to throw caution into the wind by saying that before you begin implementing mission-critical applications involving encryption, take some time to really learn about the mechanics of data encryption. Remember that in the world of data security, ignorance is certainly not bliss. For those new to the subject, take a moment to check out the links that I've included. They are widely regarded as great introductions to the many facets of encryption and data security.

E-Commerce Functions

One can hardly deny the frenzy that the advent of ecommerce has instilled into the populations of the world, not to mention the advantages and conveniences that have resulted from it. Thankfully, those of you who are interested in developing your own ecommerce sites have a number of trusted third-party applications that you can easily integrate into PHP scripts. I make brief note of some of the more popular ones in this section.

Verisign

Verisign, Inc. (http://www.verisign.com) offers a wide array of ecommerce-related products and services. PHP provides support for interfacing with Verisign's Payflow Pro service.

> **NOTE** *To use the Verisign functionality, PHP must be compiled with the —with-pfpro [=DIR] directive. Also, there are several Payflow Pro configuration directives available in the php.ini file.*

PHP's Payflow Pro functionality is extremely easy to use and requires a minimum of time and knowledge to begin performing transactions. However, just because you compile Verisign support into your PHP installation does not mean that you are capable of using the Verisign services! To do so, you must first register at the Verisign site and download Verisign's SDK package. At the time of this writing, setup of Payflow Pro involved a one-time fee of $249, in addition to a monthly fee of $59.95 for a maximum of 5,000 monthly transactions, or a monthly fee of $995 for unlimited transactions.

One further note to keep in mind: Before you purchase a Verisign account, you can test your script interface with Verisign's test account, offered free of charge. Performing test transactions with this test account will eliminate unnecessary expenditures when debugging your code. Check out the Verisign site for more information.

You can find more information regarding Verisign at:

- http://www.verisign.com

- http://www.php.net/manual/ref.pfpro.php

Cybercash

Cybercash, Inc. (http://www.cybercash.com) offers a variety of credit card authorization and transaction services and software to those wishing to incorporate these services into their Web application.

> **NOTE** *To make use of the Cybercash functionality, PHP must be compiled with the —with-cybercash=[DIR] directive.*

Cybercash provides C and Perl scripts capable of interfacing with the Cybercash transaction service. With this in mind, PHP users generally choose one or a combination of the following methods for incorporating Cybercash into their site:

- Make use of the cyberlib.php API, included in the PHP distribution. This provides you with the functionality necessary to perform the transactions. (Recommended.)

- Use the existing Perl and C scripts to interface with the Cybercash service, calling them from your own PHP scripts. (Recommended.)

- Rewrite the existing Perl and C scripts in PHP. (Not recommended.)

As with Verisign, keep in mind that just because you compile Cybercash into your PHP installation does not mean that you can use the service! Cybercash integration services are not free and can be rather costly. (The setup for the Cybercash ecommerce CashRegister service currently runs $495, in addition to a $20/month fee plus $0.20 per transaction.) However, despite these costs, many PHP developers feel that Cybercash is one of the best solutions available.

One further note: Before you purchase a Cybercash account, you can test your script interface with the Cybercash test account, offered free of charge. Performing test transactions with this test account will eliminate unnecessary expenditures when debugging your code. Check out the Cybercash site for more information.

Further information regarding Cybercash is at:

- http://www.cybercash.com

- http://www.php.net/manual/ref.cybercash.php

CCVS

CCVS, or the Credit Card Verification System, is a technology developed by Red-Hat (http://www.redhat.com) that allows you to independently process credit card transactions, directly accessing the credit card agencies rather than going through a third party (such as Cybercash). CCVS is compatible with many of the major Linux/UNIX platforms and can be easily modified since RedHat provides you with the source code to make changes as you wish.

> **NOTE** *Note: To make use of the CCVS functions, PHP must be compiled with the —with-ccvs=[DIR] directive.*

You can find more information regarding CCVS at:

- http://www.php.net/manual/ref.ccvs.php

- http://www.redhat.com/products/ccvs/support/CCVS3.3docs/ ProgPHP.html

- http://www.redhat.com/products/ccvs/

User Authentication

Just like knowing the "secret handshake" will get a person into the treehouse, knowing the correct username and password can grant a user the right to enter otherwise unauthorized server directories. These authentication systems are typically known as "challenge and response." The challenge is the prompt for the username and password, and the response is the input of a username and password combination. If the combination is correct, the user is permitted to enter the restricted directory; otherwise, the user is denied, and an appropriate message is displayed.

A pop-up authentication prompt is often used to query the user for a username and password. This prompt can be activated via calling an authentication header, shown in Listing 16-2.

Listing 16-2: Basic authentication prompt

```
<?
header('WWW-Authenticate: Basic realm="Secret Family Recipes"');
header('HTTP/1.0 401 Unauthorized');
exit;
?>
```

Executing the code in Listing 16-2 will only produce the pop-up window. The two calls to the header() function prompt the browser to display this window. This window will look similar to the one in Figure 16-1.

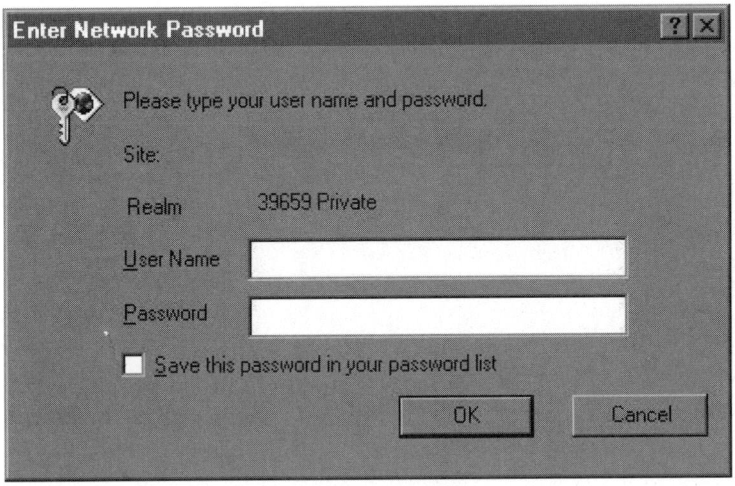

Figure 16-1. User authentication window

Now that you can set up the necessary interface, it is time to turn your attention to processing the username and password. In PHP, the login and password are stored in two global variables, namely, $PHP_AUTH_USER (username) and $PHP_AUTH_PW (password). Listing 16-3 shows how these variables can be checked for values. If they are not set, the authentication window is again displayed.

> **TIP** *As you experiment with the scripts in this section, you may find that the authentication window does not always pop up as expected after you refresh the page. This does not necessarily imply a problem with the code; rather it is a function of the browser's implementation of the authentication window. You will need to close and relaunch the browser in order to receive the prompt.*

Listing 16-3 Checking PHP's global authentication variables

```
if ( (! isset ($PHP_AUTH_USER)) || (! isset ($PHP_AUTH_PW)) ):
    header('WWW-Authenticate: Basic realm="Secret Family Recipes"');
    header('HTTP/1.0 401 Unauthorized');
    print "You are attempting to enter a restricted area. Authorization is
required.";
    exit;
endif;
```

An easy albeit rather restrictive way to set up a restricted page is to simply hardcode the username and password into the authentication script. Consider Listing 16-4, which builds on the previous example.

Listing 16-4 Hardcoding the username and password into a script

```
if ( (! isset ($PHP_AUTH_USER)) || (! isset ($PHP_AUTH_PW)) ||
   ($PHP_AUTH_USER != 'secret') || ($PHP_AUTH_PW != 'recipes') ) :

    header('WWW-Authenticate: Basic realm="Secret Family Recipes"');
    header('HTTP/1.0 401 Unauthorized');
    print "You are attempting to enter a restricted area. Authorization is
    required.";
    exit;
endif;
```

Multiple User Authentication

Although the code in Listing 16-4 may be your solution when dealing with a small, static group of people, chances are you will be interested in a more robust and flexible solution to granting access to restricted areas of your Web site. Most likely, this involves granting a separate username and password for each user that you expect to visit the restricted area. There are several methods used to accomplish this, perhaps the most common being checking authentication information against a text file or database.

Storing Information in a Text File

A very simple yet effective solution for storing user authentication information is in a text file. Each line of this text file would contain a username/password pair that can be read in and tested one by one. A text file used for these purposes might look like the one shown in Listing 16-5.

Listing 16-5: A typical authentication text file (authenticate.txt)

```
brian:snaidni00
alessia:aiggaips
gary:9avaj9
chris:poghsawcd
matt:tsoptaes
```

As you can see, each line consists of a username, followed by a password, with a colon (:) separating the two. This means that there are five potential username/password combinations that can be used to enter the restricted area for which this text file is intended. Each time a user enters a username and password via the authentication window, the text file is opened and searched methodically for a matching pair. If a match is found, the user is permitted to enter the restricted area; otherwise, the user is denied access. This authentication procedure is displayed in Listing 16-6.

Listing 16-6 Text file-based user authentication

```php
$file = "authenticate.txt";
$fp = fopen($file, "r");
$auth_file = fread ($fp, filesize($fp));
fclose($fp);

// assign each line of file as array element
$elements = explode ("\n", $auth_file);

foreach ($elements as $element) {

    list ($user, $pw) = split (":", $element);

    if (($user == $PHP_AUTH_USER) && ($pw == $PHP_AUTH_PW)) :
        $authorized = 1;
        break;
    endif;

} // end foreach

if (! $authorized) :
        header('WWW-Authenticate: Basic realm="Secret Family Recipes"');
        header('HTTP/1.0 401 Unauthorized');
        print "You are attempting to enter a restricted area. Authorization is
        required.";
        exit;
```

```
else :
        print "Welcome to the family's secret recipe collection";
endif;
```

Storing Information in a Database

Storing user authentication information in a database is advantageous for many reasons, many of them discussed in detail in Chapter 11, "Databases." Easy updating, scalability, and flexibility are just a few reasons why using a database is the logical choice for storing large amounts of user authentication data. Table 16-4 illustrates a sample database table used to store this data. After authentication lookup has successfully taken place, the user ID can then be used to tie into other tables hosting various other forms of user data and preferences. The idea of effectively quarantining related data to separate, smaller tables, rather than just grouping it all into one massive table, is known as *database normalization* and was briefly discussed in Chapter 11.

NOTE *MySQL syntax is used to illustrate the examples in this section. The code is simple enough to be easily converted to other database servers.*

Table 16-4. A sample user authentication table (user_authenticate)

USER ID	USERNAME	PASSWORD
ur1234	brian	2b877b4b825b48a9a0950dd5bd1f264d
ur1145	alessia	6f1ed002ab5595859014ebf0951522d9
ur15932	gary	122a2a1adf096fe4f93287f9da18f664
ur19042	chris	6332e88a4c7dba6f7743d3a7a0c6ea2c
ur18930	matt	9252fe5d140e19d308f2037404a0536a

Listing 16-7 will first check to see whether or not the $PHP_AUTH_USER variable has been set. If it has not, the authentication window will pop up, prompting the user to enter the necessary information. Otherwise, a connection to the MySQL server is established and the user_authenticate table is queried using the username and password entered by the user. If no match is found, the authentication window will be displayed again. Otherwise, $userid is assigned the matching user ID, essentially authenticating the user.

Listing 16-7: Authenticating a user via database lookup
```
if (!isset($PHP_AUTH_USER)):
    header('WWW-Authenticate: Basic realm="Secret Family Recipes"');
    header('HTTP/1.0 401 Unauthorized');
    exit;
```

```
else :
    // connect to the mysql database
    mysql_connect ("host", "user", "password") or die ("Can't connect to
    database!");
    mysql_select_db ("user_info") or die ("Can't select database!");

    // query the user_authenticate table for authentication match
    $query = "select userid from user_authenticate where
                                    username = '$PHP_AUTH_USER' and
                                    password = '$PHP_AUTH_PW'";

    $result = mysql_query ($query);

    // if no match found, display authentication window
    if (mysql_numrows($result) != 1) :
        header('WWW-Authenticate: Basic realm="Secret Family Recipes"');
        header('HTTP/1.0 401 Unauthorized');
        exit;
    // else, retrieve user-Id
    else :
        $userid = mysql_result (user_authenticate, 0, $result);
    endif;
endif;
```

Conclusion

This chapter introduced a wide array of topics relating to security. As you've
learned throughout this chapter, properly securing your PHP applications revolves around a combination of properly configuring your server and PHP installation, and employing prudent coding to prevent user input from wreaking havoc.
Other variables such as encryption, credit card verification, and user authentication play important roles when applicable. To recap, I briefly introduced the following topics:

- PHP's configuration issues

- Safe mode and the PHP module

- Coding issues

- Data encryption

- Ecommerce functions

- User authentication

In closing, I would like to state that properly planning the level of security that your PHP application will require is as important as, if not more so than, planning the other features of your application that will make it a success. Therefore, always take time to properly outline the security features that you must employ *before* you begin coding. In the long run, it will save you time and aid in the prevention of potential security holes in your application.

Index

The Story Behind Apress

APRESS IS AN INNOVATIVE PUBLISHING COMPANY devoted to meeting the needs of existing and potential programming professionals. Simply put, the "A" in Apress stands for the "author's press™." Our unique author-centric approach to publishing grew from con-versations between Dan Appleman and Gary Cornell, authors of best-selling, highly regarded computer books. They wanted to create a publishing company that emphasized quality above all—a company whose books would be considered the best in their market.

To accomplish this goal, they knew it was necessary to attract the very best authors—established authors whose work is already highly regarded, and new au-thors who have real-world practical experience that professional software devel-opers want in the books they buy. Dan and Gary's vision of an author-centric press has already attracted many leading software professionals—just look at the list of Apress titles on the following pages.

Would You Like
to Write for Apress?

APRESS IS RAPIDLY EXPANDING its publishing program. If you can write and refuse to com-promise on the quality of your work, if you believe in doing more then re-hashing existing documentation, and if you are looking for opportunities and re-wards that go far beyond those offered by traditional publishing houses, we want to hear from you!

Consider these innovations that we offer every one of our authors:

- Top royalties with no hidden switch statements. For example, authors typi-cally only receive half of their normal royalty rate on foreign sales. In con-trast, Apress' royalty rate remains the same for both foreign and domestic sales.

- A mechanism for authors to obtain equity in Apress. Unlike the software in-dustry, where stock options are essential to motivate and retain software professionals, the publishing industry has stuck to an outdated compensa-tion model based on royalties alone. In the spirit of most software compa-nies, Apress reserves a significant portion of its equity for authors.

- Serious treatment of the technical review process. Each Apress book has a technical reviewing team whose remuneration depends in part on the suc-cess of the book since they, too, receive a royalty. Moreover, through a part-nership with Springer-Verlag, one of the world's major publishing houses, Apress has significant venture capital behind it. Thus, Apress has the re-sources both to produce the highest quality books and to market them ag-gressively.

If you fit the model of the Apress author who can write a book that gives the "professional what he or she needs to know'," then please contact any one of our editorial directors, Gary Cornell (gary_cornell*@apress.com), Dan Appleman (dan_appleman*@apress.com), or Karen Watterson (karen_watterson*@apress.com), for more information on how to become an Apress author.